GALVINISED!

GALVINISED!
The Footballing Tale of Brothers
CHRIS & TONY
GALVIN

DAVID SAFFER

First published by Pitch Publishing, 2023

Pitch Publishing
9 Donnington Park,
85 Birdham Road,
Chichester,
West Sussex,
PO20 7AJ
www.pitchpublishing.co.uk
info@pitchpublishing.co.uk

© 2023, Chris Galvin, Tony Galvin and David Saffer

Every effort has been made to trace the copyright.
Any oversight will be rectified in future editions at the
earliest opportunity by the publisher.

All rights reserved. No part of this book may be reproduced,
sold or utilised in any form or transmitted in any form or by
any means, electronic or mechanical, including photocopying,
recording or by any information storage and retrieval system,
without prior permission in writing from the Publisher.

A CIP catalogue record is available for this book
from the British Library.

ISBN 978 1 801504 19 5

Typesetting and origination by Pitch Publishing
Printed and bound in Great Britain by TJ Books, Padstow

Contents

Acknowledgements 9
Foreword by Steve Perryman 11
Foreword by John Kaye 13
Introduction by David Saffer 15
1. Football-Crazy Kids 19
2. Apprentice Dreams 34
3. European Cup Teenage Debut 43
4. Challenging Days at Elland Road 58
5. Super Leeds! 76
6. Goole, Mr Scary and Snowy Trek to Spurs 87
7. New Era Dawns at White Hart Lane 105
8. Tottenham 'Up for the Cup' 116
9. FA Cup at the Double! 146
10. Glory, Glory Nights 164
11. Galvin 'Shuffle' Dazzles Hull 181
12. King Billy then Relegation Woes 204
13. Big Jack and the Boys in Green 230
14. Slow Boat to China 258
15. Sojourn to Civvy Street 276
16. A Final Word 302
Appendix 1: Chris Galvin's Playing Career 313
Appendix 2: Tony Galvin's Playing Career 314
Appendix 3: Tony Galvin's International Record 315
Bibliography 316

To Mum and Dad – Muriel and Thomas Galvin – for giving us such a caring and loving upbringing. They sacrificed a great deal to ensure we both had the opportunity to reach our full potential.

Acknowledgements

FIRSTLY, THANK you to Steve Perryman and John Kaye for providing forewords to *Galvinised!*

A special appreciation to football writer David Bond for his expert knowledge and contacts at Hull City FC and Goole Town FC. David provided anecdotes from Hull's John Kaye, Jeff Wealands, Bruce Bannister, Dave Roberts, Peter Fletcher, Steve Deere and Gordon Staniforth, alongside Goole's Tony Taylor, Micky Driver, Tom Wilson and club secretary Graham Wilson.

Former Goole manager Alan Turner and Chris's team-mates Jim Kelly and Chris Jackson also offered recollections. Sadly, they passed away during the writing of this book.

Thanks to Tony's former teacher and football coach at St Gregory's and All Saints School, Tony Tomlinson, for providing invaluable information from Tony's school years. And to Sir Paul Grant, a team-mate of Tony's in the University of Hull football team.

A personal thanks to Mark Manley for his introduction to Chris Galvin, Phil Goldstone for access to his football book library, Andrew 'Stats' Dalton for his meticulous Leeds United records and William Susman for his help in sorting out the photos.

Every endeavour has been made to establish copyright of photographs. Chris and Tony Galvin have provided photographs from their family collections.

Galvinised! includes credits for newspapers, match programmes, magazines, brochures and books, with a journalist and author, where possible, for match reports and article snippets. A full list of credits is included in the bibliography.

Shoot magazine was important for the 1981 and 1982 FA Cup Finals and 1982 League Cup Final. The *Tottenham Hotspur FA Cup Finalists 1981* and *Glory Glory ... Tottenham Hotspur: 1981 FA Cup 25th Anniversary* brochures were likewise invaluable.

At this juncture, thank you to Jane Camillin at Pitch Publishing for backing this book.

Last, but by no means least, thanks to my better half, Deborah, who has put up with my madcap ideas for over 40 years! I'm forever grateful to be able to indulge my various hobbies!

Foreword by Steve Perryman
(Tottenham Hotspur 1967–86)

TONY'S PATH into professional football wasn't the traditional route. He arrived at Tottenham Hotspur from non-league Goole Town and was a breath of fresh air. Tony was not a jinky-type winger but an athletic runner with the ball and he brought a genuine work ethic to the team.

Tony was a very good player on the left side of midfield. Players wanted to be in the team but not on the left. We tended to go through Ossie Ardiles, Ricky Villa, Glenn Hoddle and Micky Hazard in the middle. Whoever was on the left saw themselves as a bit-part player but Tony fitted the position perfectly. He was happy to play where selected, was naturally two-footed and turned the spot into his own. He'd pick up the ball and attack the full-back but also defend our goal, protecting Chris Hughton. We were a great team made up of different styles, attitudes and personalities.

Tony was intelligent, interesting and down to earth. He was a straightforward-talking Yorkshireman like Bill Nicholson and Keith Burkinshaw. They were all from the same ilk. Tony was proud to pull on the white shirt with cockerel on the breast of Tottenham and I always appreciated what he brought to the side. A manager picks you and captain rates you. We continually talked up Tony because the press and supporters didn't do it enough.

Tony came into an emerging team. We'd been relegated to the Second Division, managed to get back up and had been reformed with Ossie and Ricky. Steve Archibald and Garth Crooks were then brought in to score the goals. But as with any great team, you ask yourself have you got enough on the left and right, have you enough height, pace and desire to succeed? It comes down to the manager to fit all these attributes together. Tony brought his work rate, talent and consistency to the team. Opponents didn't like playing against Glenn because of his skill, Ossie because of his dash, and Tony because of his non-stop drive, energy and purpose, without being flash.

I provided width at right-back but we had genuine width with Tony and Chris on the left. We were balanced with Tony in the side. He chipped in with goals, which was great, and provided crosses for our strikers to get their share of goals. We used a moving set piece, which was a major play for us. I'd get out wide very early because normal left-wingers could be lazy. If a cross came in I knew that Ray Clemence would take it. I'd be on the touchline quicker than my opponent, would look long and cut it into Glenn, who would hit Tony. Teams knew about the tactic but found it very hard to stop.

I played in two very good Tottenham teams. The early 70s side, I was the legs to get the ball to someone who could play. I was the captain of the 80s team and enjoyed our success more because I was more of an influence. Tony was part of a very special side that won the FA Cup twice and the UEFA Cup. Tony had a consistent, purposeful, no frills, 'get on with it' attitude. I loved his mindset. Tony was a great signing for the club.

Foreword by John Kaye

(West Bromwich Albion 1963–71, Hull City 1971–74, Hull City manager 1974–77)

CHRIS ARRIVED at Hull City during the 1973/74 close season and did well under manager Terry Neill. We played together briefly before injury ended my playing days. When I took over from Terry in September 74 the team was struggling at the wrong end of the table but the lads battled away and got into the top eight. It was a great achievement and we enjoyed some outstanding results. Boothferry Park was bouncing when we defeated promotion favourites Manchester United and Sunderland. Chris was part of that team and a dangerous player. The following season I put in five or six young kids and we started off like a house on fire. We were up with the leaders but unfortunately fell away.

Chris was an individualist. He had a step-over trick to get away from opponents, which was a big advantage to us when we were on the attack, but I wasn't so keen when he did it on the edge of our own penalty area, as it was risky! Chris played wide on the left, he was very skilful on the ball and could easily get past an opponent. Chris was two-footed so able to cut inside opponents or take them on down the wing. Chris fitted into the team and his step-over made him popular with supporters.

Billy Bremner brought invaluable experience to the club when I brought him to Hull in September 1976. Chris was delighted because he'd been with Billy at Leeds for a number of years. It clearly made a big impact on him. I faced that Leeds side of the early 70s many times and they were a top team. Chris joined Leeds as an apprentice, trained with top professionals and made the first team, which was no easy task. Billy's enthusiasm on the training pitch was fantastic, he brought a lot to the side on and off the pitch. All the lads benefitted.

Chris really enjoyed the skills part of training but wasn't as keen on the running sessions! He tended to let his ability on the ball do the talking for him but was brilliant for us going forward. I couldn't fault Chris off the field. He was dry-witted, funny and one of the lads who got the banter going in the dressing room and on away trips, especially with his partner-in-crime, Peter 'Stretch' Fletcher. Chris was an easy-going lad, never gave me any trouble, was great to have in the squad and enjoyed playing football over a long professional career throughout the Football League.

Introduction by David Saffer

BROTHERS HAVE graced English Football League and Premier League clubs for decades. When the game first caught my imagination in the mid-1960s the most famous siblings were Bobby and Jack Charlton. The ensuing years have seen many footballing brothers make the grade, including members of the Clarke, Greenhoff, Latchford, Fashanu, Allen, Stein, Wallace, Neville, Ferdinand and Touré families on the domestic, European and international stage.

However, the probability of siblings playing professional football is rare. Football academies are commonplace but only a tiny percentage of starry-eyed youngsters are rewarded with a full-time contract. For one family member to come through the highly competitive academy system is incredible, for two or more is astonishing. Making the grade isn't solely down to talent. Injuries, squad strength, managerial changes, being in the right place at the right time and Lady Luck all come into play at different times. Chris and Tony Galvin experienced all these aspects and more in their respective footballing journeys.

The story behind *Galvinised!* goes back to a countryside pub chat with Chris near his home in Huddersfield in the spring of 2016, when he recalled his frustrations at trying to break into Don Revie's legendary Leeds United team of the early 70s. Chris also made an intriguing remark that at crucial points of his career he made 'bad choices' compared to his kid brother Tony, who made the 'right choices'. After a few moments it dawned on me that I had seen both play ... Chris for a 'Super Leeds XI' in Eddie Gray's testimonial at Elland Road in 1979 and Tony for Tottenham Hotspur in two FA Cup Finals at Wembley Stadium in the early 80s.

Chris, the elder Galvin by five years, was a tad taken aback by my enthusiastic ramblings about two brothers enjoying a professional career being a noteworthy tale to tell. But he agreed, nonetheless, to arrange a meeting with Tony at the same pub a few weeks later. Hearing anecdotes from Chris and Tony – who between them enjoyed representative success at schoolboy level in football, rugby union and cricket – about playing in non-league football, the Football League, European and international competition convinced me further to document their experiences. A crucial factor was Tony insisting that any publication must be about both brothers.

Chris was a talented schoolboy footballer when Revie signed him on apprentice professional terms in 1967. After a European Cup debut against Ferencváros during the 1969/70 season, Chris was a regular member of Revie's elite squad for three seasons before a lack of game time took him to Hull City, where he unveiled the 'Galvin shuffle' to Tigers fans. A six-year stint included a loan period at York City but a chronic knee problem threatened his playing days, before the collapse of a transfer to South Melbourne Hellas in Australia made him a free agent, much to the chagrin of Hull. Chris joined Stockport County to complete his Football League pyramid trek before enjoying a final hurrah in Hong Kong, where he played for a representative XI.

INTRODUCTION BY DAVID SAFFER

Over a 15-year career Chris experienced the highs and lows of the beautiful game, from playing at the Camp Nou, Old Trafford and Anfield to slugging it out at stadia no longer in the Football League, such as Hereford United's Edgar Street and Bury's Gigg Lane. Overcoming plenty of challenges, including arguments with his father regarding performances and an ongoing frustration over a lack of pace, Chris lined up alongside Leeds legends of a golden era, then battled away against hard-working journeymen footballers and legends of the game, including Bobby Moore and George Best, where he displayed his skills in front of appreciative fans.

Tony played for Goole Town FC while studying Russian at the University of Hull. Tottenham were pushing for promotion to the First Division when they snapped up Tony, who was completing a training course at Trent Polytechnic, after he impressed legendary manager Bill Nicholson while he was on a scouting mission to Buxton in January 1978. Tony broke into Keith Burkinshaw's legendary team of the early 80s on the left wing, enjoying FA Cup and UEFA Cup success, while cementing cult hero status. Domestically he faced world-class players, including Kenny Dalglish, Brian Robson, Graeme Souness and Gary Lineker in their heyday. And there were derby clashes against Arsenal, with Tony Adams and David O'Leary in their last line of defence. He played alongside Glenn Hoddle and Ossie Ardiles in midfield, with strikers Steve Archibald and Garth Crooks scoring goals galore. The great Diego Maradona even lined up for Spurs on an unforgettable night at White Hart Lane!

Eoin Hand gave Tony his Republic of Ireland debut against the Netherlands in 1982. A regular for much of the decade, under Jack Charlton he played in his nation's first major tournament at the European Championship finals in 1988, when they stunned

England and just missed out on qualification to the semi-final stage. Tony pitted his wits against all-time greats, including Ruud Gullit, Marco van Basten, Marco Tardelli, Paolo Rossi, Andoni Zubizarreta and José Antonio Camacho in a historic period for his country. After a decade at The Lane, during which he played every minute of seven Spurs appearances at Wembley, Tony ended his career with spells at Sheffield Wednesday and Swindon Town.

Football-daft kids around the globe dream of becoming professional footballers. The Galvin brothers lived that dream from 20-a-side games and kickabouts with their father to modest and iconic stadia of world football.

Chapter 1

Football-Crazy Kids

CHRIS GALVIN was born on 24 November 1951, in Huddersfield. He was the elder son of Muriel and Thomas Galvin and sport featured in his life from an early age. Growing up, his younger brother Tony would join in at every opportunity with his dad or friends.

Chris said: 'From as far back as I remember, I wanted to be a footballer. My parents were really supportive. Dad was a good amateur footballer and I enjoyed watching him play, but my main memories were having a kickabout with him and Tony in the local park. I recall having a Wembley plastic football, which was popular with kids from my era. Dad would buy me one every other week because it quickly burst with the amount we played! I'd thwack it against a wall for hours and take the ball with me everywhere in an old string bag hoping to find some mates for a game. Often it would be as many as 20-a-side until dark.

'At school we played in the playground every free moment and I was a regular for St Joseph's Primary School under-11 junior football team for a couple of years after breaking into the side at nine years of age. We played on a Saturday morning and to me there was nothing more exciting. It was brilliant catching a bus, carrying my boots and kit into town, and arriving at the ground to play a match. It didn't matter who we were playing, it was the highlight of my weekend. The team were not very successful and I was not happy with a losing streak, but one season everything came together as we won the Huddersfield School Junior Cup.

'I've no idea why I chose Wolverhampton Wanderers when it came to following a football team. Maybe it was the long club name that captured my imagination, but whatever the reason I followed their fortunes and Wolves were a great side in the 1950s. England skipper Billy Wright was captain, but Jimmy Murray, Peter Broadbent and Norman Deeley grabbed the headlines most weeks as the main goalscorers. Broadbent, though, was my hero and for football writers of the day the driving force of the team in midfield.'

Whatever the background to Chris's adoption of Wolves as his team, his allegiance emerged when they were trailblazers in Europe in addition to being a major power at home. He recalled: 'Wolves won the First Division title three times in the 50s, including back-to-back seasons, which at the time seemed the norm for a young, football-mad kid. They also won the FA Cup, defeating Blackburn Rovers at Wembley in 1960, which was a really big deal. Cup Final day was the biggest game of the season for every club because it was the only match on live television. Kids nowadays will find that astonishing, with wall-to-wall coverage, but it was a very different world.

'During this period Wolves also played prestigious friendlies against top European teams before the first European Cup competition began. Maybe glamour matches against the likes of Honvéd sparked my support for the club, but they were a top team to follow apart from the likes of Manchester United's Busby Babes. I was too young to comprehend the enormity of the Munich air disaster in 1958, but Matt Busby's legacy lives on today, which is absolutely right because that team was packed with talent. I played against Bobby Charlton and Bill Foulkes, who both survived the crash. Big Jack, Bobby's brother, was at Leeds throughout my time at the club, but rarely mentioned the tragedy.'

But then Chris came up against a barrier that stood in the way of his enjoyment of football and his potential progress in it: 'Playing football was my life, but after my 11-plus I started at St Gregory's Roman Catholic Grammar School, who played only rugby union. I was really unhappy. Not playing football regularly was unthinkable, but that was the situation, so I very reluctantly had to accept it. I made the rugby team as a scrum-half and also represented Yorkshire under-15s. I was something of an all-rounder when it came to sport because I was also a useful cricketer, but it was really tough not being able to play football. The biggest problem was that there were no local football clubs for my age group. In fact, the youngest were under-16, but I was determined to play any football, so my parents let me join Central Lads' Youth Club. My chances of getting into the side, though, were slim, but I thought I'd give it a go.

'I don't recall whether it was a surprise to make the team within six months, but playing at this level at such a young age helped me to become a decent footballer. I grew up quickly and realised that a hard tackle didn't do you any real harm, you just have to get on with it. Looking back, this benefitted me. I'm convinced it's a reason why many kids nowadays don't come through. They give up far too quickly. Kids play under-11s, under-12s, under-15s and so on, but don't have the challenge of facing bigger, stronger, older, faster, more skilful players. We produce mediocre players and this is part of the reason. It does no harm playing tougher opponents because the best will adapt.

'I played for Central Lads until I was 15, but can't remember how a chance came to play for Huddersfield Schools. I also made the schoolboy cricket team and went on tour with the Yorkshire Federation team, but football was my first-choice sport. Someone must have spotted my potential at football and told selectors that I could play a bit because my schoolteacher rang to see if I'd attend a county trial. Of course, I wanted to and did enough to get selected for the under-16 team. I'd played left-wing mainly at school, but developed my right foot by kicking a ball for hours against a wall at home.

'Playing at this level meant that scouts were at games and we had a good side so you just hoped to get spotted. Invites from clubs soon arrived to train and play an odd game, so I obviously had something. Huddersfield Town invited me to train with them twice a week at Beck Lane. This gave me the chance to develop as a player. Among the lads in our group was Frank Worthington, who stood out even at 15 and went on to become a legend at Town and Leicester City. Frank had a long career in the game and liked to entertain the crowd like Rodney Marsh, Stan Bowles, Tony Currie and Duncan McKenzie also did in this era. A transfer to Liverpool famously fell through but Frank did make the full England side when Ron Greenwood was manager. The training sessions at Town carried on through the 1966 World Cup tournament so I missed the midweek games on television but like everyone followed England's progress. And when the final came around I was glued to the television at home with the family as Bobby Moore led England to glory.

'When Leeds United offered me a trial, it was a no-brainer. Leeds were the biggest club in the area and among the best in the Football League. The club put me up at a little hotel behind the City Hall and we played a number of games during a few days. It was exciting, yet really nerve-racking. This was the first time I'd played against lads of my age. They seemed five yards quicker, which was a shock to my system, but I must have done okay because Leeds invited me back for further trials. Again, everything seemed to go fine, even though there was still a pace issue in my mind. Among the lads were some really fast kids from all over the country, including some who had played England, Wales and Scotland schools' internationals. I knew they'd be quick, but it surprised me that, no matter how much I tried, they were that bit faster. Lots of lads took part and, if they didn't come up to scratch, others were ready to try out. Leeds seemed keen, but I got a "Dear Chris" letter telling me they would not be taking things further. It was a huge blow at the time, but I didn't have a chance to feel down because out of the blue I received an invite from Bolton Wanderers.'

Tony Galvin was born in Huddersfield on 12 July 1956. Less than five years younger than his brother Chris, football formed a memorable part of their early childhood.

Tony recalled: 'Dad would take us out for a kickabout or to play cricket on playing fields not far from our home most Sundays and also on summer evenings. He was really encouraging, insisting we play at every opportunity. Dad loved his sport. On a family day trip, we always found time for football or cricket. Mum was happy to sit in the car catching up on some reading while we got on with it. They are really happy memories. The early 60s were a time of innocence, you could play on the streets without any real concern. We'd put our jumpers or coats down for goalposts and kick off. It was about 20-a-side and we'd play for hours. There were no referees, VAR, iPads, computers or satellite television – just football. It was special, the norm, nothing distracted us from having fun. Chris was the keener of the two of us, especially when

I was quite young. I loved playing but football was not the most important thing in my life. Some days I was happy to stay in with Mum, just playing, reading comics or watching television. There would usually be a Bob Hope or Elvis Presley film worth watching. I especially loved Laurel and Hardy. Also, there was not much sport on television in those days!'

Tony celebrated his tenth birthday a day after England began their quest to win the World Cup in 1966 with a 0-0 draw against Uruguay at Wembley. The Boys of 66 and tournament left an indelible impression because he insisted: 'The excitement following England was incredible. After getting through the group stage, then a fiery quarter-final encounter with Argentina and a semi-final win against Portugal, my only thought for the final was England defeating West Germany to win the World Cup. On the day our street was deserted as everyone packed around a television. The game was really exciting. There was the tension of England holding on at 2-1 before the last-minute Germany equaliser and then extra time when Geoff Hurst grabbed his hat-trick. I was never a good loser and got very upset when Germany equalised. Was Hurst's second a goal? Did the whole of the ball cross the line? I didn't care. England captain Bobby Moore lifted the World Cup after the final whistle. That's all that mattered. We ran outside to celebrate and had a huge kickabout until dark. England's win in 66 was an unforgettable experience.

'One of the disappointing things about that World Cup, though, was the treatment dished out to Pelé. Dad had told us about this amazing Brazilian footballer who had two excellent feet, was very quick, a wonderful header of the ball and scored goals of breathtaking brilliance. But Pelé in every game had little protection from the referees and was kicked out of the competition, which was a great shame. However, Pelé and Brazil got their revenge in 1970.

What a magnificent side they were! I loved that team. The other person who took the eye in 66 was Portugal's Eusébio, a powerful and stylish player who scored goals for fun. His performances were outstanding, especially the quarter-final against North Korea. Portugal were 3-0 down against the underdogs when Eusébio dragged his country back in front with four of the five goals. It was an unbelievable display, reminiscent of how Ronaldo often leads his country in key games all these years later. His impact on and off the pitch when Portugal won the Euro 2016 championships in France was incredible. As for his goalscoring record for various clubs and Portugal, it's astonishing. I doubt it will ever be matched.

'Dad's favourite English players were Jimmy Greaves and Bobby Charlton. Unfortunately, Jimmy, for me England's greatest-ever striker, got injured in the last group game against France and was unable to reclaim his place in the final, which was a tragedy for him. However, Bobby had a fantastic World Cup, scoring brilliant goals against Mexico and Portugal. Dad loved Charlton, not only because he scored sensational goals, but he could shoot with both right and left feet. That enabled him to throw a dummy and go past defenders to either side. Bobby was a joy to watch running at opponents from deep positions.

'I loved watching England winning the World Cup on home soil in 1966. Could this achievement be equalled or bettered? When the 1970 Mexico World Cup came around, I had a better understanding of football. England had a great manager in Sir Alf Ramsey and an excellent squad. Hopes were high. The Brazil clash in the group stage was a classic. Gordon Banks' save from Pelé was legendary and Moore showed why he was a world-class defender. Pelé and Moore embracing at full time is a timeless image of a classic encounter. But the quarter-final versus West Germany would go down as one of the most disappointing days for an England supporter. England should have won, having been 2-0 up. Alan Mullery and Martin Peters scored that day. Fast forward many years and the Germany clash came up whilst I was working with both as a hospitality host at the old White Hart Lane. I asked them what it was like to play in that game and was fascinated to listen to these two England legends discussing the merits of Alf's decision to replace Charlton with Colin Bell, having just conceded a goal. Both had massive respect for Bobby and Sir Alf but had differing opinions as to whether it was the right decision with the score at 2-1. I listened intently to what they had to say and kept quiet! Brazil lifted the trophy for a third time in a sensational performance against Italy, capped off by Carlos Alberto's goal in a 4-1 win.'

Tony's formative years of education were at St Joseph's Primary School and, as with Chris, he was a star in the football team. During his last year the school team defeated Bradley Voluntary in the Huddersfield School Junior Cup Final. St Joseph's also won the under-11 section A title. The double team were dubbed 'The Invincibles' in local papers.

But the times they were a-changing for the Galvin family because, Tony added: 'Mum and Dad decided to buy their first house when I moved to St Gregory's in 1967. This was a big deal and major commitment for my parents. They paid about £2,500 for the house – a pittance these days, but a fortune back then, and they lived there for the rest of their days. I'm sure they were very proud that they managed to leave their council house and buy a property. Mum and Dad worked hard to better themselves and provide Chris and me with a wonderful upbringing in a really nice neighbourhood. They were great parents who wanted the best for their kids. When we moved from Dalton to Waterloo, I tried to keep in touch with friends, but inevitably you move on to a new chapter. I had to catch two buses then take a short walk to school. I loved my bit of freedom. But actually, there was no option because Dad was at the local bus depot and Mum worked on school dinners, so both left early. Breakfast was left on the table. I locked up and began my journey to school. When I think back, how many 11-year-olds would do that nowadays?

'I've always enjoyed my own company. I've a few close friends but only a handful from my football days. Chris was far more sociable, always going out and having a good time in his fancy Ford Capri. Chris, though, was and still is a generous person. He loved his Capris and gave Dad enough money to buy one of his own. Chris was doing well at Leeds and wanted his parents to benefit from his success. I also benefitted because a window sill in his bedroom was covered in loose change, which Chris seemed to discard. Mum told me to leave it and generally I did. However, on occasion Chris would ask me to buy Mum and Dad some chocolate or other goodies and I could keep whatever was left over. For an 11-year-old, loose change was a small fortune. Well, I thought so!'

Tony followed Chris to St Gregory's after passing his 11-plus. An all-rounder at sport, there was no school football team, but Tony played stand-off for the rugby union team for three seasons.

'St Gregory's held their own against strong grammar schools. Invariably, I kicked the ball too much, but rugby did toughen me up. There was great camaraderie travelling around West Yorkshire. We were not allowed to talk back to a referee. But when it came to football, I had a problem with referees and always argued. It is amazing, looking back, that I never got sent off more often. I had a big mouth and had a habit of talking back. It's ironic that later in life I trained to be a referee. It turned out to be a disastrous move. I'm still close friends with Stephen Miskell and Stephen Kenny from my junior school. From St Gregory's, I still keep in touch with Gerard Quinn, Chris Helliwell, Gerard Wood and Tony Ward.

'Football was more popular than rugby away from school. With mates there were five-a-sides at our local YMCA gym and we eventually joined St Columcille in a Halifax junior league. A couple of games still stand out. Playing in defence against Greetland we were getting hammered, when I tried to control the ball under no pressure in my penalty box but it squirted off my foot into the goal. I am pretty sure this is my only own goal! Then in a match against Wareham Green I received a huge whack on my shins when I went into a tackle. I had no shin pads on and it really hurt. Fortunately, Gerard Quinn's dad, Joe, was in attendance with his copy of the *News of the World*. Joe dragged me to the side, rightly told me off for not wearing shin pads and proceeded to gather his newspaper up into two separate rolls. Joe told me in no uncertain terms to put them down my socks, stop crying and get back on the field. I'm pretty sure we won that game. I owe Joe one after that! Chris still thinks teams I played for always won, which is nonsense. Apart from St Columcille, who invariably lost, my worst schoolboy footballing experience was playing for Moldgreen Youth Club under-16s when we were thumped 14-0 by Upperthong Youth Club one Saturday afternoon. We were distraught, but picked ourselves up to fight, and probably lose, another day!'

St Gregory's was renowned for its educational and sporting standards. History teacher Tony Tomlinson taught Tony days after starting in September 1967 and was later seconded by head of PE Peter Loraine to help with the transition from rugby union to football as the boys' main sport. The under-15s won the local schools' cup in their inaugural 1970/71 football campaign. Tony recalled: 'Tony was a great football coach, and Pete instilled in all of us a sense of self-discipline and fair play. He also ensured we engaged in all sports.'

The *Yorkshire Post* covered the football exploits of St Gregory's during the season, including when they played in the Crowther Cup Final against Rawthorpe at Huddersfield Town's Leeds Road on 22 April 1971. Tony captained the team, scoring twice in a 3-0 win. The match followed Town losing to Wolves in a First Division fixture.

Tony remembered: 'For a kid beginning his football journey, to watch your local team play and then take part in a cup final on the same ground was amazing. Running out was brilliant. A few supporters and Town players stayed behind to watch, which was great, but the pitch was a mudheap. It was impossible to play flowing football. I played left side of midfield and struggled to get the ball to our strikers. I doubt anyone was impressed by the standard of football, but we won so it was a memorable occasion. My overriding memory was: "I'm playing at Leeds Road and getting a cup winners' medal. This is all right. I'll have some of that!" It was also memorable because Mum and Dad were there for the game.'

Cricket came to the fore during the summer and Tony was a regular at school, represented Yorkshire Schools and also joined Hall Bower Cricket Club in the Huddersfield League.

He recalled: 'Dad had captained Hall Bower for years, winning the championship, and made sure we were both well-schooled in cricket. Our sessions were competitive. In fact, I used to get upset if I got bowled out by Dad or Chris and would occasionally throw a tantrum, feeling they were ganging up on me but I made the first team at 14 and played against some formidable cricketers. It meant a lot following in their footsteps.'

The highlight for Tony was playing in a Roses battle at Old Trafford on 14 July 1972. The teams were:

Lancashire Schools XI: Mooney, Allen, Bolton, Bradshaw, Brambles, Foster, Gintry, Lewis, Peters, Ritchie, Sherlock.

Yorkshire Schools XI: Mather, Ramage, Barrett, Baxter, Stevenson, Nicholson, Galvin, Parkinson, Welch, Kirk, Brannigan.

He recalled: 'This was the only time I played on a Test cricket ground and it was an amazing experience. I took an impressive over-the-shoulder catch to dismiss a batsman and, of course, Yorkshire won! Born and bred in Yorkshire meant the summer was about cricket. I enjoyed playing but my technique needed to move to a higher level. Graham Stevenson and Alan Ramage played for Yorkshire. Graham also represented England. Alan also played professional football for Middlesbrough and Derby County. Chris Balderstone was another stalwart for Yorkshire and Leicestershire who played for England. And he played for Huddersfield Town and Carlisle United. Successful footballers and cricketers often demonstrate similar qualities – a belief in your own ability, lack of fear and a desire to work hard.'

During the summer of '72, Hall Bower reached the final of the Huddersfield League's Sykes Cup but Tony missed the big match due to a school trip to the Soviet Union. Hall Bower won, which was memorable for the village club. Tony recalled: 'Mr Chirgwin was an excellent Russian teacher. The school trip for O-level and A-level pupils was to Moscow and Leningrad – now St Petersburg. The Soviet Union were always in the media so participating could broaden our outlook. Not all of our class could go as it cost our parents a small fortune. Schoolmates joked that we were communists, but they were just jealous. I was so fortunate

Mum and Dad forked out to pay for the trip. It was the first time I had been abroad. Mind you, it was '72 so I wasn't alone there. I loved the passion older Russians had for their country. They had been through hell in World War Two and wanted to communicate to us that they hated the Germans but liked the British. The old buildings were rich in history and splendidly decorated. We visited the tourist sites. My abiding memory was enormous queues at Lenin's tomb, St Basil's Cathedral, the Winter Palace and so on. However, we bypassed them as we were foreign tourists! The locals accepted their wait was longer than ours. They were really proud we wanted to see Lenin in his tomb. We are indebted to the Soviet Union for their efforts during the war. Churchill said as much. Anyway, the trip inspired me to continue my Russian studies.'

Not every school ran A-level options in this era. Tony's choices included an unusual subject because, he explained: 'A number of pupils began careers in various industries, but I was not ready for work. Studying English, French and Russian seemed a more natural path. Very few grammar schools had a Russian option. The Soviet Union was viewed by the British government as an arch-enemy of the Cold War so there was a move in education to gain a better understanding of Soviet culture and history. We were told that the civil service was recruiting Russian graduates so there was a possible career path. But that was not my main motivation, Russian to me just seemed a logical choice.'

St Gregory's reached the Yorkshire Cup section quarter-finals of the English School Cup in 1972/73. Tony also made the Yorkshire Schools team and played in a soccer tournament in Skegness in April 1973. England School scouts attended; however, he failed to make the national team. Tony, though, was getting noticed and trained with the apprentices at Huddersfield Town during the school holidays. But it mystified him: 'Town's youth trainer took the sessions. It seemed like a good idea at the time but was an awful experience, primarily because none of the apprentices talked to me. I was treated, or so I thought, as an outsider or a possible threat. After two days I went home and told Mum I wouldn't be going back. She said fine. I am not sure that Dad was too pleased but I preferred my school environment. Ian Greaves was Town's manager at the time, and I'd later get to know him, as a good friend of mine, Gerard Quinn, married his daughter, Christine. It's a small world!

'I later played for Leeds United's youth team against Huddersfield at Beck Lane. Chris was at Elland Road so maybe they thought they'd take a look at me. A club official told Dad I'd played well, but was too old to be an apprentice. I then turned down a trial at Sheffield United. Chris being at Leeds did not spark me into aspiring to be a footballer. Although football was a huge part of my life, captaining Yorkshire Schools for the 1973/74 season was enough for me at the time.'

St Gregory's merged with St Augustine's Roman Catholic Secondary Modern School to form All Saints Comprehensive School for Tony's final academic year. Sport again featured heavily. All Saints reached the Yorkshire final of the English School Cup but, alas, Holgate Grammar School won 7-6 on penalties after a 2-2 draw at Dodworth Miners' Welfare. Tony starred for Yorkshire Schools and impressed in England trial matches, receiving a call-up for the Football Association's International Centenary Shield. England played Scotland at Manchester United's Old Trafford ground. He then faced Wales at Ninian Park, Cardiff.

He recounted: 'I loved the experience but it's ironic that I went on to play for the Republic of Ireland. You could represent a country at school level then switch at senior but that was for the future. As I approached A-levels, my mindset was not to be a footballer. Football League clubs did not want grammar school players. All the best lads were signed by 15 years of age. However, after I broke into the professional game, I never understood why A-level pupils were not viewed as good enough. You are limiting your chances of discovering talented players. I came through the non-league route and was not the only one. You only have to look at the likes of Steve Heighway, Ian Wright, Jamie Vardy and others to see that. Scouts nowadays attend games at all ages. My exams went well but I had no idea what to do in terms of a future job so took the most obvious option to study Russian. The University of Hull had a solid reputation and Chris was playing for Hull City, so it seemed a sound idea. There was a new adventure ahead and it wasn't far from home.'

Chapter 2

Apprentice Dreams

AT JUST 15 years of age Chris Galvin decided that becoming a professional footballer was to be his main aim in life and he was fortunate enough to have options available. For example, after missing out on a chance to impress Leeds United, Chris travelled to Bolton Wanderers with a view to joining them. He also had a surprising chance to join his hometown club, Huddersfield Town. Both were in the Second Division.

He explained: 'St Gregory's wanted me to join the sixth form, but could not stop me leaving if an opportunity came up after my O-levels. Trials at Leeds had not worked out, but suddenly Bolton and Town approached me. I don't recall Bolton ever watching me or how they invited me to Burnden Park, whether by letter or a phone call, but I went down with Dad and was allowed to bring Tony along. I really enjoyed the experience. Bolton must have seen me play because they offered apprentice terms without a trial. There was no money flying around like the modern game, just standard terms of £8 a week! The Sunday afternoon after the offer, Town's manager Tom Johnston turned up at my grandparents' house out of the blue. He had heard that Bolton had offered me terms and was adamant I join Town as I'd been training there. Johnston offered me the same terms but was forceful in his manner, which did take Dad and my grandad by surprise. We told him that we'd get back to him in a day or so. After he'd gone, it didn't me long to dismiss Town's offer.

'Bolton did everything to impress me and I was ready to join. However, Leeds manager Don Revie came around to our house and offered me an apprenticeship. I've no idea how it came about but it was hard not to be impressed. Leeds had yet to win a major honour, but they were a top team. Young players such as Gary Sprake, Paul Reaney, Terry Cooper, Paul Madeley, Norman Hunter, Peter Lorimer, Jimmy Greenhoff, Rod Belfitt, Eddie Gray and Terry Hibbitt had all broken through to the first team. Sprake and Hunter were internationals. Don explained how Leeds would develop me as a footballer. I thought I'd be among the next group to get a shot at the big time. Dad, though, thought I'd be better signing for Bolton because I'd get more first-team opportunities. I knew it would be tough at Leeds, but what kid wouldn't want to join a top club? My major concern was how quick some lads had been at trials. I lacked natural pace, but put it to the back of my mind. Should I sign for Leeds or Bolton? I was headstrong and believed I could make it. If you think you're good enough, and Revie did, then go for it. I joined the ground staff at Elland Road in July 1967.

'I made the short bus journey to Elland Road every day and was really excited to be with first-year apprentices Sean O'Neill, Robert Malt, Peter Hearnshaw, Andrew Danskin and Colin Smith. But if there were any thoughts of glamour, they were soon knocked out of you. Alongside second-year apprentices we cleaned the first-team and second-team players' boots every morning and then made sure kit was laid out in the dressing room. When the first-team squad went out to train, we swept the stands from top to bottom, got rid of rubbish and helped the groundsman. It was pure graft. After tidying the dressing rooms, we trained in the afternoon. Occasionally during the week we'd train with the first team as an incentive to improve our skills. In the winter, because of frost, we also cleared hay to the side of the pitch before a game and then put it back after the match to stop the pitch from freezing. That particular task ended when undersoil heating was installed, which was a relief. Duties were not difficult, but they were boring, although there was great banter with the lads. We just got on with it.'

Chris discovered that the coaching set-up at Leeds was rigorous and intense. He recalled: 'Cyril Partridge ran the junior squad and Syd Owen coached us at training sessions. Syd was an old-fashioned centre-half who played and captained Luton Town in a long career at the club. He was a hard, uncompromising coach and some of the lads felt that Syd was a bully because he kept on at them, but it didn't bother me. Syd did what I needed at the time; he'd stay late and really pushed me. Syd was genuinely keen, but you couldn't crack a joke with him, although he did tell us that the scars on his forehead were from heading a ball in the days when it had laces! The game, of course, has moved on in terms of understanding the dangers of repetitive heading of a football and the impact it can have on a player's health in later life. This is great for the welfare of modern-day footballers.

'Discipline was really important at Leeds, and Syd was a fanatic. Coaching appeared to be his life. I didn't particularly like him, but he was there to do a job. While natural pace was a problem, I made up for it in other areas. I'd continually practise passing and control. I was two-footed, which I thought all footballers should be, but that was not the case. I'd spend hours with Syd on drills. Control-pass, control-pass over and over again. Every afternoon he'd drive 30- and 40-yard balls at me to drive back at him. It was tough. It was also obvious that weaker lads mentally were not going to make it. Leeds, though, were no different from other top clubs with a youth set-up. It was a strict regime and Syd could be intimidating, but I never thought of packing it in. My mindset was that I deserved a chance. If you trained hard and progressed, Revie offered you a full-time contract at 17 years of age. You had a chance to break into the reserves and then go from there. I was desperate to make it despite my nagging doubt about pace. After training I'd do sprinting drills with Madeley to try to find an extra yard, but did struggle. The lads, though, never had a go at me, but it gnawed away. This continued throughout my career.

'We played on a Saturday morning in the Northern Intermediate League at Fullerton Park and then had first-team duties if there was a home fixture. Two lads would be on dressing-room duty in case a player needed something. Another was on hand for match officials. When opposition teams arrived, often they looked beaten, players would be white as a sheet and they hadn't kicked off! That's how intimidating it was to play Leeds at Elland Road at that particular time.'

Chris was making his way and broke into the reserves by November 1967. The first team would soon make history by winning the League Cup at Wembley in March 1968. Terry Cooper scored the only goal for a famous triumph. Chris recalled: 'Revie made sure we all got a chance to be at the game. I was allowed tickets for my parents and Tony to attend the match. I travelled down with the other apprentices, squad players and club staff on the day. It wasn't entertaining but we won and that was all that mattered. Around the club there was a sense that more trophies would follow. It was an exciting time.'

Chris witnessed many intense battles against top teams at Elland Road, including a league fixture against Tottenham

Hotspur on 17 April 1968. The *Daily Mirror* journalist Frank McGhee was at the midweek clash. It was an important match for both clubs with Leeds challenging for the title and Tottenham pushing for a Fairs Cup place. Spurs had beaten Leeds 2-1 on Good Friday at White Hart Lane so Revie's team were looking for revenge. Leeds dominated the match and just past the hour, after Pat Jennings conceded a penalty, Lorimer converted the kick. Alan Gilzean was dismissed ten minutes later for a kick at Cooper.

McGhee recorded the key passage of play:

> With their spot-kick expert, inside-left Johnny Giles, absent – he limped off in the 15th minute with Greenhoff substituting – Lorimer stepped up to take it. He waited through a nerve-testing 60 seconds, first because the ball had been blasted angrily away by Spurs skipper Dave Mackay and then because Mr Baldwin had to resort to threats to clear any lingering Tottenham rebels from the area. But he hit it so crisply and, although Jennings got a hand to it, he could not absorb enough of its force to prevent a goal.

As for the sending off, McGhee penned:

> Any chance Spurs might have had of battling back disappeared in the 73rd minute when Gilzean was dismissed. It was so blatant, so senseless it can be explained only as perhaps a lingering remnant of simmering ill feeling between the two men that started in the first half when Cooper was booked for a foul.

Chris recalled: 'It was a really feisty game. Gilzean was sent off for a dreadful challenge on Cooper when the ball was down the other end of the pitch. He looked relieved to be sent off! Greaves hardly had a kick that day.'

With Chris on the Elland Road ground staff, his family attended first-team matches. The Tottenham clash was one of the earliest that Tony recalls: 'Revie built some team. Tottenham had won the FA Cup a year earlier and had star players. I was in the West Stand with Dad and it was an exciting match. United outplayed Tottenham yet won only 1-0. Jennings was the bravest player that night, but the match is remembered for Gilzean being sent off. I'd get to know all the Tottenham lads and asked Alan about this match at a charity event. "Cooper for no reason caught me late with a tackle, the referee bottled it so I had to do something about it!" he recalled. Watching Leeds was brilliant and the atmosphere was fantastic.'

Leeds were by now an established European club and received invitations to play in international youth tournaments. Chris played in a couple and enjoyed an outstanding tournament in Lille, France. There was also a surprise approach from Italy for his services.

He explained: 'We didn't let in a goal during my first competition, but failed to reach the semi-finals because the eventual winners Sporting Lisbon knocked us out by a corner kick, which was crazy, but those were the tournament rules. In Lille we played well, but lost to AC Milan in the final. We attended a ceremony at the end of the tournament when they awarded the player of the tournament. I was sitting near Terry Yorath when the presenter announced the winner in French. I wasn't really paying attention when Terry stood up and went to collect the award, but then realised it was not for him. The presenter came up to me and told me I'd won it. The look of disbelief on Terry's face was priceless!

'I was chatting with Don in the changing rooms shortly after we got back from Lille. On his way out, Don turned around and told me about an approach from AC Milan. They had put in a bid after seeing me play in the tournament. I've no idea whether there was money involved, but he told me the club had turned it down. I was gobsmacked and nodded okay. I thought it was the norm. That was the end of the matter. Milan's approach gave me a boost of confidence but, looking back, I should have questioned it. I'd not been offered a full-time contract, but there were no agents. I was on my own. A club controlled the players so you accepted what was going on. Players left when they told you to leave. There was far too much power for a club then, but now players and agents have the power.'

In addition, Chris hit the headlines for Leeds United in the FA Youth Cup during the 1968/69 season as the first team battled for the First Division title. The cup run started with a 5-0 victory at Darlington before a hard-fought 2-1 replay win at home against Sheffield United. Leeds then defeated Rotherham United 2-1, but lost to Sunderland in a replay at Elland Road. 'Galvin fights a lone battle' was a newspaper headline.

A correspondent noted:

> One goal after 162 minutes of all-out effort settled this FA Youth Cup fourth round tie. They had drawn 0-0 at Roker and this looked odds on another goalless affair. Lathan grabbed the decider with 18 minutes left. Sunderland were strong enough to hold on in the face of frenzied Leeds assaults. Still Leeds might well have thought they should have gone through. They had a great leader in Galvin, the

outstanding player on view, who dominated the midfield, but they just could not finish.

And it was reported in the *Yorkshire Post*:

> For entertainment and excitement the match was good value and a 2,000 plus crowd showed their appreciation with constant encouragement. Even though they displayed plenty of enthusiasm, Leeds were unable to penetrate a sturdy Sunderland defence, although they had their chances to be a couple of goals in front by the interval. Galvin, a wing-half of distinct promise, dominated in midfield ball play and Danskin was a lively outside-left, but no one could put the finishing touch to some enterprising approach work.

Chris was progressing and broke into the reserve team. His dad watched him regularly but they argued about performances. He recalled: 'I've no real idea why this happened. Maybe Dad felt that by criticising me I'd become a better player. During a Sunday lunch it would continue and we'd never finish a meal. Tony would run upstairs to avoid the arguments. He's told me since that the constant arguments put him off becoming a professional footballer. But it was not only football when we had differences of opinion. It was baffling because I was also a good cricketer. Kirkburton's main rivals in the local Huddersfield League were Almondbury, who approached me to open the batting. Dad, though, hated Almondbury from when he was Hall Bower captain, so refused to watch me play. Dad was so supportive in some ways, but also had crazy traits.'

Chris could not complain about his progress in his first season at the club. And Leeds United were First Division champions.

Apprentices and reserves were present when United clinched the biggest prize in domestic football at Liverpool in April 1969. Chris recalled: 'We travelled over on the afternoon of the match and picked up our tickets at the ground. We watched the game with the Leeds fans. The atmosphere was tense, but we battled to a 0-0 draw. Don told Billy to take the lads over to the Kop and they were acclaimed as champions. It was an amazing scene to witness. Back in Leeds, the celebrations continued at the Queens Hotel. My aim now was to break into the first-team squad and play in the first XI.'

Chapter 3

European Cup Teenage Debut

LEEDS UNITED were set to play in the European Cup for the first time in their history during the 1969/70 season, and Chris Galvin was on the fringes of first-team football for the campaign. And he was determined to make the personal step up to mirror United's progress because, he insisted: 'Getting a run with the first team was my main target. I was settled at the club and part of a historic pre-season team picture of all the players at the club with the First Division championship trophy. It was an exciting time and media interest was huge.'

As the coverage of the club intensified, the First Division champions kicked off a series of articles in the *Daily Mail* as journalist Ronald Crowther captured the atmosphere at Elland Road towards the end of July 1969. He wrote:

> Leeds United started reaching for the moon at roughly the same time as America's space scientists. In soccer terms their brilliantly charted rise through the 60s has been every bit as spectacular as the space programme. It was in March 1961, a month before President John F. Kennedy set America the goal of reaching the moon by 1970, that Don Revie became manager of a near-

bankrupt club on the brink of the Third Division. Yet he and his directors dared to set Leeds the goal of Championship honours and a place in the European Cup by the end of the same epoch-making decade. Such targets seemed even to the most stoical of success-starved Leeds fans as distant as the moon. But now the Championship has been won and the European Cup is there to be claimed in 1970. Rarely, if ever, have any English club been better equipped for such a mission. In direction, determination, dedication, ability and know-how, Leeds appear to lack nothing.

Crowther overviewed Revie's all-international team and prolific supply lines that had turned out all but four of 27 professionals on the club's books: 'Revie is convinced he has the young men to follow in the footsteps of his present-day champions, players such as David Harvey, Terry Yorath, Jimmy Lumsden, Chris Galvin and even younger ones still in their apprenticeship.' Revie told Crowther that he had a great team and was certain Leeds United would become a great club.

Leeds won the FA Charity Shield, defeating FA Cup holders Manchester City 2-1, and then opened their title defence with a 3-1 victory against Tottenham Hotspur. A few days before a clash against their bitter rivals Manchester United at Elland Road, Chris was included in a party of 13 for a League Cup tie at Fulham, with Sprake, Bremner, Hunter, Clarke and Giles nursing injuries. There was speculation in local papers that Chris might get a surprise debut, and Revie's line-up was: Harvey, Reaney, Cooper, Madeley, Charlton, Gray, Lorimer, Bates, Belfitt, Jones, Hibbitt. Sub: Galvin. Leeds won 1-0 at Craven Cottage with a Charlton goal from a Hibbitt inswinging corner.

Chris was an unused substitute but it was a memorable occasion, as he recalled: 'It was great to be named in the matchday line-up. I was only 17, so it was a big deal. Being a part of the first-team set-up was important to see how they prepared for a game. What I remember most was the performance of the great Johnny Haynes who starred for England in the late 50s and captained the side in the early 60s. Haynes was the first £100-a-week footballer when the £20 maximum wage ended in 1961 and one of the first players to get advertising deals. He was at the end of his career but still had a great touch on the ball.'

Chris was on dressing-room duty when Revie named a full-strength team against their Old Trafford rivals on 6 September 1969, for a clash that marked Charlton's 500th league appearance for the club. Leeds took the lead with an own goal by David Sadler but missed numerous chances to settle the match before George Best scored twice in the second half. Billy Bremner salvaged a 2-2 draw with a brilliant overhead kick late on.

Chris recalls the match well: 'Bestie was one of my heroes as a kid and there was an extra buzz when he played because he was the biggest star in British football. United were not quite the team they had been, but it was still one of the top games of a season for players and fans. George was in town to show off his skills and he did not disappoint.

'Leeds took the lead and would normally control a game, but Bestie took centre stage. Paul Reaney had stuck with him all around the park and it looked as if Bestie didn't seem interested, but he could destroy a team on his own. The gaffer was screaming from the dugout for Reaney to get tight, but he lost concentration for a moment. Bestie started a move and then was free in the box to score. He then got a second with a 25-yard strike when again there was too much room to run at the Leeds defence. Revie was fuming in the dressing room. He had a right go at the lads because we'd switched off momentarily. Reaney was lightning quick, but he'd made a couple of mistakes. Don told him to stick to his strengths. The gaffer was always fair. He'd back you to the hilt, but would let you know in no uncertain terms when he was disappointed.'

Chris was a regular for the reserves but still available for the junior team and made the headlines when United came from behind to defeat Sheffield Wednesday 2-1 in the FA Youth Cup. A correspondent wrote: 'United's attack blended well with left-winger Galvin, who equalised Johnson's goal for Wednesday, always menacing. In Galvin manager Don Revie has a future star of outstanding ability and promise.'

Another correspondent noted: 'Just before half-time Galvin, the Leeds outside-left and the outstanding player of the game, had a shot kicked off the line. Wednesday could not hold on to their lead for long in the second half when Leeds scored twice in seven minutes. Galvin hit the equaliser and then made the second for Hearnshaw.'

The run continued against Liverpool, and Leeds won the replay 3-2 following a 0-0 draw at Anfield. Summing up the first clash, one journalist opined: 'The game produced two genuine stars, both half-backs, who are certain to make themselves very much heard-of in the future. Chris Galvin, the United left-half, gave a splendid all-round performance that was equally adept at attack or defence and John McLaughlin, the Liverpool right-half, left nobody in any doubt as to why he is a regular Central League player. These players had it all.'

Another correspondent was just as impressed with Leeds' rising star, noting: 'There is no doubt that Chris Galvin, United's left-half, was the best balanced player on the field, strong in attack and defence.'

United's youngsters then overcame Sunderland 2-0, avenging the previous season's fourth-round defeat, before losing 2-1 to Bristol City in the quarter-finals. This time it was written: 'United's tall, classy half-back Chris Galvin played a star role in midfield, cutting out home attacks and then thrusting forward to push Leeds towards the City goal.'

Journalist Herbert Gillam noted City's success but also had a word for the Leeds left-half: 'Galvin, tall, strong and a brilliant ball player, would have won the man of the match award by a big margin. He looks another Norman Hunter in the making. In the last 15 minutes Galvin pulled out all he could to save the game and shot only inches too high after scything his way through the City defence.'

Further afield, Leeds' first team thumped Lyn Oslo 16-0 on aggregate in a European Cup first-round tie before being drawn against Ferencváros in the second round. In 1967/68 Leeds had beaten them in the Fairs Cup Final. This time United held a three-goal cushion after the first leg at Elland Road as they prepared for the return at the Nep Stadium in Budapest on 26 November 1969. The next few days would be a blur as Chris received an England Youth call-up, turned 18 and enjoyed a first-team debut against the Hungarian champions. First up was a trip to Budapest. The sides were:

> Ferencváros: Géczi, Novák, Bálint, Megyesi, Juhász, Szűcs, Szőke, Branikovits, Horváth (Vajda), Németh, Katona.

> Leeds United: Sprake, Reaney, Cooper, Bremner, Charlton, Hunter, Lorimer, Madeley, Jones, Giles, Gray (Galvin).

United put on a display that had journalists eulogising after a 6-0 aggregate triumph, and one correspondent noted:

Chris Galvin, Leeds United's birthday boy of the week, will long remember his trip to Hungary. No fairytale senior debut can compare with that of this Huddersfield-born forward. Just look back on these last few days and put yourself in the place of one of United's most promising youngsters. He learned last week of his selection for the England Youth team and was then told he would be going to Budapest with the first team. Galvin was 18 on the day the party left for Hungary, a suitable celebration, complete with traditional cake, being held among the team on arrival. And to crown everything, he was sent on in the late stages against Ferencváros, thus making his debut in the world's greatest club competition before turning out in the league. What did he think? 'I'm still reliving the moment,' he said on the plane bringing the team home. 'The seniors give a junior all the help they can and make him feel part of the plan. So I didn't really have too many butterflies.' No doubt we shall be hearing a lot more of this talented boy. The way he left two Hungarian defenders sprawling near the corner-flag on the left with delightful footwork augurs well for his Elland Road future.

And it was written in the *Yorkshire Evening Post*:

In years to come, football historians will pick through the annals of English and European scenes in the 1960s and marvel at the deeds of Leeds United. They will reflect in glowing chapters relating to performances of a sufficiently high calibre to stamp the Elland Road brigade as the outstanding team of the decade. United have carved their name with pride in far-reaching corners of the Continent, but nowhere more emphatically than in the rain-drenched Nep Stadium in Budapest. There was a stunned silence as Leeds, holding a 3-0 lead from the first leg of their European Cup second round tie, ripped into the dispirited Magyars. This was the destruction of a once-famous Ferencváros, who were overwhelmingly humiliated by the sheer brilliance of the English champions. Three more goals without reply might reverberate through Hungarian sport. National honour was stripped as this huge arena, containing only 5,429 fans, witnessed the setting up of another Leeds record. Few can be left open to them, but this one will stand as something extra special for Ferencváros had not lost previously to a British side in the Nep.

Chris recalled: 'A number of players were carrying injuries, so I was added to the squad for the match with Nigel Davey and Terry Yorath. It didn't cross my mind I'd play. Don named a full-strength team. I was on the bench. On the night I came on as a substitute for Gray. Jones and Lorimer got the goals. Making my debut was memorable, it is something you don't forget, but later I had a feeling it was a thank you for missing out on a chance to speak with AC Milan. That was a regret. I was only a kid and didn't have the confidence to say anything, but Don should have at least made me think about the possibility of speaking to Milan. I never came close again to playing for a club as big as Leeds. On the journey home, though, there was great satisfaction that I'd finally made the first team and wanted more opportunities.'

England's clash against the Republic of Ireland at Tolka Park, Dublin, was an international youth tournament qualifying-round match on 14 January 1970. The squad appeared in the national press, but Chris was already aware he would not be able to play and it was the biggest disappointment to date of his fledgling career. Those selected for the England Youth squad were: Johnson (Arsenal), Tilsed (Bournemouth), Charles (West Ham), McDowell (West Ham), Whitworth (Leicester City), Hoadley (Crystal Palace), Mortimer (Coventry City), Passey (Birmingham City), Taylor (Orient), Towers (Manchester City), Allder (Millwall), Cantello (West Brom), Galvin (Leeds United), Hunt (Southend United), McCaffrey (Nottingham Forest), Perryman (Tottenham), Probert (Burnley).

Chris explained: 'The gaffer told me I'd been called up to England's squad when I was having treatment for an ankle problem. There was no time to celebrate, though, because Don said I couldn't go because of club commitments. He'd informed the England Youth team manager and wanted to know if I was fine with that. It was huge for a kid making his way to get an England call-up, but I was young and naive, so just muttered "okay". Don caught me totally by surprise, as he did when AC Milan came in for me. To say I was gobsmacked was an understatement. Looking back, I wish I'd had the nerve to challenge his decision, but the moment was over in a flash and it's a big regret.'

England won 4-1, but even though Chris had missed out against the Republic of Ireland, he did represent his country against Wales at Orient's Brisbane Road ground on 18 March 1970. Ironically, England's 18-man squad included future Tottenham team-mates of his brother Tony! Those chosen were: Daines (Tottenham), Johnson (Blackpool), Charles (West Ham), McDowell (West Ham), Whitworth (Leicester City), Hoadley (Crystal Palace), Mortimer (Coventry City), Passey (Birmingham City), Taylor (Orient), Towers (Manchester City), Allder (Millwall), Cantello (West Brom), Galvin (Leeds United), Hunt (Southend United),

McCaffrey (Nottingham Forest), Perryman (Tottenham), Phillips (Rotherham United), Probert (Burnley).

Chris reflected: 'I was delighted to play. We lost 2-1, which was disappointing, but I'm pleased I got a chance to play at that level, although it was my only international cap. Dennis Mortimer, Steve Whitworth, Tony Towers, Len Cantello and John McDowell all went on to enjoy great careers. Tony, of course, played alongside Steve Perryman and Barry Daines at Tottenham. Perryman is one of the club's greatest players and led the side to trophy success. Mortimer captained Aston Villa to a European Cup triumph and First Division title, Whitworth played for the full England team and Towers won honours with Manchester City. Looking back, it's only natural to think about what might have been.'

The 1969/70 season finished early to allow England time to prepare for the World Cup finals in Mexico and it resulted in a fixture pile-up as Leeds attempted to win an unprecedented First Division, FA Cup and European Cup treble. They faced ten matches in 22 days, including an FA Cup semi-final trilogy against Manchester United, and played Derby County, Celtic, West Ham and Burnley during a crazy six-day period. Just 48 hours before the Derby match a depleted Leeds team lost at home to Southampton. Then, in the build-up to the Derby clash, news emerged that Chris might be making his full league debut if Eddie Gray failed a test on an ankle injured in the Saints match.

Journalist Frank Clough, of *The Sun*, wrote:

> This is a match Leeds must win to keep alive their fast-dwindling hopes of retaining the title. But with the European Cup clash with Celtic only 48 hours later they cannot afford any more injuries to an already-frightening list. And that is why I expect Don Revie to call up England

Youth winger Chris Galvin for a Baseball Ground debut. Leeds had six men on the treatment table before Saturday's game against Southampton – Paul Reaney, Terry Cooper, Norman Hunter, Billy Bremner, Mick Jones and Johnny Giles. Last night they added two more to the list – Gary Sprake and Eddie Gray. Said Revie: 'The six who missed Saturday's game are improving, but we shall need another look at them in the morning before picking the team for the Derby match.' Leeds insist that the battle for the title isn't over – even though they are now five points behind Everton and even though they have arranged to play a league game against West Ham on Thursday, 24 hours after the Celtic collision.

Derby prepared for a record crowd for Leeds' visit on 30 March 1970, by calling in extra police and arranging to open their gates at noon. But Revie effectively ended United's title defence by fielding a reserve team and United were fined £5,000 by the Football Association. The line-ups were:

Derby County: Green, Webster, Robson, Durban, McFarland, Carlin, O'Hare, Hector, Hinton, Wignall, Hennessey.

Leeds United: Harvey, Davey, Peterson, Lumsden, Kennedy, Yorath, Galvin, Bates, Belfitt, Hibbitt, Johanneson.

Chris said: 'The lads experienced an incredible season, but the title race eventually caught up with them. The game at Derby's infamous ground was embarrassing. The match was a sell-out. Fans were buying black-market tickets outside the ground, but we knew on the morning of the match we'd be fielding a reserve side. The first-team lads did not travel, but we didn't board the coach thinking we were the first XI. This was a reserve XI playing a first-team fixture. Home supporters inside the ground must have been shocked, but were still delighted to win 4-1.

'The gaffer's decision to play a weakened side resulted in a fine, which was really harsh, but he had no option. Players were injured or fatigued. There was some sympathy in sections of the media, but perhaps not as much as there should have been as a result of press hostility towards the club. Leeds often had games postponed because of cup fixtures. We had reached the FA Cup Final against Chelsea, but it was exceptional having to play three games in four days. In hindsight the gaffer might have brought in squad members earlier, especially against mid-table teams when we had enough to beat them without a first-choice XI. But it was an era when teams used the same players week in, week out. However, few teams had as punishing a schedule as Leeds, because they were in for all the trophies. The first-team lads wanted to play, but Don could and should have rested them because they would have been fresher for key games. That said, playing games on consecutive days would not happen nowadays and there is also little outcry when Premier League sides make wholesale changes for games, especially in the League Cup and FA Cup. But it was a different era then.'

Left-back Nigel Davey also played. He recollected: 'For the reserve lads, it was a chance to show what we could do against a good Derby side managed by Clough, who was never short of having something to say. When we ran out there was not stunned silence from home fans as our team was not announced in the papers, but I'm sure they would rather have seen the first-teamers in action. We got on with the game and lost 4-1 but we were not battered as pundits would have predicted if they'd known such a weakened team was being played. The Football Association fine was ridiculous considering how many games the first-team lads had played in a matter of days. Don's decision was frowned upon and he received a lot of bad press when he was actually ahead of his time.'

With the league gone, Chris played against Burnley on 4 April and then the final First Division match at Ipswich Town when Revie rested players before the FA Cup Final replay. The Burnley clash has gone down in club folklore thanks to an exceptional performance by Eddie Gray. The teams were:

> Leeds United: Harvey, Yorath, Peterson, Madeley, Faulkner, Gray, Lorimer, Bates, Johanneson, Galvin, Hibbitt.

> Burnley: Mellor, Angus, O'Neill, Waldron, Todd, Thomas, Casper, Docherty, Kindon, Probert (Bellamy), Dobson.

There was praise in the media for Gray and also Revie's youngsters. For example, it was reported in the *Yorkshire Post*:

> Some weeks ago Leeds United complained that they, like other clubs, were experiencing difficulty in finding young players of high promise. In the last eight days followers of the club have been given a preview of the Leeds United team of four or five years hence. The signs are encouraging. On Saturday, Galvin looked to be the type of player who may mature into another Clarke, Peterson as though he had taken his cue from Cooper and Faulkner looked to have the temperament of Madeley. Of the other eight reserves in the team who beat Burnley, Harvey and Bates showed again, as many of us know, that Leeds United must have to exercise a deal of charming persuasion to keep them happy in the second team. These five players are capable of first team football, there is another Gray in

EUROPEAN CUP TEENAGE DEBUT

the shadows and one or two other youngsters are capable of looking after the club.

The paper noted a virtuoso display by one of United's gifted Scottish internationals:

> Gray scored two superlative goals, sinking Burnley with his own deft feet and fertile imagination. He saw that Mellor had committed himself and was unable to get back into goal and so he floated a lob from 30 yards over the goalkeeper's head when everyone expected a ground shot. Gray's second half goal was even more spectacular. Hemmed in by five players near the touchline and restricted towards the middle of the field by Johanneson writhing in pain on the ground, he weaved a tight web, the ball glued to his feet and defenders unable to get near it. Gray feinted to pass this way and that, he bobbed and ducked and finally shot past the helpless Mellor. What a goal, fully deserving to win the match!

Journalist Len Noad wrote:

> Leeds United, with only three regular first team players, gained a magnificent victory over Burnley as a heartwarming preliminary for the cup final next Saturday. With eight inexperienced reserves in the side and centre-half Faulkner making his first appearance for the club, they completely outplayed Burnley's full-strength league side, effectively overcoming the morale-shattering effects of the past few days. And equally important was the positive proof that the Leeds youngsters are far superior

to the much-vaunted Burnley youth and emphasised the splendid team-building job by Don Revie. Madeley was an outstanding figure in defence, plugging the few gaps that appeared and always being on hand to give that degree of authority to the youngsters around him.

Eighteen-year-old inside-forward Galvin in particular revealed tremendous promise of a rich future and left-back Peterson showed tenacity in everything he attempted.

As for Gray's second goal, Noad wrote:

> He gained possession inside the box and, with a series of shuffles reminiscent of Stan Matthews at his peak, evaded the lunges of six defenders before calmly turning the ball over the line. It brought him a tremendous ovation from the crowd for what was one of the finest goals seen at Elland Road in living memory.

Gray's two goals have stood the test of time, as Chris noted: 'They were superb. Eddie demonstrated his great close control with his second goal, but his first from distance when he chipped the keeper was also outstanding. When fit, Eddie was unplayable, as he showed in the FA Cup Final against Chelsea on a dreadful surface because of the Horse of the Year Show that had taken place at Wembley a few days before. And we should have won that day. Big Jack and Mick Jones gave us the lead twice, but the match went to a replay. Losing the replay after Mick opened the scoring was heartbreaking for the lads because they deserved to win something that season. We ended up winning no trophies. This was the first cup final when I travelled with the squad and watched both games from the stands. I was pleased to have made the breakthrough into the first team and hoped for more appearances, with the club playing in four competitions, although I realised how tough it would be.'

Chapter 4

Challenging Days at Elland Road

LEEDS UNITED were determined to bounce back from the treble disappointment of the previous season when the 1970/71 campaign kicked off. After the heartache experienced by the squad, United got off to a flyer to lead the way in the early fixtures. And with home attendances at an all-time record high, all was well at Elland Road, especially with the strength in depth of United's star-studded squad.

In September 1970 James Lawton of the *Daily Express* highlighted Revie's shadow superstars in an article focusing on six fringe first-team players – Terry Hibbitt, Mick Bates, David Harvey, Terry Yorath, Chris Galvin and Rod Belfitt – who had traded almost certain knowledge that they could make the first team of another senior club for the chance of a break with Leeds United. Lawton wrote:

> For Revie the backing-up operation is a bedrock to his success. His gratitude is fulsome, the debt acknowledged. He says: 'I know what goes through the minds of these boys. I know how I felt when I was a professional. I wanted first team football. When you are playing, it is natural to think first of your own career. These players are naturally

ambitious. They have my deep gratitude. They are so vital to our chances of success.'

The season is recalled for United's shock FA Cup fifth-round defeat to Colchester United and a pitch invasion against West Brom that ultimately cost them the First Division title. Sixty-four points would have clinched the title in every other season except two campaigns of the Revie era as manager. Fairs Cup success came for a second time. Chris had broken into the first-team squad as he featured in the official pre-season club photograph distributed to the press. But the campaign would be frustrating as he made just two substitute appearances, against Swindon Town in the FA Cup and Dynamo Dresden in the Fairs Cup.

Chris reflected: 'The squad that won the 1969 First Division title was beginning to change. Allan Clarke and Mick Jones were among the best spearhead attacks around, but Jimmy Greenhoff and Mike O'Grady had left to get first-team football. Terry Hibbitt and Rod Belfitt would soon move on and by my own admission I was beginning to feel impatient. Don often talked about his squad. If possible, he picked his strongest team, which was the norm in that era, but that left players like myself hoping for a run in the side hugely disappointed. Don had to manage that situation. The first-team regulars at times carried knocks and I became frustrated when lads played not fully fit. There were plenty of matches against mid-table or lower-league sides when a slightly weaker side would have been strong enough to win. This would have given lads carrying a knock a chance to be fully fit for big games. But a run-out would come only if someone were seriously injured, so I had to push my case. And I was not the only squad player to do so. Every other week I'd have a chat with Don in his office. He'd say: "Stick it out Chris, you'll get your chance."

Don would put an extra £5 in my wages as a sweetener, which may not sound a lot now, but when you're on £30 a week, a fiver was welcome. Football is a young man's game and, although up against world-class players, I could not sit back waiting for things to happen. There were squad players happy to do so, but that was not my nature.

'During the season, Bates deputised for Bremner and Giles because of long-term injuries. It was a huge disappointment from my perspective because I felt I could have offered more to the team. I'd have wanted to make things happen, whereas Mick stuck to the pattern of play. I understood Don's decision and Leeds won most weeks. Good luck to Mick, he enjoyed being a squad member, but it was not in my nature to just sit on the bench every week.'

When the league run-in came around, it was not just injuries to key players Revie had to consider, as Chris recalled: 'A number of the lads told Don they wanted to play an offside game. Don was against it because we lacked pace in the middle of defence. Big Jack and Norman were an unbelievable combination, but they could get caught out by pace. The discussion one pre-match got really heated in the players' lounge. Don was clearly annoyed. I'd not seen that situation before. He didn't like the lads telling him what to do and made it clear that if they were going to question him, then he'd be off. Revie walked out of the room, the lads sensed they had gone too far and Les Cocker was left to calm things down.

'The lads missed out on the title by a point to Arsenal, which was heartbreaking. The West Brom match at home proved to be the crucial game. I was playing for the reserves at Newcastle United that day. Everyone remembers it because of the controversial offside goal by Jeff Astle that resulted in a pitch invasion. I heard about it when we got back to Leeds and saw it on *Match of the Day*.

The lads were still angry at training on the Monday morning. Although we won the final league games it was not enough.'

There was now a real determination to win the Fairs Cup. During an eventful European campaign, United started out against Sarpsborg before facing Dynamo Dresden at home in a first-leg clash. Chris came on and helped secure a hard-fought victory, when crucially they kept a clean sheet. The teams on 21 October 1970 were:

> Leeds United: Harvey, Davey, Cooper, Bremner, Charlton, Hunter, Lorimer, Clarke, Jones, Belfitt (Galvin), Madeley.
>
> Dynamo Dresden: Kallenbach, Ganzera, Dörner, Sammer, Kern, Haustein, Zeigler, Kreische, Hemp, Heidler, Richter.

A correspondent noted:

> Leeds United's six-year-old tenure near the centre of European soccer power is lurching crazily sideways this morning. Their embarrassment comes from 90 minutes of truly incredible frustration before the massed ranks of the stern-faced defenders of Dynamo Dresden, the shock side of East German football. Leeds have to thank the sure shooting touch of Peter Lorimer who swept home the goal from a penalty in the 54th minute.

Chris recalled: 'I was glad to finally get a run-out. There was something special about European nights at Elland Road. The lads struggled to break Dynamo down but we eventually got the winner.'

Chris then travelled with the first-team squad for the return when United's preparations were hampered by travel delays. On a highly charged evening at the Rudolf Harbig Stadium, with Leeds

2-1 behind following goals by Hemp and Kreische either side of a Jones strike, a mass brawl saw the referee dismiss Bates and Dresden substitute Geyer. Sprake saved the resulting free kick to send Leeds through on away goals. Distraught home fans invaded the pitch at full time, with one attempting to strike Charlton. United then eased past Sparta Prague and Vitória Setúbal before drawing Liverpool in the semi-finals. The first leg took place a few days before the West Brom league match. Bremner had endured the longest spell of his playing career away from first-team action. Desperate for his inspirational skipper to return, Revie arranged a secret 30-minute run-out against Huddersfield Town reserves 24 hours before United's Anfield clash. Bremner returned to first-team action and grabbed the headlines!

Chris was in the squad and watched from the stands. He recalled: 'The atmosphere in the ground against Liverpool was incredible. Billy came back into the side after a long lay-off and scored the only goal. We then drew at Elland Road to have a chance of silverware in the final against Juventus.'

But before the first-team squad travelled to Turin for the first-leg clash at the Stadio Comunale in May 1971, Revie had to contend with more off-the-pitch issues. Chris recollected: 'The lads who were married persuaded Don for the first time to allow their wives to come on the trip, although they stayed in a different hotel. Revie very reluctantly agreed. After the match was abandoned because of torrential rain and rearranged for a couple of days later, the lads expected to stop over at their wives' hotel. Don was not having it because it would interfere with preparations. There was another massive argument. Don threatened to leave the hotel and, just like the offside row a few weeks earlier, he walked out of the room. Les again chased after him, and the lads eventually backed down.

'The first team had been with Don for years, but some of the lads were questioning his decisions. At the time there were rumours that Everton were pursuing Don to replace Harry Catterick, who led them to the title in 1970. Things were beginning to change at Elland Road. Don was beginning to lose some control over the more experienced lads compared with when I arrived at the club. They were fiercely loyal to Don, but on occasions wanted more of a say. We came away from the first leg against Juventus with a brilliant 2-2 draw, Bates and Madeley scored, and in front of a packed Elland Road won the final on aggregate after a 1-1 draw; Clarke got our goal. We deserved to win a major trophy. The season for me, however, had been frustrating due to a lack of opportunities to play.'

The 1971/72 campaign saw Leeds forced to play the opening three home fixtures on neutral grounds because of the fallout following the West Brom match. Revie juggled his team because of injuries during an inconsistent start by United's standards. Their attacking options in particular were limited, with Clarke and Jones sidelined. Chris would make his first starts since April 1970.

The first opportunity came against Lierse SK in a UEFA Cup first-round tie on 15 September 1971 in the competition that had succeeded the Fairs Cup. Lierse had lost 8-0 on aggregate to Manchester City two years earlier in the European Cup Winners' Cup, so Leeds, even with a depleted XI, were expected to win comfortably. The teams were:

> Lierse SK: Engelen, Dierckx, Krivitz, Michielsens, Goelen, Vermeyen, De Ceulaer, Davidovic (Mertens), Janssens, Denul, Ressel.

> Leeds United: Sprake, Reaney, Yorath, Bremner, Faulkner, Hunter, Lorimer, Galvin, Belfitt, Giles, Bates.

Correspondent Ronald Crowther of the *Daily Mail* was full of praise for Chris in his match report headlined 'GALVANISED!' after United's 2-0 triumph:

> Chris Galvin, a teenage forward who thought he had gone to Belgium just for the ride, shot Leeds United into the lead last night against UEFA Cup rivals Lierse SK. Galvin, an 11th-hour choice when Allan Clarke became the sixth international to drop out of the Leeds side, struck in the 25th minute for his first goal in Europe. And what a valuable goal it was for it took a lot of pressure off his side after a bright and aggressive start by the Belgians ... Things had looked ominous for the English side when young Galvin, with only a few league appearances behind him, covered himself with glory by changing the course of the game. Apart from the occasional flurry and long-range shots by Peter Lorimer, little had been seen of the Leeds attack to that point. Then Lorimer made his persistence pay off when in an electrifying burst on the right he rounded the sturdy Hungarian Krivitz and banged a low ball hard into the goalmouth. There was Galvin who had read the situation so well and even though he had to fight off a frantic effort by right-back Dierckx to impede him, he slotted the ball into the net from six yards. Immediately the deflated Belgians lost much of their early bounce and assurance.

Billy Bremner in his regular Saturday night sports column for the *Green Post* recognised the role of United's 'stand-ins' against Lierse. He wrote: 'The importance of having a large first team pool to keep pace with our heavy commitments was never more obvious

'... Chris Galvin did such a good job stepping in at short notice for Allan Clarke. That goal of Chris's in Lierse was his first for the senior side and doubtless the match will stick in his memory for that alone.'

Chris recalled: 'Pre-season was tough, but I was fit and raring to go. The Football Association ban was unjust and after a few games the squad appeared stretched for the first time. But at last I had a run in the side. Although I played midfield in the reserves and preferred that position because I could influence play, Don wanted me alongside Belfitt in attack against Lierse, so you get on with it because it's a chance of first-team football. The away leg was comfortable after taking the lead. It was a bonus getting my first goal for Leeds. I enjoyed the run-out against Lierse, but expected to be back in the reserves when Leeds played Liverpool on the Saturday.'

Three days later, however, Chris was selected against Liverpool when Clarke failed a late fitness test. The 'Clash of the Giants' was United's first home match since the ban, so an expectant crowd of 41,381 packed Elland Road, and they weren't disappointed. The teams were:

Leeds United: Sprake, Reaney, Cooper, Bremner, Charlton, Hunter, Lorimer, Galvin, Belfitt (Jordan), Giles, Madeley.

Liverpool: Clemence, Lawler, Lindsay, Ross, Lloyd, McLaughlin, Graham, Hall, Heighway (Boersma), Toshack, Callaghan.

Richard Ullyet, of the *Yorkshire Post*, reported:

Lorimer scored the only goal after an hour of frustration for the forwards and a minute or so later ought to have created a goal for Belfitt, but preferred to shoot instead of pass. The goal was a splendid one, taken after quick passes by Giles, Belfitt and Galvin ... It was typical of the matches between these two clubs – tough, friendly and more dour than exciting – but I am sure all the Leeds supporters thought it had been well worth waiting for and they will turn up again.

Phil Brown in the *Green Post* wrote:

United's determination was not wilting however difficult a score had been and after 62 minutes they went ahead. Giles got them a footing in Liverpool's half and there Belfitt beat a man and squared a low cross across the edge of the Liverpool area, Galvin turned it on first time to Lorimer on the right-hand side of the box and Lorimer let fly with a blazing angled drive of such velocity that Clemence was beaten all the way. A very welcome goal indeed.

Ullyet was impressed with Chris's display, going close with one opportunity and striking a post with another effort. He wrote:

Both sides had stars of the future in their teams. Galvin, sturdy and anxious for the ball, looked to have the makings of a strong inside-forward. A more experienced man might have had two goals, but no one was more eager to beat the heart of the game and no one showed better ideas as to how to use the ball ... Sir Alf Ramsey, who was at Elland Road, is likely to remember Galvin in a year or so.

Chris said: 'When Don told me that Clarke had failed a fitness test on the morning of the match, it came out of the blue, but it was great to be playing in a big game. Liverpool had a formidable team under Bill Shankly, but we played well on the day and Lorimer's strike secured a win. Playing in front of a full house was what the game was about and brought the best out of me.'

But there was no time to dwell on a fine victory over Shankly's team because an under-strength United squad, shorn of six internationals – Clarke, Jones, Madeley, Cooper, Gray and Yorath – took on Spanish giants Barcelona at the Camp Nou in a play-off match as the first and last winners of the Fairs Cup. The victors would keep the trophy. Torrential rain had caused flooding across the city. The media reported that fields around Barcelona had 'turned into lakes'. The floods had also claimed several victims. United's 16-man squad in their 54th Fairs Cup tie in five years had an unfamiliar look as Revie called on reserve players for this high-profile encounter.

Barry Foster, of the *Yorkshire Post*, wrote:

> Leeds are forced to pin their hopes on youngsters to see them through against the capable Barcelona side ... Revie's problem positions look like left-back and left-wing. Davey, an obvious choice for full-back, has had only two reserve games this season following his suspension, while Galvin, who has played on the wing for Leeds, is normally used in midfield. If the match turns out to be so close that penalties are used to find a home for the trophy, then Galvin is likely to be one of the five entrusted with the vital kicks. With him will be Giles, Bremner, Lorimer and Hunter.

Leeds battled hard but went down to a 2-1 defeat. The teams were:

> Barcelona: Sadurni, Rifé, Eladio, Torres, Gallego, Costas, Rexach, Carlos, Dueñas, Marcial, Asensi (Fusté).
>
> Leeds United: Sprake, Reaney, Davey, Bremner, Charlton, Hunter, Lorimer, Jordan, Belfitt, Giles, Galvin.

It was noted in *The Guardian*:

> It says much for Leeds' reserve strength that they were able to match Barcelona in initiative and tenacity for long periods, but as the match went on, the Spaniards gained a measure of control through their experience. Revie said, 'I was very proud of my team and the way they played against Barcelona, who are currently Spain's top club and one of the best we have met in Europe. You can assess our performance by imagining what Leeds would be expected to do if the Spaniards came to Elland Road without six top men.'

Chris said: 'This was my biggest game yet, even though it was a high-profile friendly. Playing Barcelona was a huge boost, but I struggled with the pace of the game and it was a big disappointment to lose. However, it was a memorable experience.'

Returning to domestic action, United, playing in red, took on Huddersfield Town. Chris led the line alongside Belfitt again, with Clarke and Jones still injured. The derby clash attracted an attendance of 26,340 at Leeds Road on 25 September. The sides were:

> Huddersfield Town: Lawson D., Clarke, McGill, Hutt, Ellam, Cherry, Smith, Chapman, Hoy, Worthington, Lawson J.
>
> Leeds United: Sprake, Reaney (Edwards), Cooper, Bremner, Charlton, Hunter, Lorimer, Galvin, Belfitt, Giles, Madeley.

Town struck early with a scissor-kick from Jimmy Lawson. Charlton levelled for Leeds before half-time, but Roy Ellam grabbed the headlines following a corner kick when he lashed home a rebound after Sprake had saved from Lawson just before the hour, to give Town a 2-1 win.

United had injury woes for the return leg at home to Lierse on 29 September but their two-goal advantage meant that they were overwhelming favourites to advance against the Belgian minnows at Elland Road. The line-ups were:

> Leeds United: Shaw (Sprake), Reaney, Cooper, Yorath, Faulkner, Madeley, Lorimer, Mann (Hunter), Belfitt, Bates, Galvin.
>
> Lierse SK: Engelen, Dierckx, Krivitz, Michielsens, Goelen, Vermeyen, De Ceulaer, Davidovic, Janssens, Denul, Ressel.

Lierse sent shock waves around Europe with a 4-0 victory to win 4-2 on aggregate. It was reported in *The Guardian*:

> Don Revie calculated that a largely inexperienced side, who were bound to take time to capture any rhythm or method, could protect a two-goal lead. He must regret not starting with his strongest side and calling off his more valued players when the match was won. Theories, however, are all very well, but they tend to fall apart in practice when the human element is involved and no one could have legislated for the unfortunate error by Shaw, the third-choice goalkeeper, which cost the third goal and not only dealt Leeds a severe blow, but convinced the Belgians that their mission was far from impossible.

Chris reflected: 'The Huddersfield result was really disappointing, but we were confident of advancing in the Fairs Cup. Don made changes, but we should have had enough to beat Lierse. John Shaw and Jimmy Mann made European debuts, but were replaced after we'd shipped three goals by half-time. We went for it in the second half, but they caught us on the break. Our away win counted for nothing after our defeat. All the papers rightly slammed us. The result was a real shock.'

Chris's mini-run in the team ended with a goalless draw against West Ham at Elland Road. Following a 3-1 defeat at Coventry City, Leeds bounced back with consecutive wins against Manchester City, Everton and Manchester United, but the headline news was of Revie signing West Bromwich Albion midfield man Asa Hartford for a club-record £177,000 in November 1971. The local press anticipated the 21-year-old teaming up with Bremner and Giles in midfield, with Madeley moving to right-back in preference to Reaney.

Chris said: 'I was disappointed to be dropped, but expected a recall during the season. What happened with the Hartford transfer, though, made me realise I'd never be able to prove myself at Leeds. Don strengthened the squad by signing Asa, whose transfer was headline news. He was looking to the future. Since promotion in 1964 the gaffer had brought through young players alongside only two major signings, Jones and Clarke. Asa immediately joined the first-team squad for training before our home game against Leicester City. You could not spend so much money on a player and not play him. Where would Hartford slot in?

'Before a Saturday match we would have a full-blown practice game. Before the Leicester game Don pulled me aside. He said: "Chris, you've nagged and nagged, well, things are changing." I was down to play alongside Asa in the practice match for the first team. Eddie had just returned to the side and was carrying a knock so I played on the left side, with Billy and Asa in the middle. As usual Don told us to hold back on challenges to avoid injuries, but the games were competitive. Don was switching things around. I really thought I'd finally been given a chance to break into the first team. This was my big opportunity, but during the workout I took a swing at Giles when he caught me with a late challenge. Don dragged me off before I totally lost it and told me to get changed. He'd see me after training. I got a rollicking, but Don told me Giles was also out of order. Asa would partner Billy in midfield, I was in the side against Leicester for Eddie, and I left Don's office really fired up.

'I was one of the first players down at the ground on the Saturday but, when I went into the dressing room, Hartford was sitting on a bench, clearly upset. Asa would not tell me what had happened, but said I'd find out. After the lads had rolled in, Don called a meeting and told us Asa had failed his medical. The club would not be going ahead with the transfer, but he wouldn't go into details. Don announced the same team as the last match against Manchester United. Giles and Gray played and I was substitute. At that moment I realised Don would not build another team. His comments to me about change weren't going to happen. Don was going to get as much as he could out of his senior lads and I was not part of the plans. We later discovered the transfer collapsed three hours before kick-off because medical tests on Asa detected a heart abnormality.'

Hartford's transfer collapse made headline news, with questions being asked about whether Asa would ever play again. He did, playing hundreds of times in a top-class career for West Brom, Manchester City and Scotland. Leeds, meantime, found their form and chased a First Division and FA Cup double. For Chris, while he was integral to the squad, it was a difficult time.

He recalled: 'The lads enjoyed an incredible run. Everyone remembers the 5-1 win against Manchester United and 7-0 rout against Southampton; however, there were other terrific displays during the remainder of the campaign, with a number of exceptional performances. But it was tough not getting a chance to play. Our Bristol Rovers FA Cup third-round tie in January 1972 was a classic example of not getting an opportunity. Big Jack was out so Madeley switched to centre-half and Reaney slotted in at right-back. Clarke and Jones were out so Bates and Jordan came in. I was on the bench. Don preferred Mick, I just had to accept it. I was on the bench and came on for Joe during the game for a cameo role.'

Chris set up Lorimer for his second goal against Rovers in a 4-1 victory. A member of United's matchday squads against Liverpool, Cardiff City, Tottenham Hotspur and Birmingham City on the road to Wembley, Chris was involved in the build-up as Leeds prepared to play Arsenal in the Centenary final. It was the era of the cup final song, tailored suits and a players' pool. Chris featured in Leeds' souvenir brochure and song 'Leeds, Leeds, Leeds' by Les Reed and Barry Mason, which is still sung today by fans. The brochure included facts about United's squad. Chris said that George Best was the player he most admired, his favourite team and ground was Manchester United and Old Trafford. Aside from driving a Ford Capri and playing cricket, he enjoyed westerns, like many team-mates, while the West Indies was his choice for a holiday. Chris also revealed that steak and chips was his favourite meal and he began the day with Shredded Wheat!

He recollected: 'I was with the lads when we recorded the cup final song and was also in the official Wembley brochure, but you are not really part of it because I knew that I'd not be playing. We travelled down on the Thursday and visited Wembley the day before. Going down Wembley Way on matchday the crowds were enormous. I watched the game with the reserves from the bench so was close to the action. Clarke scored the only goal of the match and it was great to see Billy lift the famous old trophy. Beating Arsenal at Wembley was a brilliant occasion.

'Nowadays the matchday squad is bigger so I'd have received a cup winners' medal, which would have been special, looking back, as a reminder of being in the squad during this period. The lads and fans had waited a long time for this moment. The dressing room was jubilant after our win. Sadly, we didn't get a chance to celebrate at the cup final banquet as we went straight to our hotel to prepare for the last league game at Wolves, just two days later. There was a stark contrast in the dressing room at Molineux when we missed the double. Dubious decisions in a 2-1 defeat made headline news. The match should not have been played so soon after the final. It would not happen now. The Football League were out of order because they should have given the lads an extra day's rest, as they would have secured the double, which that team deserved. But the lads did win the FA Cup for the first time in the club's history, which is still the only time. Later in the week, thousands of supporters lined the streets as we celebrated winning the cup in an open-top bus parade to City Square then to a packed Elland Road. Fans were everywhere, the scenes were incredible. At Elland Road we paraded the trophy and we also gave a rendition of our cup final song, which went down well.'

Chris was frustrated by a lack of opportunities and these feelings intensified after just three appearances in 1972/73. United's penultimate league match at Birmingham City would turn out to be his last for the club. Leeds lost in the FA Cup Final that season to Sunderland. Chris was a non-playing substitute when AC Milan controversially won the European Cup Winners' Cup Final in Salonika. In what was a black day for European football, UEFA and the Greek federation suspended referee Christos Michas after the worst officiating of a match in the Revie era.

Chris reflected: 'My match fitness was suffering because I was playing only occasionally in the Central League. The only way you could get a game was if a player had a bad injury or there was nothing to play for at the end of a season, which happened with the Birmingham game. I didn't get a look-in. Nobody wants a fellow professional to get injured, but that's the harsh side of the game. As a door shuts for someone, then you get a chance. That's how Joe Jordan got in when Jones started getting injuries that led him to retire eventually. The major issue for me was, no matter how a first-team player performed, they never seemed in danger of being dropped, even with a run of bad games. Come what may, Don had his first XI and stuck with them. And you can't argue because they were so successful, but if he had given them a rest for some clashes, in my view they would have won more major trophies. The lads were involved to the end of every season; a rest would have helped their sharpness.

'We were overwhelming favourites to beat Sunderland and Don led me to believe that I would be substitute on this occasion. After the build-up that surrounds a Wembley final, for whatever reason Don changed his mind and Terry Yorath was given the number 12 shirt, which was a huge disappointment for me personally. Of course, Sunderland caused a huge shock by winning. When I reflect on this game, Eddie had missed much of the latter part of the season through injury and I'd have been an ideal replacement for him in the final when we were chasing the game, rather than Yorath. Don's decision again left me feeling frustrated.

'There were a few injuries and suspensions against Milan, so I thought that I might have a shout of playing. But Bates, Yorath and Frank Gray came in for Bremner, Giles and Eddie. I was on the bench, but disillusioned. In the second half we were a goal down when Don told me to get stripped. I was waiting on the sideline to go on, with Don, who told Norman Hunter to come off but he refused. Don told me to sit down. I could not believe it. I'll never know if I'd have made a difference, but it would have been great to help the lads. It was farcical. Hunter was sent off late in the game, but it was over by then.

'Throughout the match I've never seen a more biased referee. There were rumours we might have issues with the referee, but you never really believe such blatant bias might happen in a final. It did. The lads were devastated. There was no way we were going to get anything from the referee, who was banned from officiating. In the build-up to the final there were again rumours that Everton wanted Don. The board persuaded the gaffer to stay another season but the campaign left me feeling I'd never get a run in the side.'

Chris returned for pre-season training in July 1973, but a new challenge quickly emerged when Revie informed him that Hull City and Wolves had put in bids shortly after the 1973/74 squad picture was taken. A new journey was about to begin.

Chapter 5

Super Leeds!

CHRIS PLAYED a total of 16 first team matches for Leeds United, including five as a substitute, scoring one goal. He witnessed the club during its glory days win a First Division title, FA Cup, Football League Cup, Fairs Cup twice and the FA Charity Shield at close quarters. They also finished runners-up in the league during three consecutive seasons and were twice FA Cup finalists.

Chris recalled: 'Football fans often ask about my time at Leeds and without fail always recite Don's legendary XI ... Sprake, Reaney, Cooper, Bremner, Charlton, Hunter, Lorimer, Clarke, Jones, Giles, Gray. Most don't believe me when I tell them this line-up played only one match, against Mansfield Town in the FA Cup, because Paul Madeley was always in the side!

'The first team picked themselves week in, week out. Apart from being unassuming as a person, Paul was an exceptional footballer and would fill in at centre-half, full-back or midfield if there were an injury. For lads hoping to get a chance, you got a run-out only if more than one change was needed because Paul was a brilliant player who could adapt. The only time I thought I'd be more involved was when Asa Hartford signed from West Brom but the transfer collapsed and the gaffer went back to his trusted line-up, which was demotivating. I was frustrated, but you couldn't argue with the gaffer's thinking because the lads won trophies, so his decision was justified.'

Chris is reluctant to be critical of Revie, while remaining well aware of the competition for places at Leeds that made it so hard for a youngster to break through as a regular in league football. He said: 'Don was a tremendous manager and his record speaks for itself, but in the early 60s he did have an exceptional crop of players on the ground staff who came through together. Eventually Harvey replaced Sprake, and Yorath came in during Don's final seasons, but from my apprentice group only Frank Gray broke through and Leeds had the pick of kids around the country. I've always believed that with a decent run of games I could have retained a place in the side, but playing odd games was no way to show what you could do. Travelling up and down the country and in Europe with the first-team squad, I saw places I'd never been to and occasionally I'd be substitute. I was not match-fit, even with a run-out. My sharpness was affected without regular games. Not playing took a yard off my pace that I could not afford to lose. I was on half and then full bonus money but that was not enough in the end. I needed first-team football and things ground to a halt. It was a privilege being part of the set-up, but it got to a point when I could not carry on.

'The gaffer built one of the best club sides in Europe, if not the world. Their standing didn't really cross my mind at the time because I was so desperate to play, but I was a small part of it, which supporters appreciate all these years on. From the bench or sitting with squad players on the sidelines, I saw the lads play every week. The period from winning the league in 1969 to just missing out on the 1972 double, they were the best club team around. Billy and the boys had an inner strength, skill and a cutting edge that were brilliant to watch from close quarters. They knew each other's game inside out, could anticipate where they'd be on the pitch and never overcomplicated things.

'A topic that always comes up with fans is how "hard" were this Leeds team compared with other top sides of the era? We had a tough, uncompromising side, but every top club – Liverpool, Arsenal, Everton, Chelsea, Manchester United and Manchester City – had players who would put in crunching tackles. We had players who could dish it out. Hunter had a reputation, but I never heard the gaffer say, "Share it around," although he did turn a blind eye at times. Big Jack went into print about his infamous "black book", but opponents feared Giles, Bremner, Clarke, Reaney and Charlton. Tony played with lads who came up against Leeds and they all said that Giles could be pretty ruthless, although he was a wonderful player. Billy had the worst reputation in some ways, but he never left a foot in like some lads. Billy wasn't scared of anyone and he'd put in horrible tackles, but they were late or clumsy, not malicious.

'Being at Leeds during this period was an amazing time. Fixture congestion hampered the treble bid in 1969/70 and the Football Association cost them a double in 1971/72, but they should have won more major honours. I've always felt that. If Don had rotated the team, they would have. But you cannot argue with what Don achieved and the fans have never forgotten what the club accomplished. I've been to a number of anniversary dinners where the affection of supporters for the whole squad is amazing and I'm always surprised how many ask me for an autograph. They recognise the part fringe players made. For a period, Leeds were almost unbeatable and one of the best club sides of all time. Apart from the fans, the city has never forgotten what the club did and in 2018 acknowledged it formally when the team was awarded the

Freedom of the City. It was a wonderful occasion to be a part of on a memorable day.'

Chris had one big supporter when he opted for Leeds – his brother. United were becoming a major force in football and Tony followed their fortunes during Chris's time at Elland Road. And he witnessed many ups and downs during a golden era for Super Leeds.

Tony said: 'When Chris joined Leeds, it was exciting to think that he was at the best Football League club in the country. I remember scouts coming to our house to speak with Chris when he was about 14 years of age. I also vividly recall travelling to Bolton Wanderers and walking around the changing rooms before a game at Burnden Park. You could not help but be impressed. Chris was really close to signing for Bolton. We all thought that's where he was going as an apprentice. Goalkeeper Eddie Hopkinson and winger Gordon Taylor, later the Professional Football Association's chief executive, chatted with us before the game. It looked done and dusted, but then Don Revie came on the scene.

'Chris would have had more first-team chances with Bolton but, equally, if you turn a club such as Leeds down, not everyone would understand that decision. "Leeds not good enough for you, Chris?" was the type of comment that was a hard one to ignore for a kid. Leeds were regularly on television and they had loads of household names among the players so it was natural to join a club of that stature. Dad thought Chris had made the wrong choice; he saw the bigger picture and would ultimately be proved right. But I understood Chris's decision. He was confident in his ability and believed he'd break through.

'When Chris signed for Leeds, they had a young squad with years ahead of them. By the time he was being considered for a debut, Bremner, Giles and Gray played in midfield, then there was Madeley, who could play anywhere and, if a chance came up in attack, there were Lorimer, Clarke or Jones. Most were international players and a number were already world class. There were no agents offering advice. Signing for a club was down to Chris, although he could chat things through with Mum and Dad. Revie told Chris how kids had made it from the apprentices and he was in the next crop. It's easy to understand why he chose Leeds.

'The family fully supported Chris trying to make it at Leeds. I went with Dad to watch the juniors and then reserves. There was real pride seeing Chris run out in the famous white shirt of Leeds United at Elland Road for a Central League game. We sat in the West Stand with a few hundred diehard fans on a Saturday afternoon. Unfortunately, my main memories of Chris playing for Leeds were when he made a mistake, because Dad would get really wound up. Chris had loads of skill but was not naturally quick. If he beat a man, he'd momentarily wait to do something with the ball and, if nothing was on, he'd try to beat his opponent again. Chris wanted to make his opponent look stupid, knock the ball through his legs and this frustrated Dad because he might lose possession. Dad felt Chris was not making the most of his talent. There were also moans from fans when Chris made a mistake, as with any other player. I was only a kid and didn't like it because he was my elder brother and proud of him.

'Unfortunately, Chris and Dad had rows over Sunday lunch after what seemed like every game. It would carry on until one of them stormed off. I couldn't add anything to the arguments so pretended it was not happening. I'd run off to watch television. Over the years we've discussed our relationship with Dad and it was different for us both. Dad wasn't one to hand out lots of praise. I think that's a Yorkshire thing! Dad was desperate for Chris to make it, possibly because he did not make it as a footballer, maybe that's why he gave him such a hard time. Even now I don't know quite why it got so heated because he helped to develop us and I'm sure he just wanted to help. But he showed it in an odd way. Chris getting criticised did impact on me. Luckily, I had it far easier. Dad didn't watch me play as much as Chris, which I understood as he was making his way at Leeds. But occasionally, he'd come and there was some criticism, but not to the same degree that came Chris's way. I tried not to let it get me down. I had time to develop. It was not so easy for Chris.'

The 1967/68 season was historic for Leeds United because they won the Football League Cup. Tony was at Wembley and witnessed many other big occasions. He reminisced: 'I quickly became a fan. Revie always made sure families were included for big games and Leeds got to a number of cup finals at Wembley. I remember standing on a box beside Leeds fans behind the goal when they defeated Arsenal with a Terry Cooper goal to win their first major trophy. It was a bit scary and a horrible game to watch, but an important win. A couple of years later Leeds should have beaten Chelsea in the FA Cup Final before losing the replay. Leeds played brilliantly at Wembley, especially Eddie Gray, who tore David Webb to shreds on the wing. I'll never know how they did not win. But Gary Sprake let in a howler from Peter Houseman just before half-time to allow Chelsea back in the game. We were behind that goal when the shot squirmed in, but Leeds still had enough chances to win the game.

'A few days before the Chelsea final, Leeds played Celtic in a European Cup semi-final at Elland Road. What a game! Jimmy Johnstone had an absolute blinder and tore Cooper inside out. I'd never seen a team rip Leeds apart as Celtic did that night. Leeds had an aura about them, especially at home, but Celtic, and "Jinky" in particular, were outstanding. Sprakey didn't have a chance with the only goal of the game and he was a top keeper, but did have his moments. At Liverpool he once threw the ball into his own net!

'I saw Leeds play some of their greatest games. There were really tough wins over Arsenal and Chelsea, uncompromising games when they kicked hell out of each other. It was also a privilege to see Leeds play against star players such as Bestie, Denis Law and Bobby Charlton in their pomp for Manchester United. It was amazing watching Leeds, but how on earth that team did not win more trophies is hard to understand because they got close on so many occasions. They were five times First Division runners-up and three times FA Cup finalists, which was an amazing record. I've often wondered why they consistently got so close only to fall at that last hurdle. Maybe they were mentally shattered because they rarely rested players. Sometimes lads need a week or so off to recharge or rest injuries. By the time you get to the end of April, fatigue catches up with you when really big crucial games come along. But Leeds got to more finals than other teams in that era and won their share of honours.

'I understood the siege mentality engendered by Revie. At times it seemed the whole world was against the club. Leeds could annihilate any team on their day, but there were occasional days when they dominated and then conceded against the run of play, which proved costly. One game that illustrated this best was a defeat against West Brom that almost caused a riot at Elland Road in April 1971. Back then there were score flashes on *Grandstand* and *World of Sport* on a Saturday afternoon, not minute-by-minute scores as you now see on Sky Sports. I was not at the game, but remember seeing the final score on *Grandstand*. Then we heard all about the controversy concerning the offside goal. *Match of the Day* commentator Barry Davies could not believe that referee Ray Tinkler allowed West Brom's second goal. When I saw the goal that night, I didn't know what to say. Leeds were victims of a dreadful decision. Davies's commentary was superb on a clear injustice. The result cost Leeds the title as Arsenal went on the win the double that season. The crowd invasion after the goal meant Leeds had to play three home games on neutral ground the following season, which was another disadvantage. Leeds lost the 1971/72 title by a point, this time to Derby County, on the final day of the campaign against Wolves when again they were victims of dodgy refereeing decisions. Fans still talk about both games and rightly so.'

At least there was some compensation on the horizon because, as Tony added: 'Leeds did win the FA Cup and I was there to witness it. Leeds played well against Arsenal and deserved to lift the trophy with a Clarke header. Chris was in the squad, but there was only one substitute allowed. He did get to experience the bus parade and civic celebrations with ecstatic supporters but nowadays he'd have picked up a winners' medal, which would have been deserved for his loyalty to the club.'

Football throws up bizarre coincidences and the Galvin brothers can lay claim to one around the FA Cup Final. Wolves overcame Ferencváros in a UEFA Cup semi-final on aggregate a couple of weeks before Tony was cheering on Leeds at Wembley. Wolves then controversially denied Leeds the title and double two days after Wembley. Chris was in United's cup final and Wolves squads. Either side of the Leeds vs Wolves match, Tottenham Hotspur defeated Wolves in the UEFA Cup Final. Chris made his Leeds debut against Ferencváros and Tony would win the UEFA Cup with Tottenham!

Tony surmised: 'As Jimmy Greaves used to quip: "Football is a funny old game." The sequence of games was obviously a quirk of fate, but it's nice to look back on this fact in that way. Leeds winning the FA Cup was great, but the Football Association should have let them play Wolves later the following week. Another 24 or 48 hours and they would have recovered enough to win the league. They were really unfortunate. This type of situation thankfully would not happen now. It was such a massive game.

'A year later I was back at Wembley when Sunderland shocked the footballing world in the final. Leeds should have battered them, but it was an awful match. Ian Porterfield scored in the first half, then Sunderland defended and Jim Montgomery pulled off a wonder save from Lorimer. If that had gone in, Leeds would have won, but it wasn't to be. A few days later Leeds were robbed of winning the European Cup Winners' Cup against AC Milan when Chris was a non-playing substitute. Chris had been getting frustrated because of a lack of opportunities and this was the final straw. Soon after, Chris joined Hull City to get a chance of regular first-team football. Overnight, my days following the club ended, although I still look out for their results with interest and it's great they are back in the Premier League.'

Tony's allegiance to Leeds was played out against the backcloth of Chris's time with the club as he strove to become an accepted regular among some of the best players in the country. And the emotions are mixed. Tony said: 'It's clear Chris rarely got an opportunity of first-team football, which was such a shame. He was frustrated about not getting much game time and seeing the progress of players such as Mick Bates, who, he felt, had less skill, getting regular opportunities. It must have been tough to experience, but Bates had been at Leeds longer and did as Revie instructed when he came in for Bremner, Giles or Gray, whereas Chris wanted to make his mark and show what he could offer. When the Asa Hartford deal fell through and Chris was out of the frame, he'd had enough. Within a year of Chris joining

Hull, Revie became England manager. Would Chris have been given a run-out by Brian Clough? He liked wide players. Look at how well John Robertson did at Nottingham Forest. Chris might have got a chance. But you make decisions and accept the consequences. Competing alongside world-class players was really tough. Chris didn't get the breaks. Timing is important in football and he was at Leeds at the wrong time, but he did have a special insight into the club during an incredible period and that cannot be taken away.

'Bremner was a magnificent player, probably the best of the lot. I would have to say he is one of the greatest midfielders I have ever seen. Dad loved his invention and clever passing. I remember when Dad and I watched a game at Spurs not long after I had joined the club. After the game he said Ossie Ardiles reminded him of Bremner. Dad was a good judge and I couldn't disagree. Ossie was world class and so was Billy. I always liked Cooper, who was an unusual player because he used to bomb up the wing and get crosses in like wing-backs of the modern era. There were not many players of that type around and he was the best.

'Eddie Gray was also great to watch. He was unplayable on his day. At the back of my mind, though, Eddie played in the same position as Chris so was keeping him out of the side. When Chris played against Burnley, as Leeds chased the treble, it was one of the few times I saw him in a first-team game, and he played well. I'm really pleased it's still a memorable match for Leeds fans and, of course, they remember Eddie's two goals. His 40-yard chip was outstanding but there are no words to adequately describe his dribble for the second. When you look back at the footage of the goals, apart from the state of the pitch, which hardly had a blade of grass on it, it's hard to believe how understated Eddie's celebrations were for what were world-class finishes by any standard.

'Teams would often be beaten before Leeds came on the pitch. Chris used to say: "You should see the look on players' faces." They just wanted to get the match over and done with. Revie's Leeds were a tremendous side, but could be over-physical. However, all the top teams had players who could put their foot in when the situation called for it. But opponents feared Leeds and it was a privilege to watch a great side. On their day, home or away, Leeds could be ruthless and majestic. Revie might have rotated his squad more and let his team play more freely but, putting those discussion points aside, they were one of the best club teams in the world for a period. You cannot get away from that fact. Teams nowadays prioritise possession of the ball as a key aspect of the game. Leeds were masters of this tactic, pulling teams out of position and then finding a way to thread a ball through for the strikers to pounce. Revie was in some ways ahead of his time and created a wonderful side in their pomp.'

Chapter 6

Goole, Mr Scary and Snowy Trek to Spurs

EVEN THOUGH Tony Galvin initially chose the academic life after leaving school, sport was never far from his thoughts. And he immediately took an interest in the game after he had started his studies at Hull University. In practical terms he was able to get the best of both worlds.

Tony reflected: 'After moving into student accommodation in a great big, old house, I signed up for the university football team during freshers' week and quickly made the first XI. My surname probably helped me because the guy running them was a Hull City supporter called Mally Maguire. Whatever the reason, I was not complaining, because other first-year lads played in the second XI, so it was great for the development of my game.

'Academically I wasn't a high flyer on my course, but worked hard. We studied Russian culture, literature, history and politics. I was reasonably competent as a Russian speaker by the time I had graduated and could hold my own in a conversation. The university visit to the Soviet Union was somewhat different to my school experience. We studied intensively at a Moscow institute for a month, mainly the language, but there were efforts to teach us about the great achievements of the Soviet's. The institute was fairly basic, the hotel was spartan, in a poor area, so we saw the murkier side of Moscow life. The Cold War was part of everyday life and it opened my mind. We were allowed to wander off because there weren't enough guides or tutors to monitor all of us. Before the trip we were told there was a camera or a listening device in every room and people would be watching us. We were also told that you got amazing rates if you changed dollars into roubles but, if you got caught, you risked the chance of being arrested. We didn't really take in the warnings but, after exchanging some money, it made me feel on edge. There was a sense of people acting suspiciously in the corner and watching you, so you were continually looking over your shoulder. A number of lads made plenty of roubles for their shirts and jeans, but you could spend your money on only beer and vodka, so you proceeded to get inebriated and ended up having to buy new clothes when you got back home!

'Students were from various backgrounds, but we were all well aware of the American–Soviet political scene. English lecturers who accompanied us gave us a balanced viewpoint. There were lefties among the lecturers and rumours that they were being watched by British secret agents. We were told that, if you did a Russian studies degree, you would automatically be on a list, but, as long as you did not do anything dodgy, then you were fine. The British government were worried about Communist Party sympathisers and closely monitored anyone writing for extreme left-wing publications. It was a bit disconcerting, but I wanted to enrol on the course because it sounded interesting, and three years down the line I had developed a much better understanding of the Soviet culture, politics and history. From the Czars to Lenin, Stalin and now Putin, it's a country with a fascinating history. But at this juncture, I must note that Vladimir Putin's illegal invasion of Ukraine in February 2022 and the appalling misery he has inflicted on that country is incomprehensible. It is reassuring that our government is leading the way in responding to the invasion by providing financial and military support to Ukraine. We don't know what the outcome will be but let us hope and pray that in the not too distant future Putin is defeated and that he is ultimately replaced by a leader that seeks to engage positively, both with Ukraine and the West.'

Away from his studies and university football, Tony watched Chris play for Hull with several mates. But attending English football in the 1970s was not much fun because, he remembered: 'I recall in particular when Hull played Manchester United in a Second Division game during my first term at university. The atmosphere was heated and Hull won 2-0, but then what seemed one side of the ground invaded the pitch at full time. United fans ran on to the pitch towards us in the home end and there was only a handful of police. It was frightening as we tried to get out of the ground. Hooliganism was a big issue inside and outside grounds. Every team had an element of fans intent on making trouble and that was one game which illustrated it. Even growing up and watching Huddersfield Town and Leeds in the late 60s and early 70s, there was often a feeling at games that violence could erupt, because every team had a small section of what you could describe only as mindless thugs. On this particular day, when the United fans ran across the pitch, the only sensible move was to get out of the ground. There just weren't enough police on duty to control these thugs. It was a sad period in terms of crowd behaviour. The grounds, unlike now, were not particularly family friendly in terms of safety and facilities.'

Snippets appeared in the press that Goole Town and Bridlington Town were interested in signing Tony because he had impressed for Hull University's first team. Goole played in the

Northern Premier League and manager Alan Turner was aware that Tony was performing well for Hull in the university league.

Turner recalled: 'I used to go all over the place in local non-league football in East Yorkshire to look for players and I first watched Tony when he was playing at the university's ground in Inglemire Lane. I was so impressed by him and knew that someone else would come in and pinch him if I didn't sign him straightaway. After all, his brother Chris was already at Hull City and I was concerned that they might just pick up him up if I wasn't quick enough. We went to the Haworth Arms, not far from the ground, for talks after the game. I think I got him for ten bob and offered him £5 a week! Tony was still only 18, but he was nearly six foot tall and had pace. He was very quiet, but a strong lad. And he was just what we wanted because he scored and made goals.'

Tony reflected on his arrival at the club: 'Goole were a decent side. Playing didn't interfere with my studies, so I signed. The contract was not really worth the paper it was written on, but I was happy as it was a step up. I was on a student grant, so the money helped. Alan was great. I could continue playing for the university team as long as I did not get injured.'

Tony made his debut two days after signing on 15 February 1975, with Goole's squad down to 'the bare bones' according to Turner. He was handed the No. 6 shirt for a trip to Stafford Rangers. Goole lost 5-2. He recalled: 'The university played in a midweek league and also in the East Riding League on a Saturday. After signing for Goole, I was allowed to miss the Saturday match. Although I occasionally missed an afternoon lecture, I kept up to date with my studies and however late we got back from a long trek I always made the 9am lectures the following day. I played on the right of midfield for Goole and pushed wide in a 4-4-2 formation. Although we lost against Stafford, the manager

GOOLE, MR SCARY AND SNOWY TREK TO SPURS

felt I'd done well. It was a tough place to go and play, the pitch was appalling, so I was chuffed with my efforts. Stafford had an old-fashioned-style centre-forward called John Ritchie, which was a surprise because I saw him play for Stoke alongside Jimmy Greenhoff and Terry Conroy against Leeds United. Ritchie held his own against Charlton and Hunter in their pomp, so I found it sad that professional players had to carry on playing until their legs fell off! The match ended a hectic few days.'

Turner was putting together a squad based on stability and experience. The league provided a platform for emerging players to find out whether they could adjust to higher levels of football. Goole finished eighth in 1974/75, but the highlight was a run to the quarter-finals of the FA Trophy before losing at home to eventual winners Matlock Town, managed by former Sheffield Wednesday and England international Peter Swan. Goole played nine ties.

Tony recalled: 'There were experienced players throughout the league and a number had played in the Football League. Swan was an England regular and a member of the 1962 World Cup squad in Chile but missed out on playing due to illness. Sadly he became involved in a betting scandal soon after the finals when Wednesday lost to Ipswich Town. He was not the ringleader but received a four-month jail sentence and life ban that was subsequently overturned. Swan was tipped to be in the 1966 World Cup, which must have been hard to come to terms with. He came back into the game and I recall him as a tough old pro at Matlock, where he is fondly remembered.

'One of my favourite teams during the early 60s was Burnley so it was great playing against their former keeper Adam Blacklaw, who won the First Division title in 1959/60 and then played against Tottenham in the FA Cup Final a couple of seasons later. Blacklaw played for Great Harwood at a dilapidated old ground. Swan and

Blacklaw were top players in their day but had to continue to earn a few quid because they'd not earned a lot playing professional football. These guys toughened you up and we had to respect their achievements.

'You'd get comments all the time from players with less skill, threatening to break your legs and so on, but you had to ignore them. The scariest player I faced was legendary hardman John King, who played for Wigan at the old Springfield Park ground. He was really intimidating, threatened me a few times and on one occasion stared me out. I was genuinely frightened. He looked at me: "If you come near me again and do that, I'm gonna have you." Looking at him, I said to myself: "I think he means it." I stayed well away from him for the remainder of the game and amazingly we won against the best team in the league.

'I had never been as afraid on a football field as I was that day, but it was a valuable experience and I was determined that I would never allow myself to be so intimidated again. Back in the dressing room I realised King never meant it, but you'd get that in the non-league game. You were young and lively so old pros thought you were taking the mick out of them. I had pace, I'd knock the ball past them and leave them behind, so it was not uncommon for opponents to threaten something. Physically it was very tough and, as a person, I was a bit soft in my university days. The league shocked me how physical and aggressive it was to play in. It could be brutal and uncompromising football. Non-league football hardened me as a player and as an individual. Playing at the back were Tom Wilson and Harold Wilcockson, who both kept an eye out for me, which I really appreciated. Both would sort out any opponent who gave me verbal and physical stick during a game!'

Goole finished tenth in the league and had another fine run in the FA Trophy in 1975/76. Micky Driver, a central-midfield player who could also operate at full-back, saw Tony's increasing impact. He recalled: 'Against Stafford one evening Tony was having a quiet game on the right-hand side of midfield. Then suddenly he went on a run, knocked the ball past one opponent, then another and finally got to the byline to whip in a great cross. We realised he'd got a bit of everything. He kept making those runs, he wasn't scared of a challenge and just got better and better.'

Tony was attracting attention from Football League clubs, while balancing his studies and football obligations. Hull City and Blackburn Rovers were among the first to register an interest when he scored ten times in 50 appearances during the season: 'Goole nearly always played on a Tuesday so I was able to play for the university the following day. Alan was happy as it kept me sharp. By now I was on £10 a game so could afford a few luxuries! Dad used to come and watch me play. Neither he nor Chris pushed me to become a professional footballer but it was around this time I began to think about possibly getting a shot. I'd heard Hull had watched me play and in the local paper there were always snippets saying clubs were watching a few lads. Hearing that Sheffield United, Scunthorpe United, Grimsby Town and Lincoln City might be interested was encouraging, but there were no official approaches to Goole.'

Tony enjoyed his share of positive press coverage that was no doubt picked up by Football League clubs. For example, the headline 'Galvin stars as Goole clinch second double' appeared when they won 1-0 at Gainsborough Trinity. Correspondent Bob Kernohan covered Goole FC for the *Hull Daily Mail*, and wrote:

> Galvin was superb at times and 20 minutes from the end he collected the ball in his own half to set off on a 60-yard run in which he beat five players. As he reached the 18-

yard box, Galvin paused before bending a shot past Rose. It struck the top of a post and flew back across goal where Thompson forced home the winner. A few minutes later Galvin repeated that incredible run and this time his 20-yard shot was saved by Rose. Galvin's skills were almost unbelievable at times.

Tony had also toughened up to the demands of the league. He received a three-match suspension after being sent off late on in Goole's match at Bangor City. Town lost 2-1 and it was reported: 'Galvin's sending off was a miserable affair. He was shielding the ball on the touchline while two Bangor players hacked at his legs. Amid the flailing boots Galvin kicked one leg out backwards and the referee, right on the spot, took advice from the linesman 15 to 20 yards away before sending him off.'

But the best was yet to come. The catalyst was an FA Cup run to the third round in 1976/77 when Goole finished sixth in the league. Goole competed with just 15 regular players. The FA Cup run comprised a club-record nine ties, beginning in the first qualifying round with a 4-1 win at Farsley Celtic before a 1-0 victory in a replay at home to Appleby-Frodingham. Tony came in for some rough treatment in the first meeting, a goalless draw at Brumby Hall, his boot being split in one challenge. After Goole's 7-1 home win over Mexborough Town they were nearly knocked out by Howard Wilkinson's Boston United in a 1-1 draw. Goole won the replay 3-1 at York Street to reach the first round and move into the limelight, where they were drawn away to league rivals Barrow. The tie at Holker Street ended in a 2-0 win and became known in Goole as the 'Battle of Barrow'.

Winger Tony Taylor recalled: 'It was a long trek and not a particularly nice place. It was a really tight game. When I scored about ten minutes from the end the crowd invaded the pitch to try to get the game stopped. Tony and I were standing fairly close to each other when one fan came on and straight-armed him across the face, poleaxing him. But even though he'd been knocked off his feet, Tony typically just got up and carried on, although our trainer, Stan Steadman, who was a great bloke, came on and gave him the magic sponge! We got on our way straight after the match and had a police escort out of Barrow, but I seem to think that we still got a brick through the coach window.'

The second round saw Town drawn at high-flying Third Division Wrexham in a plum tie. Their squad included a strike force of Bill Ashcroft, Bobby Shinton and Graham Whittle, plus Welsh internationals Brian Lloyd, John Roberts, Arfon Griffiths and Mickey Thomas. Turner discussed Tony's future in the build-up, as he had been watched by Southampton and Bury. He was quietly hoping that no one came in for him. The tie provided an ideal showpiece for Tony's talents as Goole upset the odds by drawing 1-1 at the Racecourse Ground, when substitute Jim Kelly cancelled out a controversial strike by Whittle. Goole's exploits resulted in national media coverage. Correspondent Brian North chose Tony as Goole's star player in his ratings. The third-round draw offered the possibility of a visit to 1973 FA Cup winners Sunderland. But Goole lost the replay to a goal by Shinton in front of a 4,200 crowd, including Wales manager Mike Smith. Only a string of saves by Wrexham keeper Brian Lloyd denied Goole a deserved equaliser.

Alan Turner recalled: 'We knew that it was going to be difficult, but it was cold and the dressing rooms had stone floors, so we thought that perhaps Wrexham would not relish the battle. I was very pleased with the way we played, but really disappointed because during the two games we deserved to have won. We proved what a good footballing side we had at Goole at the time.

It was a misty night, the atmosphere was terrific and in many ways it was the highlight of my time at Goole.'

In the midst of Goole's FA Cup adventure, Tony was a member of Hull's team that won the national Universities Athletics Union Cup in 1977. He recalled: 'Hull City's Malcolm Lord coached our side. For a university not known for sporting achievements, we had a very good team. We triumphed against universities with much larger student numbers, such as Leeds, Durham, Exeter and then Aston in the final. Our greatest achievement during the UAU Cup run was beating Loughborough 2-1 in the semi-final, a university famed for its sporting prowess.'

Sir Paul Grant is President of the University of Hull Alumni and was one of Tony's teammates in the victorious Hull side.

He recalled: 'We had a good set of players but without Tony would not have triumphed. Playing on the left of midfield he terrorised the opposition with his marvellous left foot, robust tackling and dribbling ability. Tony had a goal in him, never shirked a challenge and was a warrior. We came through a difficult group with Durham, Sheffield, Newcastle and York. Home advantage was huge. Durham had an excellent side but we came from behind to beat them 3-2 and then dispatched Sheffield 5-1. We eventually faced Exeter and everyone wanted to be in the starting XI. Competition was fierce. Exeter put us under heavy pressure in front of a big crowd that hugged the touchline. It was very close but Tony came to town again and we nicked a win in extra time. The match against Loughborough was an epic encounter. They were professionals in all but name and led with a superb free kick but Tony crashed in a superb equaliser. Ian Lindsay got the winner. Aston were the weakest team since the group stage and we comfortably won the final 2-0. I really enjoyed Tony's company, he was always humble and supportive of others.'

Tony's performances earned him a call-up for England Universities' representative team in Dublin against Irish universities but it was not the most memorable of occasions as he was substituted before half-time.

Towards the end of his degree course Tony applied to Trent Polytechnic in Nottingham to explore the possibility of teaching PE alongside Russian: 'The college offered a combination course for a year. I could have signed for a local non-league side, but Goole wanted me to carry on playing for them and would pay my expenses, so it was ideal.'

Interest in Tony was significant in 1977/78. Goole played seven FA Cup ties before losing at Spennymoor United in the first round. Sheffield Wednesday, Grimsby Town and Scunthorpe United watched him when Goole beat Worksop Town 3-1 at Doncaster Rovers' old Belle Vue Ground in an FA Cup replay. When Goole drew 2-2 at home to Northwich Victoria it was revealed that Sheffield United and Wimbledon had watched him. Turner told reporters: 'Some of these scouts must be blind to risk losing out on such a rare talent.'

Tottenham Hotspur, Bolton Wanderers and Scunthorpe watched Tony in Goole's 1-0 home defeat by Gainsborough Trinity on Boxing Day 1977. There were no bids by the end of the year but speculation about Tony reached fever pitch when Tottenham's Bill Nicholson watched him in Goole's 1-0 defeat against Buxton at snow-bound High Peak on 10 January 1978. It was the quiet before the transfer storm. A verbal offer of £3,000, rising to £10,000 after Tony had played ten first-team matches was turned down. Tottenham then made a firm bid of £5,000 for Goole's board to consider at a meeting on 17 January. Extra options were mooted, the only one that applied being £5,000 after Tony made ten senior appearances. A further £10,000 if Tony became a full international and 10 per cent of a future transfer fee were lost in the mists of time.

Tony made his final appearance for Goole in a 3-2 defeat at Mossley on 21 January, wearing what had become his customary No. 7 shirt. During four seasons at Goole, he made 163 appearances, scoring 23 goals. Tony's move to Spurs was finalised, with talks brought forward by two days to foil late interest from a certain Brian Clough. Tony's transfer made front-page news in the *Huddersfield Daily Examiner* on 26 January 1978, under the headline 'Talented Galvin is £5,000 Spurs bargain'. Alan Turner was saddened that no Yorkshire club had come in for his gifted winger.

Turner never doubted Tony's ability to make the transition to the top flight.

He recalled: 'I was looking for a winger and needed only ten minutes to realise that Tony was special. We had some good players at Goole and managed to get some useful ones in but Tony was my best signing as a manager without a doubt. He became a great player for Goole. Tony was a strong, marauding winger. He really seemed to enjoy it at Goole. In fact, he was sheer magic, and the rest, as they say, is history.'

Tony is fondly remembered by Goole team-mates. Tom Wilson said: 'Tony was deceptive. He could go past people, get in crosses and also posed danger when he'd cut in and shoot with his left foot. He was a good outlet because he'd stay out wide and I used to like to try to find him from the back. Tony found himself up against experienced players like myself who had dropped out of the Football League. But, fortunately, he was a quick learner. Tony always seemed to have his head in a book on the team coach. Usually he was quiet on the pitch too, and wouldn't say boo to a goose until the opposition upset him. But he knew how to look after himself.'

Tony Taylor recollected: 'On the ball Tony was deceptively fast for a big guy and difficult to tackle because he was strong and covered it well with his body. He was good at centring the ball and he had a good shot.'

Chris Jackson added: 'It was a joy to play with him. I was usually at right-back and normally Tony did half of your defending for you. He made the job easier for you because of all the good work he did going up and down the line. Tony had a long, loping stride, but was very quick once he got into it. It was no surprise to me when he went on to great things.'

Jim Kelly recounted: 'Micky Driver and I often used to pick up Tony in Mirfield to take him to home games. We had a good team spirit at Goole, we were all friends and there were no stars. A few young lads would be a bit too cocky, but Tony wasn't. He listened to what Alan Turner and senior players told him and took it on board. He took a back seat until he got on to the pitch and then he became a hell of a good player. Tony gave us quality in midfield and I thought that he could do well in a central position because he was so strong. But I always remember Phil Neal saying that Tony would give him the hardest games he had when he was a full-back at Liverpool.'

Club official Graeme Wilson recalled two cracking goals among Tony's collection: 'One was against Mossley at Goole on a day when it was backs to the wall against a good side. Goole had the experience and knew how to defend well against the elements deep into the second half, but Tony ran 90 yards from one end to the other and cut inside just outside the area to send a left-foot drive into the top corner. Then one night at Gateshead's International Stadium he did something similar, although conditions were far more mundane.'

Tony recalled the transfer saga: 'Snippets appeared in the papers but you do wonder if an opportunity will come along.

Deep down the odds are against it so Alan Turner and Chris advised me to keep my head down until a firm bid came in. I'd signed a new contract so was on £20 a week. It was a frustrating time but I was realistic; it was important to qualify as a teacher in case an offer never came. A few weeks before Christmas I received a phone call to play in a trial match at Sheffield United. I was in the middle of teaching practice. The course head was not happy because he had no idea I played football. But after explaining everything I was allowed to play. However, the game was postponed because of bad weather. It was so frustrating but a few days later I heard a Tottenham scout was coming to watch me play at Buxton.

'Tottenham had been relegated to the Second Division but were on target for an immediate return to the top flight. I was well aware of the club's history so was excited about the prospect. The team were being rebuilt, so it was a massive opportunity to impress. Naturally I was nervous, but to make things worse it was a really wintry, snowy night, bitterly cold with a strong wind on a surface caked in mud. Nowadays the game would have been postponed. Dad travelled to the game but struggled to get there because roads had been blocked. Chatting to Dad beforehand, we felt sure nobody would come because the conditions were awful. But I had to try to put that to the back of my mind, which was not easy, and it was one of those nights when it was not possible for anyone to shine.

'Next thing, Goole rang to tell me Tottenham wanted to sign me. I felt a mixture of disbelief and huge excitement. I later heard that the scout turned out to be the great Bill Nicholson, who did get to the match with his wife. After joining the club, I soon found out what a legend Bill was at Spurs. It was typical of him as chief scout to battle through awful weather to see me play. Bill loved the club and if he agreed to check out a player nothing would get in his way. I'm certain that other scouts would have turned back. I will always be grateful that Bill made the effort. The game ended 0-0. Bill obviously saw something and recommended that the club sign me. It was my lucky day. Goole told me to keep things quiet until everything was agreed. They arranged for me to travel to London on a Monday afternoon after lectures to meet Tottenham manager Keith Burkinshaw. I had to pay for my own ticket and claim it back on expenses. Can you imagine that happening nowadays?

'Just before travelling to London for the most important meeting of my life, I received an urgent message from Nottingham Forest to call manager Brian Clough's main scout, Ronnie Fenton. The message read "Don't go to Tottenham. Talk to us first", or words to that effect. I could not believe it. Why now, after I've been on Forest's doorstep for months? They'd obviously got wind that I was talking to Tottenham and thought maybe they'd missed something. Cloughie had a knack of picking up lads from lower leagues and turning them into great players and this was a time when Forest were really on the up. From struggling in the Second Division they'd got promotion, won the League Cup and were on the way to becoming First Division champions. Who knows what would have happened if I'd met Cloughie, because he liked wide players. Forest played with Martin O'Neill on the right wing and John Robertson on the left wing. In my mind there was no way I'd force my way past either, I'd be in the reserves. I was satisfied with my decision and I've never been one to look back, even though they went on to win the European Cup twice.'

Tony wasn't for turning: 'The way Forest acted summed up football clubs. They sat back until the last moment and expected me to jump with no guarantees. Tottenham had gone out of their way to watch me play and I was confident they'd soon be back in top-flight football. However, Cloughie obviously didn't realise I had signed for Spurs because he turned up for the next Goole game. Apparently, he asked a club official if I was playing. He was told no, because I'd already signed for Spurs. Cloughie was not best pleased! He said thanks for letting me know, promptly turned around and left the ground.'

Tottenham were a team that Tony enjoyed watching growing up: 'Jimmy Greaves was my favourite player in the early 60s after seeing him play, watching football on television and reading about him. Greavsie might not look interested, but would suddenly pounce. He was the most naturally gifted striker of his generation for me. His goals-to-games ratio for club and country was exceptional. Jimmy was a star and the thought of playing for the club, even though I'd never been to London, was too big a pull. Jimmy told me stories about playing teams such as Leeds away from home, when you rarely got a chance as a striker. He did score at Elland Road, but at White Hart Lane it was a different kettle of fish. Leeds struggled to stop him. Greavsie was the best and scored so many goals. My favourite was a solo effort I saw on BBC's *Match of the Day* against Manchester United when Jimmy seemed to beat the entire team for a brilliant goal in a 5-1 win.

'It is almost beyond belief that his incredible goalscoring record has now been passed by the amazing Harry Kane. What an unbelievable achievement. Harry will go down in Spurs folklore and I can say with confidence that his final tally will not be beaten. I just hope he wins a major honour to cement his career at the club.

'When Jimmy passed away in 2021 the many tributes showed the esteem he was held in by the footballing world but also the impact he had after his playing days, on television with Ian St

John, who we also lost the same year. ITV's *Saint & Greavsie* was an iconic show in its time for players and fans alike.'

Tottenham's assistant manager Peter Shreeve met Tony at King's Cross station. Tony recalled: 'We went straight to White Hart Lane to meet manager Keith Burkinshaw. He sat me down and got straight to the point. He said, "I've never seen you play, so I don't know what you are like, but if you are good enough for Bill, then that'll do for me." We chatted briefly about my teacher training and Keith felt it would be best to finish the course, which did make sense, although there was a part of me that hoped I'd just sign on full-time terms. I would not be able to train full time with the squad until my studies were complete, so they could judge me properly only after a full pre-season. Keith insisted during holidays from college that I'd come down to train and get a feel for things. The club would organise digs. Keith offered me £50 a week with a view to signing a full contract in the summer after my exams. There was no discussion about the money. Basically, he said take it or leave it. There was nothing to consider. I signed my first professional contract in January 1978.'

The move meant a change in Tony's general lifestyle: 'I travelled down from Nottingham on a Saturday morning to play for Tottenham reserves in the Football Combination League and travelled back after the game. Looking back, football was a different world all those years ago and I have to credit Keith for the way he operated. Training at Tottenham was a real eye-opener, especially in terms of fitness and skill levels. But having an opportunity with a big club at 21 years of age was amazing, although I knew I'd be on the periphery. Even so, I had my big break so was hugely excited, although nervous in equal measure as I prepared to move south.

'Peter managed the reserves and was really encouraging, but he could be scary and had a wicked sense of humour. Of course, there was a lot of mickey-taking because of my studies and student-like appearance from lads such as Mark Falco, Chris Hughton and Paul Miller. But I quickly got used to the jibes and gave some verbals back. I was a bit raw in terms of the football, but the main gulf in class was training. During a game I was not overawed and got my crosses in as instructed. But when you saw some of the lads in training, a number were technically better than me. I had a lot to work on, especially my first touch, control, passing and getting my head up when on a run, but it was great to be at a club with such a rich history in English football. It was an exciting time as Tottenham battled for promotion with Bolton Wanderers, Southampton and Brighton. First-team regulars included Steve Perryman, Glenn Hoddle, Peter Taylor and John Pratt. Tottenham did go up, but only on goal average ahead of Brighton. Bolton won the title, a point clear of Southampton, who were a point ahead of Tottenham and Brighton. It was that close. With Spurs being back in the big time, breaking into the first team would be more difficult, but I relished the challenge.'

Chapter 7

New Era Dawns at White Hart Lane

TONY GALVIN had made a giant leap in footballing terms when he swapped non-league life with Goole Town for a chance to play for Tottenham Hotspur, one of the biggest, most prestigious clubs in the United Kingdom. He had served his apprenticeship in the lower reaches but Spurs were on the way back to the top flight after one season in the old Second Division and a lot was expected as they strove to re-establish themselves among the top echelons. The pressure was on them as a club and that in turn was passed down to the individual players to succeed.

Tony reflected: 'Spurs signed me on a full-time contract during the close season. Top teams didn't often take a punt on a 21-year-old they were hoping to develop, but I fell into that category and was determined to give it everything. The club used numerous bed and breakfast places and put me up in digs in a house in Enfield, close to the ground, but the situation didn't suit me because the landlord was rather old-fashioned. I had to get out and found a room in a flat that a Tottenham supporter was renting out in Ware, just off the A10. I liked being more independent because it did not feel like digs and I got on well with John the landlord. I was also able to provide him complimentary Spurs tickets, which of course delighted him, so the arrangement worked well.

'There was great anticipation for the new season at White Hart Lane, which sky-rocketed to another level following the arrival of Ossie Ardiles and Ricky Villa, who had just helped Argentina to win the 1978 World Cup. The media frenzy was incredible. I watched the World Cup finals in Argentina on television, but was not prepared for the signings of Ardiles and Villa a few days after I had joined the club full time. It was a shock and surprise, not only to me but the football world. Ossie had been one of the stars at the tournament. Spurs wanted to make an immediate impact in the First Division. It was a massive statement of intent but a huge gamble for the club, shelling out a lot of money, as it was in those days.

'When Ossie and Ricky arrived, it really struck home that this was serious business and it did cross my mind on numerous occasions that I was miles away from the quality of some of these players. Would I ever play for the first team? In the end, the way I looked at it was that I had nothing to lose because I had never set out to be a professional footballer. I would get reasonable money for a year or two and take it from there. If it did not work out at Spurs, I would probably get a shot elsewhere because I was at a top-flight club. I joined the first-team squad on occasions for pre-season training, but mainly trained with the reserves. Of course, you hope at some stage to get a chance of a first-team appearance, but it was no great surprise that I never broke through in that first full season.

'My pre-season experiences had been at Goole so I was not sure what to expect at Spurs. I'd previously been told, "You won't see a ball for a week or so." It would be all endurance work. Not at Spurs. On the first day, after running drills in the morning, the balls came out for the afternoon session. I was shocked but it told me about the club's philosophy. The reserves would line up in practice games against the first team, normally on a Thursday.

Peter Shreeve was a really good coach and his team was well-drilled to make it as hard as possible for the first team. I loved these games. It gave me a chance to show my stuff against the senior players. It was also an opportunity to get stuck in and let players know you weren't a pushover. In these games I'd prefer it if things got a bit lively and maybe a little physical. I would be up against Jimmy Holmes, John Gorman and sometimes John Pratt, all experienced First Division players. John in particular was a Spurs stalwart who was rarely out of the first team. John often says to me that in these practice games the best way to deal with me was to be pleasant and say, "Hello." The mistake would be to kick me and get me riled up!

'We did a lot of technical work with the ball. A couple of afternoons a week we'd work on a variety of skills and technique in the ball court. To begin with I was useless at these sessions, but improved over time. I'd never taken part in such practice drills. Apprentices had been doing it for years so were far superior to me. I remember Mark Falco and Gary Brooke ribbing me about my ineptness. They weren't wrong, but Shreeve wouldn't allow you to get changed unless you completed your final task, which may have involved volleying the ball three times into a circle on the wall. You had to work on your technique and improve. I was inferior technically but had natural pace, was two-footed, strong and fearless. I was not scared to get stuck in and was always a reasonable crosser of a ball, whether on the right or left wing. Spurs were a ball-playing team, so good technical ability was important. I had the basics but was lacking in terms of some technical elements. But that was no surprise. My starting point was non-league football. I had to improve this aspect of my game and achieved it through persistence and hard work, despite the mickey-taking of colleagues.

'The reserves played in the Football Combination League and I rarely missed a game. I never got a sense of being close to the first team. On one occasion I was 13th man against Ipswich Town, but there was only one substitute and Stuart Beavon was handed the number 12 shirt. But experiencing a matchday preparation was important and being part of the squad entitled me to bonuses! The reserve team would win the Combination League two years running. Chris Hughton, Mark Falco, Micky Hazard, Chris Jones, Paul Miller and Terry Naylor were regulars alongside players returning from injuries. Although I was slightly intimidated on a technical level, playing non-league had toughened me up. During training games, on a physical level I could hold my own and I was often guilty of getting stuck in. I could be a little cumbersome and occasionally injured fellow players, but I just believed that was how you should approach training. I wanted to impress and always felt that it was nonsense to apologise for a late challenge because all I was doing was going for the ball.

'Ricky Villa, however, saw it differently and always tells stories about his early training sessions against me. Apparently, according to him, I used to kick him more than any other player! He thought I was out to hurt him, but I was oblivious to it all and in my eyes was being enthusiastic. That was my job. Ricky complained to Keith but it invariably fell on deaf ears. Keith just told him to get on with it and never really criticised me for being over-physical in training. Knowing Keith, a Yorkshireman, he probably thought it would toughen Ricky up in preparation for some of the league's more aggressive players, Tommy Smith and Kenny Burns to name but two. Ricky was a very talented player and on his day was as good as anyone I played alongside, as proven by his amazing, mazy dribble which created arguably still the greatest goal ever scored in a cup final. But that was for the future!

'It was a privilege to train with top professionals. Glenn Hoddle was such a gifted footballer with a wonderful technique. He was excellent with both feet and had incredible vision. In training I used to avoid getting too close to him and preferred to admire him from afar. Funnily enough, he was one player I would never kick! Ossie was equally outstanding but in a different way. He had a superb first touch, was incredibly quick over five yards and was almost impossible to tackle because he always seemed to get to the ball just before you did. He was an instinctive thinker and could sense when someone had a heavy touch and would nick the ball off a player in an instant. In these days of the high press he would have excelled. Ossie was fearless at home and away, and in any conditions. Nothing fazed him. He'd pop up and do something special in both penalty areas. I never felt in awe of any of the lads but, when it came to technique, I was miles off Ossie and Glenn. Both were sensational players.'

As for Tottenham's captain, Tony added: 'Steve Perryman was a born leader on and off the pitch. An excellent communicator, sublime first touch and incredibly accurate short-passer of the ball. He was of course a fierce competitor and ferocious tackler. What these three players had in common was that they came alive in any sort of training that involved competitive games. They all had a burning desire to compete and to win. Their standards were high and this meant you had to work hard to compete. Glenn, Ossie and Steve were three different but outstanding professionals and it was a pleasure to have trained and played with them.

'Steve had been at the club for years. He was captain and could excel in defence or midfield, but more importantly he was a leader. Glenn was the star player. Comfortable on the ball, Glenn controlled games and scored spectacular goals. He was an incredibly talented footballer but sometimes would find it difficult because opponents put two players on him and he'd get overpowered. The tactic was to play him out of the game. Glenn, though, was still young and coming into his peak years. The way he'd pick a 30- or 40-yard pass out was unbelievable, left or right foot, and he could ghost past players before striking a ball with power and accuracy. Glenn on his day was the best passer of a ball I played alongside.'

Spurs were a match for anyone on their day but were inconsistent. They were easy on the eye and often featured on *Match of the Day* or *The Big Match*. But thoughts of being on television during the 1978/79 campaign would be for the future as Tony got used to life at Tottenham. He got a chance to play for Spurs abroad in friendly matches, including a 4-2 win against a Saudi Arabian XI in Jeddah and 7-0 triumph over Al Nassr. The matches enabled young players to spend time with the first-team squad on and off the pitch.

Tottenham had made an inconsistent start and their poor form was noted in an FA Cup fourth-round matchday programme when Spurs played Wrexham as a 'growing concern' following Tony's first-team debut for the club against Manchester City on 3 February 1979. Tottenham went into the First Division match on a run of one win in eight matches but City hadn't won for 13 matches. The line-ups were:

> Tottenham Hotspur: Kendall, McAllister, Holmes, Hoddle, Lacy, Perryman, Galvin, Ardiles, Armstrong, Beavon, Taylor. Sub: Pratt.

> Manchester City: Corrigan, Donachie, Power, Owen, Watson (Deyna), Futcher, Channon, Bell, Kidd, Hartford, Barnes.

A Brian Kidd penalty, spectacular Peter Barnes strike and Mike Channon header sealed a 3-0 away win.

The *Tottenham Weekly Herald* didn't hold back in its report after an inauspicious display: 'Spurs started this game with high hopes, but finished with their pride buried deep in the White Hart Lane mud and the knowledge that there's a great deal of work still to be done.'

Tony recalled: 'Keith brought Stuart Beavon, Jimmy Holmes and myself in for a home game against City. Sometimes a manager thinks, "Let's throw a few in and see how it goes." We were told the day before the game. I was delighted to get a chance, but it came as a shock. Naturally, though, I was excited. Family and friends wished me well. These were the days before texts, tweets and emails so it was great to receive good luck telegrams, including one from my old manager at Goole, Alan Turner, on the day of the game. But I wasn't ready for first-team action. My debut turned into a disaster. I was playing right-wing in the reserves so was up against Paul Power, an experienced player, and got nowhere. It was awful. I couldn't get near him and picked up a booking for fouling Colin Bell, who was one of my favourite players as a teenager. He was past his best because of injuries but too good for me on the day. City had great players, including left-winger Barnes, who had a blinder. He tore our defence to pieces and scored a goal. We got hammered 3-0. Keith came over to me on the Monday and told me he didn't think I was ready. I didn't get a rollicking, I just mumbled that it could have gone better, which was an understatement! Nerves got to me, but it didn't help that the team played poorly. I was back in the reserves for the remainder of the season; it was a deflating experience.'

An interesting newcomer arrived during the 1979/80 close season as Tottenham signed a familiar face to Tony – Terry Yorath, who played many times with Chris at Leeds United in the reserves. Tony recalled: 'Terry broke through to Revie's team but had joined Coventry City. He was never quite accepted by Leeds fans as a Revie legend. Terry got stick from a section of supporters, which was ridiculous because he was a good player, but succeeding the likes of Bremner and Giles was an impossible task. Thankfully he is now regarded as a Revie legend, as it's deserved. Terry and Chris got on well at Leeds because they experienced the same frustrations breaking into the first team. And we hit it off straightaway. Terry was down to earth and a good influence on the Tottenham side. An experienced Welsh international, he knew the game, was a tough lad, got stuck in and had a wise head in terms of attitude and tactics. Bringing Yorath to the club was shrewd by Burkinshaw.'

Tony featured in several pre-season matches. Two days before the start of the campaign there were injury concerns, with Ardiles and Villa struggling to be fit. Peter Taylor was also injured, which brought media speculation that Tony would get another first-team opportunity in the season's opener against Middlesbrough. Alas, he didn't make the 'Boro clash. But a brief north London derby appearance at Highbury followed when Tony came off the bench in a 1-0 loss. Then there were cameo appearances as Tottenham defeated Stoke City at home and then he scored his first senior Football League goal in a 2-1 defeat at Derby County on 23 February 1980. But Tottenham's performance against a Derby team without a win in 13 previous attempts was pilloried in the press.

Tottenham were competitive and illustrated that when they defeated Manchester United against the odds in an FA Cup replay at Old Trafford with an Ardiles goal, prior to the Derby clash. Liverpool ended their FA Cup dreams in the quarter-finals, although Spurs avenged the defeat with a 2-0 victory at the end of March. All that was left to play for was pride. Tony came back into the first team for a seven-match run, which was a chance to shine, starting with a trip to Molineux against Wolves, who had lifted the Football League Cup against Nottingham Forest at Wembley. The line-ups were:

Wolves: Bradshaw, Palmer, Parkin, Atkinson, Hughes, Berry, Brazier, Carr, Gray, Richards (Clarke), Eves.

Tottenham Hotspur: Daines, Yorath, Hughton, Miller, McAllister, Perryman, Ardiles, Jones, Galvin, Hoddle, Pratt. Sub: Armstrong.

Tony enjoyed a day to remember, scoring the winner in a 2-1 triumph and grabbing the Sunday newspaper headlines. One read 'Galvinised ... Spurs' new boy nails Wolves'. The *Sunday People* was entitled 'Galvin's golden one-two'. Correspondent Pat Collins wrote:

> Erratic Spurs – you never know what they'll do next – can thank new striker Tony Galvin for a good win at Molineux. In only his second full game Galvin linked up forcefully with Chris Jones to sink Wolves with the old one-two. One – Galvin crossed and Jones volleyed powerfully home when both teams were still warming up. Two – the pair had another get-together just after the half-hour and this time Galvin swept home a low pass from Jones.

Recalling the flurry of matches, Tony said: 'Keith Burkinshaw told me before a training match I'd be playing up front against Wolves, even though I'd never played that role in my life. I was not going to refuse the opportunity. I was a runner, Keith wanted me to make runs down the channels. I'd be playing alongside Chris Jones. He'd go for the ball and I should peel off into space left behind. Glenn would hit the ball in there. That's all I had to do – be wary of being caught offside. It was not about me scoring. I'd be running at the defence from an inside-right or inside-left position. Glenn had two choices, pass it in to Chris's feet or go long for me to make a run. With Glenn there were lots of options, but we kept it simple. I'd hold the line and if I made a run on the bend, keep onside, I was in and Glenn would find me.

'It worked a treat against Wolves. Emlyn Hughes in his heyday at Liverpool would have had Tommy Smith or Phil Thompson beside him so it would not have been so easy, but we ran him ragged at his new club. Hughes was past his best and got frustrated. We played well and it was special to score the winner. I wore the number 9 shirt for the first time, which was crazy because I was not a centre-forward, but nobody wanted to wear it. Nowadays players wear all sorts of numbers that have no reflection on where they are playing. Gerry Armstrong had led the line for most of the season but struggled for goals. Hoddle dwarfed his total of eight by finishing top scorer on 22 goals, which was a superb effort. When Armstrong was not in the side, Colin Lee, Jones or Falco led the attack. Tottenham had a great tradition for goalscorers. Following in the footsteps of legends such as Bobby Smith, Jimmy Greaves, Alan Gilzean and Martin Chivers was no easy task.'

Tony was progressing but a derby defeat against Arsenal followed, before a 4-1 defeat at Manchester United: 'Running out against Arsenal at a packed White Hart Lane, I sensed the occasion even though we were struggling. From the day I joined Tottenham I was aware of the fierce rivalry. Even playing for the reserves, particularly at home, we'd get solid crowds and the players would be kicking lumps out of each other. In this game, I hardly got a kick against Willie Young and David O'Leary in the Arsenal defence. There was no space and I constantly had an opponent tight against my backside, so I couldn't get into the game. In my first ever game at Old Trafford we got thumped. It was a really disappointing result, but going to Liverpool and United in those days you wouldn't see the ball too often and the game could pass you by. This time I played up front but struggled to get in the game. Andy Ritchie scored a hat-trick and Ray Wilkins finished us off. Ritchie had just got into the team as a teenager and had a blinder. He was seen as the next "big thing" but, for whatever reason, it never worked out for him at United. But he did enjoy a long career at Oldham Athletic and then at Leeds United.'

Despite the defeats, Tony remained in the team but was moved to a left-midfield role and scored his first home goal – reported as a 'low, swerving shot' in the *News of the World* – in a 3-0 win against Everton. He also hit the target in a 2-2 draw with Wolves. The season ended with a goalless draw at home to Bristol City.

Tony said: 'I was pleased to have had a run in the first team, even though it was as a striker. When Burkinshaw moved me to midfield, it suited my game more. I now had something to build on for the new season.'

Chapter 8

Tottenham 'Up for the Cup'

JUST AS Tony Galvin was making solid progress with Tottenham Hotspur, he developed a major problem with his pelvis that threatened his professional career just as it had started.

Tony outlined his plight: 'Coming into the 1980/81 pre-season, I'd played a few games and was on the fringes of the first team, waiting for an extended run to cement a spot. I felt part of the squad but had a nagging groin strain, which unknown to me was putting my career in the balance. I continually felt something pulling in the groin area, which took half a yard off my sprinting, especially on sharp sprints away from opponents. I mentioned it to the physio, Mike Varney, without realising something was really wrong. I had several massages in the area, but the club doctor, Brian Curtin, referred me to a specialist who would hopefully be able to diagnose the issue. The Doc, as we used to call him, was great with the players. He'd been there for years and was there throughout my time at Spurs. Sadly, he passed away a few years ago. The Doc was held in great esteem by the club.

'I had a serious pelvic injury and could have carried on playing, but the wear and tear injury was taking an edge off my running game. Where the hips joined, the bone had eroded away so the specialist wanted to fuse it together. I could have an operation, but there was a risk it might not work. Thinking through my options, I decided to have the procedure. The club, fortunately for my career, were happy to go with it and pay for the operation. This was long before players were insured for massive amounts of money. When the club agreed to pay for what was a tricky and expensive operation for a player who had played only a handful of first-team games, I believed from that point I owed the club something in return. Hopefully I repaid their trust and investment in me.

'I'd broken into the side while not fully fit, so if an operation could make a difference to my sprinting ability I'd have a better chance of regular first-team football. The worst scenario was that I'd be at the same level, which might end my Tottenham career. I had to give myself the best chance of making it, even though I knew my recuperation would be between six and nine months, which meant the whole season could be wiped out. This might affect my chances of getting a new contract but, from my point of view, I believed I would return fitter and stronger, which would benefit all parties. I remained positive about the future.'

Tottenham manager Keith Burkinshaw didn't forget about Tony while he was on the sidelines. He went to see him soon after the operation and Tony discovered how Spurs had made great efforts to strengthen their squad and make progress during the campaign.

Tony said: 'I was sitting up in bed at the hospital when Keith came to see me following the first game of the season against Nottingham Forest, featuring new signings Steve Archibald and Garth Crooks in a 2-0 win. Garth scored our second goal. The club had shelled out big money for them. Their arrival was a major statement of intent by the club following the signings of Ossie and Ricky Villa, although without the same media circus. They'd signed quality strikers. It was very kind of Keith to take time out to come and visit me in hospital after the game. It said a lot about him as a man. We then defeated Crystal Palace at Selhurst Park, when both scored. Garth hit the target again in a draw at home to Brighton. Keith realised we'd had a problem in attack, but now it seemed that, by signing these two top strikers, scoring goals would not be a problem.'

Tony's injury marred any sense of continuity for him within the Spurs framework, but his aspirations were aided by his powers of recovery. In addition, Tottenham failed to capitalise on a promising opening to the campaign. He reflected: 'The operation took place in July 1980 and it was going to be tough getting back, but I returned to the reserves in record time for this procedure and have to credit the club physio, who helped me back to full fitness. I'd always had a good pair of lungs but by my return I felt at least 20 per cent fitter. At this point I have to acknowledge not only the excellence of my surgeon but also the support provided by Mike. He was a hard taskmaster but instilled in me the belief that I could return to full fitness and be in a position to compete for a place in the first team. Time was running out on my football career as a consequence of my injury and subsequent operation. I was 24 years old and in football terms that was pretty old. I'll always be grateful to Mike for his encouragement during what was a pretty dark period. Also, my first wife, Julie, visited me in hospital on a regular basis and also provided the necessary support during my recuperation to ensure I was ready and able to resume full-time training. Any professional sportsperson relies heavily on support mechanisms around them. They cannot succeed without that support. Mike and Julie were really important in my recovery.

'The first team started the season well, but from the middle of November they became inconsistent again. Approaching the New Year I was pushing for first-team selection and my timing was fortuitous because we'd been on a bad run. Apart from a couple of wins against Manchester City and Ipswich Town we'd shipped a shedload of goals. Our attitude seemed to be that we could outscore the opposition, because we'd beaten Ipswich 5-3 then drawn 4-4 with Southampton and 2-2 against Norwich City during the festive fixtures. In this period I had played only a couple of reserve team games, one of which was a midweek game at Southampton, which bizarrely also ended 4-4. It was momentous because it featured Kevin Keegan's return to England. The Saints game went well and I was close to full fitness.'

In the FA Cup the road to Wembley started out when Tottenham drew Second Division Queens Park Rangers at Loftus Road. Burkinshaw had to resolve a goalkeeping crisis, with Barry Daines doubtful. Youth player Tony Parks was set to stand in after Milija Aleksic needed 15 stitches in a horrific leg wound after colliding with a net support at Norwich. But in the end Daines was able to play. Tony came on for Ricky Villa in a tense draw and played in the replay because Villa had a knee injury. Crooks, Tony and Hoddle scored in front of a 39,294 crowd at The Lane.

Burkinshaw told the *Evening Standard*: 'Tony has made a remarkably swift recovery from his operation and is obviously making the most of his chance now that he is back in the first team. He's a tenacious type of lad who never knows when he's beaten. He's got tremendous pace, two good feet and I believe he's the type of player who wins you things.'

Tony recalled: 'Keith wanted to know if I could travel with the first-team squad for the third-round tie. Mike Varney said I was ready. Loftus Road was a tight ground. You were close to the spectators and the atmosphere would be electric. Ossie had been out injured so Gary Brooke had come into midfield alongside Glenn and Ricky, who was playing on the left, but hated the position and was carrying a knock. Keith wanted me on the bench. It was a bit early, but I felt confident I'd not let the team down. I played okay in a tough 0-0 draw. It felt great to be back and Keith kept me in the side for the replay. I was really buzzing. Garth opened the scoring, then put me in for our second goal in a 3-1 win. The team needed someone comfortable on the left in midfield and from my point of view I was that man. I'd joined Spurs as a right-winger but, because Dad had insisted that both me and Chris should kick with both feet, I was comfortable playing on the left. I had done so at school and university. I was just happy to get on that field. I could do the job and, once I was in the team, I believed it would take a good man to displace me.'

Tony played his third match in a week a few days later and made his first league appearance of the season. Crooks scored in a comfortable 1-0 win against Birmingham City. Spurs were unbeaten in five matches and correspondent Reg Drury of the *News of the World* reported:

> Galvin, who has deputised for Villa, was the star turn in this match. He posed all kinds of problems for the Birmingham defence and was desperately unlucky not to score after 47 minutes. Galvin swerved his way past two opponents and beat 'keeper Jeff Wealands with a shot which rebounded from the face of the bar. In that moment I fancy he may have booked his spot against Arsenal.

And journalist James Dobson wrote:

> Galvin was particularly impressive, ever dangerous on the flanks and creating problem after problem for the Birmingham defence.

TOTTENHAM 'UP FOR THE CUP'

At Highbury, an Archibald brace won a hard-fought derby. Spurs were six matches unbeaten but there were some tensions off the pitch as Ardiles was dropped for this clash because he was late back from playing for Argentina against Uruguay in the Gold Cup. Ardiles had also not agreed a new contract but Burkinshaw named him to face Hull City in an FA Cup fourth-round clash. However, Spurs struggled to break down the third-tier team. Brooke came on for Ardiles and opened the scoring six minutes from time. Archibald made it 2-0 for the win. Ardiles, though, was soon back on song and scored as Tottenham eased past Coventry City in the fifth round. Archibald and Hughton also scored in a 3-1 victory. Spurs then drew Third Division giant-killers Exeter City, who were in the quarter-finals for only the second time in their history, after stunning victories against top-flight Leicester City and then Second Division Newcastle United. Despite the West Stand being demolished for renovations, 40,000 fans packed White Hart Lane, where Roberts and Miller scored second-half goals in a 2-0 win that took Spurs into the semi-finals.

Tony reflected: 'After a few good performances I became a fixture on the left side of the team for the rest of an unforgettable season. I was a good crosser of the ball, I had a good engine and a reasonable sense of how to defend when the opposition was in possession. Chris Hughton was left-back and we established a good rapport, allowing him to break forward and me to provide the necessary cover when he did so. He was a superb full-back, quick, alert and two-footed. A wonderful player to have as a team-mate. I think between us we nailed that left side for the next few years. The only bizarre thing was nobody wanted the number 9 shirt. So I played on the left wing in Ricky's number

9 shirt because Archie wore 8 and Garth had taken the number 11 jersey. Ricky wore the number 5 shirt.

'Coming back into the side was fortuitous because no player wants a team-mate to get injured, but it's part of the game and you have to take your chance when it comes. It just so happened that Ricky was playing on the left at the time. For whatever reason he seemed to have a mental block and much preferred to play in the middle of the park. If opponents passed Ricky, he was awful running back. He was fit but didn't have the mentality to chase back. Glenn preferred to play on the right. Ossie played either in front of the back four or just behind the front two in the hole, as they now call it, and that was probably his best position. I just ran up and down the left, getting crosses in or protecting Chris as best I could. That was, to put it simply, my job. I was happy to run up and down the left side for 90 minutes for the benefit of the team.

'I was acutely aware that nobody else in the squad wanted to play on the left. I had no problem with it. I was two-footed … thanks Dad! – so why not play on the left, despite the fact that for the majority of my amateur, non-league and Spurs reserves career I had played on the right? "Go with it" was my view. Nobody had settled in the left-sided position. Terry Yorath, Peter Taylor and Ricky had played there but now I had the slot and was not going to let it go. I could cut in or take a player on. Maybe Keith's plan all along was to try me in that position, which was my good fortune. My role was clear to me. While I was not expected to be scoring regularly, I brought balance to the left flank. Offensively we created lots of chances but, because we had a lightweight midfield, we'd come up against teams who dominated us. When I got to know Ronnie Whelan with Ireland, he told me that Liverpool knew that if they closed down Ossie and Glenn they'd win the midfield battle and the game. They felt Tottenham had a soft centre in midfield. Keith put me in to bring some defensive solidity to the team. I'd tuck in and support Chris, who bombed forward at every opportunity. I was happy to chase back and we had more options down the left flank. After a few games I couldn't see Ricky coming back in front of me. We had a team full of flair players. Ricky did not offer what I gave to the side.

'Keith needed someone who could do the defensive duties. Only I could lose my place in the side. Keith wanted me to stick to what I was good at. If I did that, then I'd stay in the team. And the lads were behind the move in those early days. Steve Perryman was always behind me, urging me on and telling me to keep on top of it. At times we'd row because I could be quite stubborn, but deep down he knew best and it was his job as captain to keep on at me and improve me as a player. All the lads respected Steve; all top teams need a player of his type. Keith was not on the field so Steve's job was to pester, cajole and encourage you. He was very good at that! A wonderful leader who was incredibly loyal to Spurs, Steve might have won more trophies and England caps if he had moved elsewhere. He didn't. He loved Spurs. For him there was no other club.'

Tottenham since 1960/61, when they won the coveted double, had enjoyed a reputation for being a strong cup team rather than one that had the consistency to win a league title. Clubs then refrained from playing weakened line-ups in the FA Cup because of its importance. A cup run also kept interest for fans when their team wasn't challenging for the league. This was the case in 1981 for Spurs' huge support, although a run to the last four hadn't been anticipated.

Tony observed: 'The FA Cup was massive in that era but we were inconsistent, so it didn't cross my mind we might win the cup. You just take it game by game. The draw was going our way. We beat Coventry City, on a ridiculously icy pitch at White Hart Lane. Ossie demonstrated incredible balance and expertise on the day, proving what a world-class player we had in our ranks, but there was no talk of winning the cup. From my point of view, I was happy to be in the team and make my contributions. Then we got another home draw, this time against Exeter. At this point you just thought: "Maybe, just maybe." QPR had been tough, but we'd won in a replay and then had three home draws. It was a massive opportunity. Exeter played well but we were now in the semi-finals. Interestingly, I hadn't played well in the game and felt under the weather. I went home and straight to bed. I felt so tired. At training on the Monday the Doc inspected me and said I had a swelling in my mouth. I was sent to the club dentist. I was diagnosed as having a serious tooth abscess and I was prescribed strong antibiotics. This clearly explained why I felt so under par on the Saturday versus Exeter! I recovered within days.

'For me it was now panic stations. Which side would we get … Manchester City, Ipswich Town or Wolves? Ossie had won the World Cup. Steve and Archie had played in cup finals, but the rest of us had not been in any major final. We started to sense pressure because the club had done nothing for years. Tottenham's last cup triumphs had been under Bill Nicholson when they won the FA Cup, League Cup and UEFA Cup in the late 60s and early 70s. But now it was our turn and there was an edge and nervousness in the dressing room. The semi-final was a massive occasion for the club.

'Ipswich were favourites with the bookmakers. They had a very strong team so were the side to avoid. Apart from battling for the First Division with Liverpool and Manchester United, they'd had outstanding results in the UEFA Cup, a trophy that was really tough to win because it was an era when only the league champions participated in the European Cup, so they came up against strong teams. Manager Bobby Robson had assembled a great squad, that included Paul Mariner, Kevin Beattie, Mick Mills, John Wark, Terry Butcher, Alan Brazil, Frans Thijssen, Arnold Mühren and Eric Gates. Ipswich went on to win the UEFA Cup and finished third in the league, as Liverpool retained their title. Manchester City had flair players but had been inconsistent in the league, like ourselves. As it turned out, Ipswich drew City and we pulled Wolves out of "the hat". Neither of us had a chance of getting into Europe via the league, so winning the cup was the only target. We fancied our chances in a one-off game to reach Wembley.

'After a brief injury I was back for a home win against Aston Villa and then victory at Coventry. We then drew 2-2 with Everton, a match when I opened the scoring. By now Aleksic had replaced Daines in goal, who earlier in the season had taken over from Kendall. No key players picked up an injury against Everton so we were all set for the Wolves clash at Hillsborough.'

With 1981 being the Chinese Year of the Cockerel there were many writers predicting that Tottenham's name was on the cup. And there were predictions from pundits, including a quartet of 1966 World Cup winners in the matchday programme. Jack and Bobby Charlton both fancied Wolves, but Martin Peters, who helped Tottenham to defeat Wolves in the 1972 UEFA Cup Final and League Cup at Wembley a year later, unsurprisingly, backed his former club. Boys of 66 skipper Bobby Moore commented: 'Neither of the sides is an out-and-out favourite, but without a doubt Spurs have the more talented players in midfield and up front.' John Fennelly wrote in the *Tottenham Weekly Herald*:

> If Spurs win the FA Cup this year many people will say that it was in the stars. But the players and supporters at White Hart Lane have many other reasons for feeling confident. With this the Chinese Year of the Cockerel and the fact that the year ends in the figure one – when the club historically seem to do well – the more romantic among us are already convinced about whose name will be going to the official engravers. But the man on the terraces does not need such omens and will point to just one thing – the quality of players on the pitch.

Come the semi-final, Tony recounted: 'We were raring to go. In Ossie and Glenn, we had top players, and Archie and Garth were scoring regularly. Keith brought Ricky back into the team after injury. We were well aware how massive the game was, not only for us but also for our supporters who had been starved of success since 1973.'

The semi-final took place at Hillsborough on 11 April 1981 and the teams lined up as:

> Tottenham Hotspur: Aleksic, Hughton, Miller, Villa (Brooke, 107), Roberts, Perryman, Ardiles, Archibald, Galvin, Hoddle, Crooks.

> Wolverhampton Wanderers: Bradshaw, Palmer, Parkin, Clarke (Bell, 78), McAlle, Berry, Hibbitt, Carr, Gray, Richards, Hughes.

But this meeting ended in a controversial 2-2 draw. Robert Oxby, from the *Daily Telegraph*, summed up the view of many correspondents when he wrote:

Tottenham were robbed of victory by a 90th-minute penalty that should never have been. Mr Thomas's erratic control marred a magnificent contest and, having booked nearly a third of the players, it is as well that he will not be in charge of the replay. In the short interval before extra time Keith Burkinshaw had physically to restrain some of his players as members of his staff consoled others.

Tony reflected: 'For whatever reason we didn't kill off Wolves. Archie tucked away one of my crosses to give us an early lead, but Kenny Hibbitt equalised. Glenn put us back in front from a superb free kick on the edge of the penalty box, which we thought should have been a penalty. We looked home and dry when Glenn was deemed to have fouled Hibbitt in the box. Glenn and Hibbitt came together. Hibbitt went down, as you would in the last minute, and Thomas, who was known for giving harsh decisions, fell for it. We felt really hard done by when Thomas pointed to the spot. There was a lot of protesting but the penalty was put away by Willie Carr. The decision knocked us back and we were hanging on during extra time. Towards the end a number of the lads' legs had gone so instructions came to give me the ball. The bench kept yelling at me to run the ball towards the corner flag to kill time, which I did. Back in the dressing room we felt deflated. There was a feeling that maybe our chance to reach Wembley had gone. A replay of the incident on television showed Glenn had clearly played the ball and Hibbitt acknowledged it was not a foul, which made it worse. We felt robbed, but snapped out of it, especially when we heard that City had defeated Ipswich. We thought this might be our year. Thomas's decision gave us extra motivation. We could beat Wolves.

'Apart from Thomas's decision, the match is remembered for crowd issues at the Leppings Lane end of the ground. Tottenham fans were on the edge of the pitch close to the touchline but I had no idea why until later, when I found out there were too many of them in the stand. Supporters complained about being crushed and were moved to the opposite end of the stadium. With crowd trouble an ongoing issue, fencing was put in and, tragically, eight years later 96 Liverpool fans died at the same end in a semi-final against Nottingham Forest. Sadly, a 97th died from his injuries in 2021. The Hillsborough disaster brought long-term ramifications. Thankfully we now have all-seater stadiums, but it took far too long for bereaved families to get justice. This was a footballing tragedy that should never have happened and must never be forgotten.'

New FA Cup rules stipulated that a different referee would officiate from the original game, so George Courtney handled the replay four days later and Spurs made no mistake, comfortably winning 3-0, with Villa giving a hint of what was to come in the final.

Tony said: 'Tottenham fans packed Highbury and roared us on to Wembley in a one-sided affair. It was strange playing a semi-final at Highbury but it was a ground used to holding semis. We were still smarting from the injustice of the penalty and were determined to start on the front foot against Wolves. Glenn and Garth linked up superbly for the first two goals in the first half. Ricky then scored a magnificent long-distance goal to clinch victory. For Spurs fans it was a memorable evening, particularly because it was at the home of their local rivals. Some say it made up for Arsenal clinching the double at White Hart Lane in 1971. Anyway, Spurs were on their way to Wembley!

'Ricky had his best game for the club and was outstanding on a memorable night. Ricky had been at the club for nearly three seasons and was the type of player who got stronger when we were on top. Ossie played deeper, allowing Ricky to have a free role with no defensive responsibilities. It took time for Keith to get the best out of Ossie, Glenn and Ricky in midfield. They could play as a three together, especially when we were on top of teams, as we were that night. . We passed and moved the ball around; we played some lovely football.'

With a Wembley final on the horizon, Tony took time out to contemplate how far his football journey had come: 'The turnaround in my career had been startling and I did have to pinch myself at times. My weekly salary had increased from about £100 to £150, which sounds a pittance nowadays, but it was a lot to me then. There were also bonuses for appearances, wins and so on. After the semi-final draw there was talk of a players' pool if we got to Wembley. But I was so naive, I didn't have a clue that there may be one, so just went with the flow. Suddenly all the talk was about Wembley and something had to give. Although you say all the right things in the press, our minds were firmly on winning the cup.

'Our build-up to the final was terrible because we didn't win a game. Whether we admitted it or not, our heads had turned. I don't recall changing my game, but there was clearly a dip from the side in general. Apart from myself, only Steve Perryman and Paul Miller of our cup final side started the five remaining league games. Behind the scenes there had been a shift in focus, but we drew our last home game with Liverpool, who were marching to another title, so we put a shift in. We rested a number of lads for the last league game at West Brom to make sure they were fit for Wembley. We were mid-table, not going anywhere but we were embarrassing. West Brom were always strong at home. Peter Barnes, Laurie Cunningham and Cyrille Regis were unplayable. They battered us 4-2 and I felt sorry for our travelling fans. We let them down that day.'

For professional footballers of Tony's generation, the FA Cup Final at Wembley was the biggest match of the season. It was one every player hoped to be a part of one day. It was an era before satellite television; the FA Cup Final and England vs Scotland Home International fixture were the only matches shown live on terrestrial television. There were just three stations – BBC1, BBC2 and ITV. Channel 4 would be launched in 1982. It was also an era before play-off finals, so most players never played at Wembley. The occasion was not lost on Tony and, during the Wembley build-up, the players got involved in all sorts of bizarre events. The highlight for most of the lads was making a cup final record.

Chas Hodges recalled how the song 'Ossie's Dream' came about in the 25th anniversary celebration brochure *Glory Glory ... Tottenham Hotspur*. The story goes that a club official approached Chas & Dave's manager, Bob England, who was a Spurs fanatic. Ardiles playing in a cup final had been in the media, which formed a theme. Dave Peacock produced a demo, then gathered the squad to record the song.

Chas recounted: 'We had the backing track laid down before the semi-final against Wolves. The day after we won that we got all the boys into the studio. We went over the road to the pub and came back with a few bottles of beer and finished the whole thing at about two or three o'clock in the morning. The lads were very professional and they really went for it. It was all good fun, a great afternoon. Ossie was messing about with a klaxon horn that he found. We took him aside to tell him that his line in the song was "… in the cup for Tott-ing-ham". He said, "It's okay, I can say Tottenham now." But we said, "No, no, no. Say Tott-ing-ham." He did it first take. I must say that we were surprised by the success of the song. At first, we were thinking that if it made the Top 20 then that would be a big success. But it kept going up and then, of course, the phone wouldn't stop ringing and we went on BBC's *Top of the Pops*. The players were like little kids that day – they seemed to be more excited there than they were out on the pitch.'

Tony enjoyed the whole experience of being a pop star. He recalled: 'Chas, who sadly is no longer with us, and Dave were popular entertainers and fanatical Tottenham supporters. Every club had a catchy cup final song and they were keen to do it. It was part of the fun associated with a final. To our great surprise it reached number 5 in the UK Singles Chart. We even went on *Top of the Pops*! Chas & Dave were excellent songwriters and performers. "Ossie's Dream" is still a cult hit with Spurs supporters. Ossie was not keen on doing his solo line "… in the cup for Tott-ing-ham" but he did after a bit of arm twisting! We still tease him, especially the way he pronounced the line.'

All manner of publications by newspapers and football magazines came out for the final. From the Tottenham perspective there was also a lot in the media about their successes that had come with a year ending in the figure one. Football fans are known to be superstitious by nature so they were doubtless delighted to read about FA Cup successes in 1901 and 1921, the First Division title in 1951, the famous double of 1961 and the League Cup in 1971. There was also the fact that Tottenham, under Bill Nicholson, had never lost at Wembley, winning the FA Cup in 1961, 1962 and 1967, in addition to the Football League Cup in 1971 and 1973.

Tony featured in an article headed 'Hero with a dash of Russian!' for winning the *Daily Mirror* footballer of the month award. He received a statuette, £100 cheque and framed drawing of himself. *Shoot* magazine's FA Cup Final special included managers and players predicting the winner. Spurs come out on top 11-7, with two sitting on the fence. Alan Sunderland (Arsenal), Alan Mullery (Brighton), Allan Clarke (Leeds United) and Alan Kennedy (Liverpool) were in the Tottenham camp. Alan Brazil (Ipswich), Mick Lyons (Everton), Arthur Albiston (Manchester United) and Peter Shilton (Nottingham Forest) backed City. No one predicted a draw!

Tony's parents, Tommy and Muriel, were looking forward to the big match. Interviewed by the *Yorkshire Post*, Tommy said, 'Obviously I hope it goes Tony's way, but it's an even-money game.' As for Tony's wife, Julie, she was hoping the match wouldn't go to a replay because she was due to take a group of schoolchildren to France the day after the final!

As for FA Cup Final week, Tony recounted: 'It was really special, but nerve-wracking because you didn't want to get injured during training. Then there was a day when they invited the press to training, so it was totally different from the norm. I'd done the odd interview, but the press were everywhere. Barring last-minute injuries, we knew the team would be the same as against Wolves. Everyone wants tickets for the big game. We had an allocation as players, so I sorted tickets for my parents, wife Julie and friends. The squad stayed at the Ponsbourne Hotel, close to our training ground at Cheshunt. I roomed with Graham Roberts. You get lots of advice but it doesn't matter how they prepared you for the big day, you were going to be nervous. It was a case of trying to contain your nerves and perform.'

The matchday programme for the final was a lavish publication. There was material about players, past finals, memories and the various cup runs. Spurs arrived at Wembley having overcome QPR, Hull City, Coventry City, Exeter City and Wolves. Manchester City had defeated Crystal Palace and Norwich City at home, Peterborough United in a tricky away fixture, Everton in a replay at Maine Road and Ipswich Town at Villa Park. A detailed itinerary was set in stone:

> Music by the massed bands of the Royal Marines (1.10pm to 1.35pm)
>
> A display by the Wonderwings (1.35pm to 2pm)
>
> Pitch inspection and walkabout by the two teams (2pm to 2.10pm)
>
> Introduction of captains of past winning finalists (2.10pm to 2.30pm)
>
> Music by the massed bands of the Royal Marines (2.30pm to 2.45pm)
>
> Singing of 'Abide with Me' accompanied by the Derek Taverner Singers (2.45pm)
>
> Presentation of the teams to Her Majesty the Queen Mother (2.50pm)
>
> Kick-off (3pm)
>
> Half-time marching display by the massed bands of the Royal Marines (3.45pm)
>
> Presentation of the FA Cup and medals by Her Majesty after full or extra time.

Tottenham had come a long way since manager Keith Burkinshaw took the helm at White Hart Lane in the summer of 1976. Following relegation and immediate promotion back to top-flight football, the team had been completely rebuilt, with Perryman and Hoddle regulars from the previous era.

Looking ahead to the cup final, Tony recalled: 'I'd watched the final on television for as long as I could remember. It seemed as if the whole country watched this match. Cup final day was massive. Everything stopped. All the family packed around the television to see who would lift the famous old trophy. The first final that I recall was 1964 when West Ham beat Preston 3-2. Howard Kendall was the final's youngest-ever player. Liverpool beat Leeds United a year later, then Everton came from behind for a thrilling 3-2 win against Sheffield Wednesday in 66. There's footage of the goal action but as famous is an Everton fan, Eddie Cavanagh, running on the pitch with police chasing him. They eventually carried Eddie off to great cheers from the crowd, but it was not hooliganism, just euphoria. When Spurs won in 67 we were delighted because Jimmy Greaves was a huge hero in our house. Then things became personal because Chris was at Leeds. When they reached the 1968 League Cup Final against Arsenal, it was played in the March so did not have the hype of the FA Cup, but it was still a big game as the club had not won a major honour. I went down with Mum and Dad. Seeing the Twin Towers and walking up Wembley Way for the first time was incredible. Supporters mingled, there were scarves and rosettes on sale. Leeds won, which made it a really memorable day. I then went to three FA Cup finals in the early 70s. Leeds defeated Arsenal in 1972. They should have beaten Chelsea a couple of years earlier, then lost to Sunderland in a huge shock. Winning is far better, the journey home goes quicker!

'Now I was a part of it and I'd never played in such a big match. I didn't sleep well the night before the game. Everything was stage-managed. After breakfast we got changed and then there were television cameras at the hotel to film us boarding the coach trip for Wembley. I was not one of the card players sitting at the back, so was in the middle of the coach. Everywhere you looked there were Tottenham supporters en route to the ground. There were nerves but they disappeared going down Wembley Way and seeing all the supporters. It was an unbelievable sight.

All I wanted to do was to get into the stadium, walk around the pitch, take in the atmosphere and then change for the game. Being involved was surreal, but pulling into the stadium, you knew that this was it.

'The manager tried to play it down throughout the week so we didn't get ahead of ourselves, but this was massive for all the lads and club. Tottenham had not won the FA Cup since 1967 so it really was a chance to imprint our names on the club's history. Even Ossie, who had played in a World Cup Final, seemed nervous. He'd experienced the biggest stage but was not the star focus of that Argentina team, whereas since his arrival at Tottenham he'd been the focus, certainly more than Ricky, in terms of media attention. Everyone was edgy and that's no surprise because the FA Cup Final was such a special occasion.

'Even though so much had happened to me in a short space of time from breaking into the first team after the New Year, I was very conscious this game would be a highlight in my career. Unlike the modern era when the same teams generally win the FA Cup, numerous clubs had won the trophy in the previous two decades. Tottenham and West Ham led the way with three triumphs since the 60s; Arsenal, Manchester United and Liverpool had achieved the feat on a couple of occasions and then a host of clubs had one win apiece. This match was massive and you never knew what was around the corner. The media always pointed out famous players such as George Best who had never won the FA Cup, so you had to make the most of this opportunity.

'The dressing room was not that big or the most luxurious but had an aura about it. We'd been to Wembley the day before to get a feel of the ground, but when we went out for our walkabout to take in the atmosphere, it was breathtaking, although nowhere near full. You think to yourself: "This will be full in the next hour," so the nerves kick in again. We got changed and went out for a little warm-up, although we were restricted to where we could go, but it was good to get out there. Back in the dressing room everyone was a little bit on edge. We'd had our team meeting on tactics but all these years later I haven't a clue what Keith said. He was always a positive person but not over-emotional in the way he came across. No doubt he'd have told us not to get over-excited or intimidated by the atmosphere, but to be brave enough to express ourselves, play as we normally did and not to play with fear.'

The final against Manchester City was the 100th in the FA Cup's history. The teams on 9 May 1981 were:

> Manchester City: Corrigan, Ranson, McDonald, Reid, Power, Caton, Bennett, Gow, MacKenzie, Hutchison (Henry, 105), Reeves.

> Tottenham Hotspur: Aleksic, Hughton, Miller, Roberts, Villa (Brooke, 68), Perryman, Ardiles, Archibald, Galvin, Hoddle, Crooks.

The match wasn't a classic but had talking points for a capacity crowd and television audiences. City's Tommy Hutchison scored for both teams in a 1-1 draw after extra time. A replay four days later would determine the winner. James Mossop of the *Sunday Express* offered a crisp summary:

> Players were collapsing dramatically, their muscles seized by the agonies of cramp, as they stripped their tie-ups and discarded their shin pads, as they took the 100th FA Cup Final lurching through the tension of extra time towards a replay on the same stage on Thursday. Sheer courage saw them through, but the celebration of more than a century of tradition could never quite lift itself to the pageant of artistic fluency these grand old clubs had promised.

Tony remembered: 'Walking out, I was behind Steve and Milija Aleksic. There were lots of shouts of encouragement from the lads but, quite frankly, you're too nervous, all you want is to get on with the game. Waiting in the tunnel for formalities to finish seemed an eternity, then suddenly as you walk up the incline towards the pitch there's no noise, but the anticipation is huge. Then as you come out of the tunnel, an explosion of noise hits you and that's the moment that has stayed with me all these years. It's an incredible feeling. You are sheltered from the noise inside the stadium in the tunnel and I'd heard lads talk about this moment, but until you experience it for yourself, you have no sense whatsoever of what it's like. The crowd are waiting with great anticipation and then they see you walking out; there are 100,000 spectators in the stadium and the noise erupts and is absolutely deafening. The whole occasion then hits you. I didn't look around. I focused straight ahead in this haze of noise. All I wanted to do was to run about, because I was really nervous. But then you think, "I've now got to play a game of football." After meeting the Queen Mother, which was a great honour, all you want to do is get on with the game.

'Lining up, I looked around and my first thought was that the pitch was enormous. It looked almost square. From the kick-off it was a tense game. We didn't express ourselves in the way we could and lacked penetration. We seemed to play within ourselves. We were too safe and tentative. Gerrie Gow was putting himself about in midfield and City players were sliding into tackles, which seemed to unnerve Ossie and Ricky in particular. Ricky failed to make an impact on the game. City certainly did a job on him. For all our tentative play, we had our chances. Joe Corrigan saved a long-range effort from Glenn and then made a great save from Graham Roberts. But City also went close when Paul Power headed on a corner that flew across our penalty box. I didn't have many opportunities to run at their defence, but I eventually cut in on my left before shooting, which forced Corrigan into a save.

'City took the lead on 30 minutes when Ray Ranson crossed for Hutchison to score with a flying header into the top corner. Aleksic had no chance. When that goal went in, it felt as if we were in trouble, but Garth had a great effort that went wide and then almost put Ossie in on goal. I knew we could create chances but City were a dangerous side on the counter and we had a real let-off when Steve MacKenzie couldn't wrap his left boot round the ball fully, so hit the wrong side of a post from a tight angle. Just before we made a substitution I had a knock. I was okay to continue so Gary Brooke replaced Ricky, who disconsolately walked off around the pitch to the dressing room instead of watching from our bench. We were desperate for an equaliser and Archie set up Brooke, but he couldn't force the ball home. Ossie then won a free kick on the right side of the penalty box and we finally got a lucky break. Glenn was always going to try to whip it round the wall and chipped it goalwards. It seemed to fly in from where I was standing. Immediately I saluted the goal as Glenn ran off to celebrate. It was only later when I saw it on television that I realised Hutchison had peeled off the wall and deflected Glenn's shot past Corrigan. Seeing the replay, I thought what was Hutchison doing? Why was he stood there? If he'd have stayed with the wall or just let it go then it would have gone straight into Corrigan's hands.

'The goal handed us a lifeline and it was a huge relief to be back in the game but, as the match wore on, there was a feeling we were getting a bit desperate. There was a lot of nervous energy. A few lads went down with cramp but we had to stay in it. MacKenzie had a late effort before the match went into extra time. There were few chances in the extra period. Brooke fired over before

Gow missed a great chance at the far post. As the game petered out, Hutchison was substituted and must have had mixed feelings. The match ended 1-1. It was the first cup final to end in a draw since the 1970 final when Leeds and Chelsea drew. It is bizarre as I was at the final when Leeds outplayed Chelsea then lost in the replay. We didn't outplay City but had we missed our chance, or were we given another chance?

'City had enjoyed the better of that first game, but we'd dug deep and it was strange going up to the Royal Box to shake hands with dignitaries and then take part in a lap of honour with no trophy. Back in the dressing room there was a feeling that we'd got away with it. The message from Keith was simple. He just said that the game has gone and we'd not lost. It had not been a great game and we hadn't played well, so the message was "let's regroup and look forward to the replay". The ridiculous thing was that, after changing, we had to troop off to a celebration dinner in central London. But we did unwind. We had a few drinks, got the game out of our system and enjoyed a late night.'

Tottenham's attention turned to the replay, which would be their ninth FA Cup tie of the season. Tony recalled: 'On the Sunday the lads had a free day so we went around London Zoo with some friends. I'd never been there before and it seemed a good idea at the time, but can you imagine that happening now with social media and so on? What I should have been doing was having my feet up and resting. We got together again on the Monday, but it was just light training. A few of us had strains so it was just a case of building up to the replay a few days later. The big decision was whether Ricky would play. Keith had already told him he'd be playing because he believed in him with his ability. But it was a big call. Steve has told me since that as captain he advised Keith not to play Ricky in the replay. He didn't think Ricky would be mentally right after the disappointment of being substituted. But Keith was adamant that Ricky would play and would be a different player in the replay. How right he was!

'The replay was on a Thursday night, so the build-up was far less intense. We'd have far more fans in the stadium than City because a lot of tickets were made available to Wembley, so Tottenham fans bought most of them. A number of our lads, including me, were far better for the Wembley experience first time around. We knew what to expect in terms of the atmosphere, even though it would be a midweek game. We stayed at the same hotel, did a bit of light training on the morning of the game and had a spot of lunch then rest in the afternoon, before making our way back to Wembley for what was the first FA Cup Final replay at the stadium. The same team was named and, going into the replay, there was a sense that we had to play better. "Let's get in front" was our attitude and see how City react this time.

'I'd taken my shirt home after the first match and they gave us another for the replay. Tottenham were miserly when it came to strips in those days, they'd tell us not to swap our shirts after European games so they didn't have to buy another. If we did swap, then our kitman Johnny Wallace would go wild! He'd yell: "If you swap, you won't have one for Saturday," but we knew he was winding us up. Arriving at the stadium we were more relaxed. It was a nice, bright night, not as drizzly and wet. The atmosphere was not as tense because we'd been through everything a few days earlier. But the deafening noise was still there when we walked out of the Wembley tunnel.'

Both starting line-ups were unchanged for the replay, although City had Dennis Tueart, who came on for Bobby McDonald, on the bench. Tottenham knew that they were capable of improvement, but they again had to come from behind to win.

David Lacey of *The Guardian* described the replay as the 'game of the century'. He wrote:

> Before last night the 1948 final between Manchester United and Blackpool had been regarded as the outstanding example of attacking play to be seen at Wembley. Blackpool's 4-3 victory over Bolton in 1953, the Matthews final, has always been regarded as the best dramatised match. Last night's borrowed something from the yellowing scripts of both of these and put them into a modern setting with Latin American accompaniment.

The match has gone down in FA Cup folklore. For Tony it was unforgettable: 'We got off on the front foot from the kick-off. Ossie and Ricky were really lively. Gow had been earmarked to put them out of the game, but we passed the ball better around the park. Archie had a shot blocked by Corrigan, and Ricky put in the rebound for the lead early on, before MacKenzie equalised with a magnificent volley. I was quite close to him when he hit it and I thought instinctively that it was going over the top, but it rocketed into the top corner. That strike in any other final would have been remembered possibly as one of the best of all time, but Ricky went close again and had his moment of magic later in the game. Glenn hit a post and I had a shot at goal saved, but it was level at half-time. We'd been the better side so had to re-establish ourselves again. But when Dave Bennett went down in the box under a challenge the referee gave a penalty. I could not believe it, just as in the semi against Wolves. Kevin Reeves slotted it home. We were deflated, but it was an open game so had to react. Looking back, this was a big moment for the team because we did respond when Garth pounced on a loose ball to poke home the equaliser. It was a typical goal by him because he had quick, sharp reactions. We were back in the game.

'Ricky then scored, and what a goal to win an FA Cup Final! Graham stopped MacKenzie in his tracks and passed the ball to me out of defence. I remember running from our own half, covering about 50 yards, looked up and passed the ball to Ricky, who went on his mazy dribble. At the time I didn't recall the run being so good because you're involved in the match. Garth was screaming for a pass but Ricky had one thing on his mind after getting past the first man. He went in and out of a few players and slotted it in! However, when I saw it back on television, I thought: "How on earth did he do that?" He could have shot twice before firing home. But that was Ricky, he did do unpredicable, instinctive things. Ricky could be infuriating but it went in. When the ball nestled in the net, I felt relief because we'd been under pressure. It's one of the finest ever FA Cup Final goals. After celebrating and lining up again, I felt we'd won the cup. There was no way back for City. Ricky might have played briefly for Argentina in a World Cup but this was the moment that changed his life.

'At full time there was a huge feeling of relief that it was over and euphoria that we'd won. We had shown character coming from behind, which made the victory more satisfying for everyone. It was a really special feeling. Keith made a brave decision keeping Ricky in the side but it paid off. Ricky rightly grabbed the headlines but it was a great team performance. Nowadays losing fans leave, so the ground is half-empty, but Spurs supporters were in three-quarters of the stadium so the atmosphere was amazing. I don't recall much about collecting our medals and trophy. Steve picked up the cup and showed it off to the fans but he didn't pass it down the line as they do now. Then we had the traditional photograph with the trophy and lap of honour. Running around Wembley, I wanted to get the trophy in my hands, but one or two lads always hog it. Finally, to get my hands on the famous old trophy was special. I'd dreamt of this moment as a kid, so to experience it was incredible. Then the post-match celebrations in the dressing room were unbelievable. Everyone was hugging each other, passing the cup round and drinking champagne. We even managed to dent the iconic trophy when Ossie threw it in the air as he jumped into the bath and it hit the ceiling. In team pictures after, we had to cover the dent until it was fixed!

'Because everything was so informal compared with the first game, we went back to White Hart Lane after changing and then to the Chanticleer restaurant. The atmosphere was fantastic, with our families, close friends and Chas & Dave. The best thing back at our ground was Tottenham supporters were rammed outside. Being in your own environment made it a special night. A few days later there was an open-top bus and civic reception at Tottenham Town Hall. Our fans had craved success but it took me by surprise that so many supporters turned out. It was an unforgettable experience.'

After a short post-season to Bahrain, Kuwait and Turkey, Tony could unwind and reflect on what had been an incredible second half of the season. He had married Julie, who he met at university, in June 1980 in Scunthorpe and was living in a small, detached house in Standon, Hertfordshire. Following a major operation, with his career in the balance, Tony had been a part of a cup final that is talked about over four decades on.

The players and management have reunited over the years to celebrate a timeless triumph for the club, including for the 25th anniversary at the Dorchester Hotel in central London. Burkinshaw masterminded the victory. In a brochure for the evening called *Glory Glory ... Tottenham Hotspur* he recollected putting the team together over five years. He said: 'I wanted a team that was entertaining and at the same time capable of winning something. That was the way I felt Tottenham should play. I wanted us to be the team everyone loved to watch.'

The Spurs boss recalled that Hoddle had an 'amazing' performance in the replay. But it was Villa who ultimately created history. Regarding the Argentine's change of fortunes over the two matches, Burkinshaw reflected: 'Ricky didn't play well in the first game. I took him off and he felt he'd been humiliated because there was such a lot of interest in that game from Argentina. He went straight to the dressing room instead of staying to support the team from the sidelines, which is what was required. I don't know what it was, when I got to the dressing room I just had a sixth sense that he'd have a big part to play. He was down in the dumps, so I said, "Ricky, get your head up, you're playing on Thursday." He was so happy.'

Of course, Villa grabbed the headlines. His winner was voted Wembley's Goal of the Century in 2001. Villa reflected: 'When I received the ball from Tony Galvin my objective was not immediately to score a goal – if it had been then I would have put myself under pressure and I don't think I would have scored. I looked up and saw a defender as my first obstacle so I went around him. Then another approached and I went around him as well and suddenly found myself nearer the goal. It was all happening so quickly that I nearly lost the ball but I still managed to score. It was totally a South American goal. With respect, I'm not sure that an English player would have tried to score such a goal because it's maybe not in his makeup. It was like a dream.

'I'm always overwhelmed by the reaction of the people when I go back to England – I get recognised here more than I do in Argentina. I get stopped in the street and everyone wants to talk about a goal that I scored so long ago. But I never get fed up with it. It's great that everyone remembers this wonderful moment in the club's history. Wherever I am in England, when people recognise me they always say, "I've seen your goal – it was fantastic." And it's not just Spurs fans – it's Manchester United, Liverpool and even Arsenal supporters. That really means a lot to me. It obviously means a lot to Spurs fans but the fact that the whole footballing public can remember the goal is amazing. It is a great honour to have played such a part in the history of English football.'

For Tony, it had been a whirlwind few months: 'When I recall the 1981 FA Cup Final the occasion goes over your head at the time. It was a lot to take in. I'd been playing non-league football three years earlier. It had been some journey from Goole Town to Wembley and brings back great memories. I had a slice of luck getting to play on the left-hand side of midfield but slotted in and didn't look back. Journalists labelled us a "sleeping giant" because we had not won the trophy since 1967. The fact that it was the 100th final didn't impact on me at the time. I was just starting out but, of course, that first triumph was really important. We had a good side that could compete and beat any team on our day. The squad was full of anticipation for what awaited us. And the ball would soon start rolling with the Republic of Ireland!'

Chapter 9

FA Cup at the Double!

TONY GALVIN began his first season as a league regular with Tottenham Hotspur after playing in a 2-2 draw against league champions Aston Villa in the FA Charity Shield at Wembley. Peter Withe and Mark Falco scored a brace apiece in an entertaining clash at the Twin Towers. The teams for the Wembley curtain-raiser on 22 August 1981 were:

Aston Villa: Rimmer, Swain, Gibson, Evans, McNaught, Mortimer (Blair), Bremner, Geddis, Withe, Cowans, Morley.

Tottenham Hotspur: Clemence, Hughton, Miller, Roberts, Villa, Perryman, Ardiles, Archibald, Galvin, Hoddle, Falco.

Tony recalled: 'After our historic FA Cup Final victory it was great to go back to Wembley against Villa. In those days this game was a major event that always filled the stadium. There were plenty of tickets for fans, unlike in the Manchester City final. There was not the pressure of a final. It was an enjoyable game to play in and a fair result. There were no penalty shoot-outs in those days so both teams shared the trophy.'

There was then an opening-day league win at Middlesbrough, followed by home defeats to West Ham United and defending champions Villa. But Tony missed the Villa fixture because he received tragic news on the morning of the match: 'I received an urgent phone call from home that Dad had been rushed to hospital after a suspected heart attack. This came as a massive shock because neither Chris, who was by now playing in Hong Kong, nor I were aware of any issues with his heart. He was only 55 years old, so still young. Mum was in total shock. A couple of hours later I received the dreaded news that he had been confirmed dead on arrival at the hospital. I had to get home immediately. I rang Keith and, of course, he told me to go home to Huddersfield. Julie and I packed a few things and set off. What an awful drive. Mum was in a terrible state. Apparently, he'd had a problem with his arteries but didn't get to hospital quickly enough. No one saw it coming so we were stunned. Keith told me to stay up to organise and attend the funeral. Chris was playing for Tseun Wan in Hong Kong and his club were superb in getting him on the first flight home. We were very grateful. I remember having an impromptu training session with my old schoolmate Chris Helliwell to maintain some level of fitness. After the funeral I trained Friday morning with the team and travelled up to Wolves for the game the next day.'

Spurs got the boost of a 1-0 victory at Molineux when Ardiles chipped the ball over the Wolves defence for Tony to run through and tap it over the head of goalkeeper Bradshaw midway through the second half. Tony recalled: 'In a very small way the goal was my thank you to Dad for all he had done for me over the years. Those endless hours in the fields learning to use both feet, as well as improving other skills, had paid off. My parents came to a few games when I joined Tottenham but Dad missed most of my career, which was such a shame. Mum did say that Dad was incredibly proud of me for playing in that memorable FA Cup

Final and it was a blessing of sorts that he lived to watch me play at Wembley. I know he would have taken great pleasure from me winning that medal. To support Mum I tried to get home more, but it was not easy with my Tottenham and Ireland commitments. After Dad's death, Chris and I got closer. We never fell out; our careers just took us on different paths for a while. We are as close now as we were as kids.'

The triumph sparked a return to form as Spurs picked up six wins in eight league matches, including successive victories against Manchester City, Nottingham Forest, Stoke City and Sunderland. Spurs were among the favourites in the cups. It was especially so after they defeated Manchester United 1-0 at home in the second round of the League Cup. Archibald and Hazard struck in the 2-0 aggregate win. Home wins over Wrexham and Fulham set up a tough-looking quarter-final home clash against Nottingham Forest. A goal by Ardiles took Spurs into the semi-finals, where they would face West Brom.

Correspondent Frank Wiechula wrote:

> Not only do Tottenham look as safe as houses, but also who would bank against a side in such devastating cup form from reaching Wembley for the second year running? And although only one goal separated these two First Division rivals, anyone with a lot of money would almost certainly put it on Tottenham. Only the brilliant Peter Shilton stood between Spurs and a hatful of goals.

Shilton's heroics culminated in a thrice-taken penalty on 35 minutes. After Shilton saved Hoddle's first attempt, the referee ordered the kick to be retaken as Forest players had encroached into the area. Hoddle scored the second attempt, only for a Spurs player to encroach. Shilton saved the final attempt but couldn't stop the winner on the hour. A correspondent wrote:

> Full-back Hughton hit a pass out of defence and it seemed destined to cross the left touchline, but energetic man of the match Galvin chased after it and just kept the ball in, whipping over a long cross. The ball went for a corner and, as it came out, Galvin hit a cracking left-footer which Shilton did well to turn aside, but Ardiles followed up and slid the ball home from five yards.

Tony recalled: 'Our performance at Old Trafford was one of our best that season but Forest were a really tough team. Cloughie played two wingers, which created a lot of space in the middle of the pitch. Robertson was an unbelievable footballer, O'Neill was a clever player and then midfielders such as Archie Gemmill raced through to support attacks. Liverpool had an incredible line-up but even they struggled against Forest in their pomp. Liverpool played Forest in a European Cup tie and Cloughie's team overran them. It helped that Forest had Shilton in goal but Cloughie had a thing about playing the ball on the deck and they surprised a lot of teams. For a provincial club to win the league and consecutive European Cups won't happen now, although Leicester City stunned the football world with a Premier League title. You can never say never, but I doubt it will happen again. The Forest game was very tight and played in front of a near-capacity crowd. We played really well and Ossie managed to get the winner.'

After a goalless draw at The Hawthorns, a goal by Hazard at White Hart Lane took Tottenham to the League Cup Final at Wembley, where they would face Liverpool on 13 March 1982. In the first leg against the Baggies, which was televised live, Tony and Martin Jol were sent off in the second half. Tony recounted: 'Unfortunately, I got involved in an altercation with Jol, who later managed Spurs. When Jol pulled me back, I instinctively swung an arm and barely caught him. Jol made a meal of it. The decision was incredibly harsh and I made my feelings known to the referee. If anything, I was impeded. Initially, I refused to leave the field but ultimately had no option but to make what seemed a very long walk to the dressing room. Apart from being jeered by West Brom fans, I knew friends and family would be watching on television. In the tunnel, I heard shouting behind me so turned round and to my pleasant surprise realised that Jol had also been dismissed. This made me feel better because he'd been winding me up throughout the game and I thought he had got away with it. Ossie almost won us the match but we edged through to the final.'

The build-up to Wembley included coverage in newspapers and football magazines but not on the same scale as the FA Cup. Liverpool were in the midst of a golden decade of success, having won four league titles, two European Cups and an FA Cup since 1973. Bob Paisley's team had lifted the League Cup in 1981 with Ray Clemence in goal and were expected by most pundits to be too strong for Tottenham. Clemence was now at Tottenham and made an impact from the start, as Tony recalled: 'Ray was a top goalkeeper and had a winning attitude. Early on he told me that every pre-season at Liverpool Bill Shankly and then Paisley would say: "Forget about the medals you won last year. They don't matter now. This season is what counts." In other words, get your attitude right, otherwise its "bye, bye". Ray was a great signing, not only because of his goalkeeping ability but his mindset.'

Shoot magazine's League Cup Final special differed, predicting a hat-trick of wins for the north London team after success in 1971 and 1973. 'It's Spurs' Cup – But Only Just!' was the headline in the cup special. Assessing the strengths of both teams and marking each player out of 10, Tottenham edged Liverpool 89-86, according to experts. Of Galvin, they wrote: 'Tony's powerful surges down the left could upset Neal's composure. Well supplied by Hoddle and Ardiles, he runs as straight as an arrow if he spots an opening. Loves to get to the byline and set up openings for strikers.' Other *Shoot* features included a crosstalk with Steve Archibald and Phil Thompson, alongside interviews with captains Graeme Souness and Steve Perryman, and keepers Bruce Grobbelaar and Ray Clemence. *Shoot* also spoke with Ossie Ardiles, who would join the Argentina World Cup squad after an FA Cup semi-final versus Leicester City to prepare for the 1982 World Cup finals.

Tony appeared in *Shoot* magazine's 'Super Focus', answering football and non-football questions. He informed readers that fish and chips along with a pint of Tetley's mild was his favourite food and drink, he drove a Triumph Acclaim and read *The Guardian*. Jimmy Greaves, Huddersfield Town and Wembley were his football hero, favourite other team and best stadium. Among likes were modern music and *Tiswas*; dislikes included gardening and shopping. Blackpool was his 'favourite holiday resort', while Neil Kinnock MP was the person in the world he'd most like to meet. Few readers could question Bruce Springsteen, John Hurt, *The Elephant Man* and *Monty Python's Flying Circus* as music, acting, best film and television selections. Like most footballers, winning a league title and international honours were personal ambitions. Tony nominated Goole Town manager Alan Turner and his father as the biggest influences of his career. As for a 'Best Ever All-Time XI' he selected Banks, Kaltz, Cooper, Beckenbauer, Passarella, Bremner, Ardiles, Giles, Pelé, Greaves, Best. Sub: Kempes.

Match Weekly ran a similar feature with many of the same responses. Tony nominated a goal against Ajax in a European

Cup tie earlier in the season as his best, with Eddie Gray's solo effort for Leeds United against Burnley in 1970 as the greatest he'd seen. Winning the FA Cup was his 'Magic Moment' in football and the semi-final win over Wolves at Hillsborough was his favourite match. France was the best country he had visited and the Olympic Stadium, Tokyo the best stadium he'd played in. Tony's pre-match meal was a cheese omelette. Away from football, Roger Waters of Pink Floyd was selected as a favourite pop star, and television shows switched off were *Spiderman* and *Give Us a Clue*. Tony's 'Best All-Time British team' was Banks, Perryman, Cooper, Bremner, Charlton J., Moore, Hoddle, Giles, Best, Greaves, Heighway. Sub: Hutchison.

The teams for the final lined up as:

Liverpool: Grobbelaar, Neal, Lawrenson, Kennedy, Whelan, Thompson, Dalglish, Lee, Rush, McDermott (Johnson), Souness.

Tottenham Hotspur: Clemence, Hughton, Miller, Price, Hazard (Villa), Perryman, Ardiles, Archibald, Galvin, Hoddle, Crooks.

Tottenham weren't overawed and opened the scoring through Archibald. Liverpool captain Graeme Souness had a fierce reputation as a player. A player of undoubted skill, he was also a ferocious tackler and caught Tony in a 50-50 challenge midway through the first half. The challenge still rankles with Tony, who recalls the incident as a key moment of the match. Ronnie Whelan equalised three minutes from time before an Ian Rush brace in extra time secured victory. Liverpool went on to also lift the League Cup in 1983 and 1984.

Tony recalled: 'We didn't have the best of records against Liverpool but were quietly confident, although they were the bookies' favourites. We were on top of our game at the time against arguably the best club team in the world. The game started well and Archie put us ahead. We were on top and I was causing problems down the left flank. That was until Micky Hazard passed me a slightly under-hit ball. Micky loved a first-time pass but this one invited an over-the-top tackle from Souness. It was an appalling challenge and I am sure Souness agrees. Incredibly, the referee allowed play to continue. I was in agony. It was at least a yellow, probably a red, even in those days. Today it's a nailed-on red card. If I was being kind to the referee, he gave Souness the benefit of his doubt. All these years later, I've no idea why. Mike Varney, our physio, was appalled when he looked at my shin, and I had shin pads on! Ray came over and told me Souness had "done" me. Ray knew the game and told the referee but he took no notice. I only received attention because the ball went out of play. If one thing has improved in the modern game it's that tackles like that result in a straight red and referees are all over them. Souness got away with it. Despite this I have the utmost respect for him and I must say he was one of the greatest players of his era.

'Mike insisted that I should be taken off at half-time but Keith was concerned about not making a substitution too early as we only had one substitute. In the end, I played the rest of the game but contributed little in the second half. Archie missed a great chance to put us 2-0 up near the end, Whelan equalised late on and the rest is history. How I carried on until the end of extra time is beyond me. My leg was in such a mess I refused to look at it after the game. If I was playing now my season would have been over. The celebration dinner with our wives after the final in a London hotel was like a wake. It was miserable and I was in so much pain.'

A 50-50 tackle was a part of the game. Nowadays if a player gets the timing wrong it's a red card but Tony played in an era when often an opponent could 'get one in' and often even escaped a booking. Liverpool had a team packed with world-class players but they also had a ruthless edge to their game. Paul Miller recalled in *The Boys from White Hart Lane* by Martin Cloake and Adam Powley that Tony was considered the dangerman in the final: 'Liverpool regarded Tony as our best player – always. Tony was the one player in that team you could never replace – you ask anyone and they'll tell you. He very rarely got injured – fantastic player. Souness done him early on, he lasted but he wasn't really at the races.'

Tottenham, although disappointed at not landing another trophy, had no time to be too despondent as there was a European Cup Winners' Cup quarter-final against Eintracht Frankfurt coming up a few days later. And there was an opportunity to return to the Twin Towers for a second successive FA Cup Final. The run started against Arsenal and then Leeds United. Garth Crooks scored in 1-0 victories. Mark Falco notched the winner against Aston Villa at the fifth-round stage. Tottenham travelled for the quarter-finals when Archibald, Hoddle and Hazard ensured a 3-2 win at Chelsea.

Tony recalled: 'As holders we were looking forward to having another go in 82. The season was going well; however, the draw put us up against Arsenal, but we had the home draw. There was great expectation. It was a close, feisty affair played in a feverish atmosphere. I recall Arsenal right-back Stuart Robson and me kicking seven bells out of each other. Such as it was in those days! Surprisingly we both remained on the pitch. Garth scored past Pat Jennings, Spurs' greatest-ever goalkeeper. How ironic. Leeds and Villa provided tough opposition. The Villa game was of the highest quality. Of course, they had an excellent team and would go on to win the European Cup that season by beating Bayern Munich in the final. Going into the Chelsea clash, I was warned that playing at Stamford Bridge would be intimidating, even though they were then in the Second Division. There was fierce rivalry between the clubs and tackles would fly in. I had played there for the reserves but only a few hundred attended on a bleak Wednesday afternoon. Walking out on to the pitch I couldn't believe the amount of abuse we received from Chelsea fans. Despite going behind, which raised the atmosphere even more, we recovered well for a hard-fought victory.'

The Archibald–Crooks strike force offered a cutting edge to Tottenham. Tony recalled: 'They were great signings at the right time. Archibald had come from an Aberdeen team who had been really successful under Alex Ferguson (before his knighthood). As a person he was a little aloof and full of self-confidence. He wasn't what you would call one of the lads, but did mellow. Archie and I weren't the greatest of friends, but that was no big deal. I knew that he was a magnificent striker, arguably world class. Archie contributed greatly to Spurs' success and would later score lots of goals for Barcelona. But he was a difficult character at times. Before a game and at half-time Keith would ask him to help to defend corners. I recall one particular match when he refused. "You've bought me to score goals," was his argument. Keith insisted he helped the team out with defensive duties, but Archie refused. There was a terrible atmosphere. After Keith dropped Archie there was a stand-off for a while when he brought him back. The lads tried to help to resolve the issue but neither was stupid. Keith needed Archie in the side but Archie knew he had to deliver. It was not the best way to foster team unity.

'Crooks was a very good player and an instinctive footballer. If you hit Garth when he was running forward, defenders could not catch him. Garth was laid-back, and loyal to Archie. It was the typical centre-forwards' union, they stuck together, any criticism of one and the other defended him! On an end-of-season tour I became engaged in a heated discussion with Garth and Archie late at night. When they described me as a bricklayer because I laid foundations for them to be successful, I took exception to the comments. It would have been a sign of weakness otherwise, but they were probably right. Both did the most difficult thing in football ... score goals. What I should have said was that as a team we succeed together and are all winners. But I stood my corner; I was never easily intimidated by anyone!'

Tottenham shared the spoils with Arsenal in a 2-2 draw at White Hart Lane prior to their cup clash with Leicester at Villa Park. As in the League Cup Final, a massive occasion followed as Spurs faced Barcelona in the European Cup Winners' Cup semi-finals. That match, though, was to come as they headed to the Midlands. The teams on 2 April 1982 were:

> Tottenham Hotspur: Clemence, Hughton, Roberts (Miller), Price, Hazard, Perryman, Ardiles, Archibald, Galvin, Hoddle, Crooks.

> Leicester City: Wallington, O'Neill, Williams, May, Friar, Kelly, Peake, Wilson, Lineker, Young (Melrose), Lynex.

The match against Leicester took place at the start of the Falklands War. Indeed, Argentina invaded the Falkland Islands in the South Atlantic on the day of the match. Leicester were a goal down when full-back Tommy Williams broke a leg in a tackle with Tony. Having already made a substitution they played the remainder of the match with ten men. Tottenham won with goals from Crooks and an Ian Wilson own goal. The semi-final was already scheduled to be Ardiles' last outing of the season as he was about to join Argentina's World Cup squad. Meanwhile, the Falklands conflict lasted until 14 June, before an Argentinian surrender.

Ardiles, after a loan spell at Paris Saint-Germain, would return to the club during the 1983/84 season.

Tony recalled: 'There was tension because of the Falklands conflict. Ossie was booed throughout by Leicester fans. It was a unique situation for all of us, especially Ossie, but as players, you have to play through it. Leicester provided tough opposition, including a promising young striker called Gary Lineker. Garth scored the first following a cleverly worked corner involving Glenn and Ossie. The second was a bizarre own goal from Wilson following a slightly misplaced cross from yours truly.'

Tottenham faced Terry Venables' Queens Park Rangers at Wembley. Clive Allen, son of Spurs' 1961 double legend Les Allen, had scored from the fourth round, hitting four in a 5-1 win against Blackpool, another in a 3-1 triumph against Grimsby Town, before the only goal to account for Crystal Palace then West Brom in the semis at Highbury.

Before the final, Tottenham faced 14 league and two European matches, not to forget a possible Cup Winners' Cup Final, due to a backlog of fixtures. Barcelona employed cynical tactics to draw a controversial encounter at The Lane. Dusting themselves off, the squad played seven matches in 19 days in April, starting with a home win over Ipswich Town and a 3-1 triumph at Arsenal. A draw with Sunderland followed before a defeat at Manchester United. Sadly, it was not to be in Europe as Barcelona reached the final. Tony then opened the scoring in a 3-1 win against Notts County, before a draw with Birmingham, but faced a battle to be fit for Wembley after being substituted against Coventry City on 1 May, just three weeks before the big day.

Fixture congestion was taking its toll on Tottenham in a season where they had gained many plaudits. The Highfield Road match ended goalless and was the first of eight league fixtures in 17 days. The final matches of the league campaign saw three consecutive defeats and a fourth-placed finish behind champions Liverpool, who sealed the title with a 3-1 win at home to Spurs in the penultimate match. Seven players made over 50 appearances in Tottenham's 66 domestic and European matches in 1981/82. Perryman was ever-present, Clemence played 62, Hughton 57, Hoddle and Miller 58, Galvin 56 and Roberts 51.

Tony recalled: 'After the Barcelona defeat there was a significant number of games still to play. I remember Keith arguing with the Football League about forcing us to play them all before the end of the league season, which had to finish before the FA Cup Final. It was a ridiculous situation. The club was playing games almost every two days. In fact, there was one particular match where the club was fined for playing an under-strength team, something that wouldn't happen in the modern game with much bigger squads. I now appreciated what Chris used to say about Leeds United when they missed out on a possible treble and double in their pomp. We had extended runs in both cups, 24 games including the Charity Shield, so it was only right Keith wanted to rest players before the final, particularly after going so close in the league and Europe. Clubs were penalised for being successful, which was crazy, but football was a different world then.

'I got injured at Coventry and missed the run-in. Keith had wanted to play the cup final team for the last match at Ipswich but his plans were scrapped by injury and illness to a number of the lads. Unfortunately, overnight at the hotel I was violently sick and the Doc decided I was unfit to play. To make sure I was isolated from the team, a car took me straight home to recover. It was a bug or food poisoning but meant a few days' recuperation. I was not allowed to return to the training ground until the Doc was sure I'd recovered. But I had just enough time to get myself fit for the cup final.'

Tottenham's squad revelled in the Wembley build-up. Chas & Dave were back on board with 'Tottenham, Tottenham', which reached number 19 in the UK Singles Chart. Again, it was a great surprise but shows the popularity of the annual event. The club featured in newspapers and football magazines in preparation for an all-London affair.

Tottenham were the bookies' favourites but *Shoot* magazine pointed out in '*Shoot* view!' that Burkinshaw's team would underestimate QPR at their peril, as Second Division teams had shocked First Division opponents in recent seasons. The feature recalled Sunderland stunning Leeds in 1973, Southampton overcoming Manchester United in 1976 and West Ham surprising Arsenal in 1980. *Shoot* highlighted QPR's Tony Currie, Clive Allen and Mick Flanagan as players with something to prove to silence critics. There were also interviews with Hoddle, the captains, managers and strikers.

Princess Anne was scheduled to present the trophy to the winners but there was political pressure on Tottenham regarding Ricky Villa playing as it would have been inappropriate due to the Falklands conflict. Burkinshaw in the end decided to leave Villa out of his cup final line-up.

Tony was among numerous players who had an injection to be fit: 'Reaching the final again was great but we had a number of players carrying knocks. I was well aware that you have to make the most of each occasion. Of course, a major talking point was the fact that there was no Ricky or Ossie because of the Falklands War and we felt under some pressure to deliver without them. It did feel a little strange to be back at Wembley after the events of 81. It was rare for players to play twice in a Wembley cup final in successive seasons but we were confident and determined to win. QPR were going great guns in the league so there was no way we would underestimate them. It was also a London derby, which are always tough games, whoever the opponent.

'Terry Venables was a young manager impressing everyone in the game with his attractive brand of football. Rangers were unfortunate to just miss out on promotion to the First Division, possibly as a consequence of their great run. Having beaten West Brom in the semis we knew they would be very dangerous opponents, particularly with the highly experienced and outstanding Currie in midfield. Then, of course, there was the issue of our team suffering from an element of burnout after playing so many games over the season. Spurs were under pressure to deliver a trophy after going so close in all competitions.'

Tottenham faced Queens Park Rangers at Wembley on 22 May 1982. The teams were:

> Tottenham Hotspur: Clemence, Hughton, Miller, Price, Hazard (Brooke), Perryman, Roberts, Archibald, Galvin, Hoddle, Crooks.

> QPR: Hucker, Fenwick, Gillard, Waddock, Hazell, Roeder, Currie, Flanagan, Allen (Micklewhite), Stainrod, Gregory.

Rangers keeper Peter Hucker stood firm throughout the match, saving from Hazard, Archibald and Brooke, until Hoddle's deflected shot off Currie deceived him in the first period of extra time. Hoddle then set up 'Footballer of the Year' Perryman, only for Hucker to save bravely, before Terry Fenwick equalised from a long throw by Simon Stainrod to send the match to a replay. Allen led the Rangers attack but was injured after ten minutes, eventually being substituted in the second half. The teams would return on the Thursday night.

FA CUP AT THE DOUBLE!

Ken Jones of the *Sunday Mirror* summarised the match: 'It wasn't that either team broke any promises, but simply that they weren't able to play well enough on the day.' Regarding Galvin's display, he wrote: 'Much of Spurs' early hopes rested with Galvin's pace and he had to be pulled down in full flight on the edge of the area, leaving Hoddle with a chance to employ his skills at a free kick. The shot skipped just wide of the near post.'

Tony recalled: 'The first game was a typically tight affair. We had the better of things, with Hucker nominated man of the match. When Glenn fired us ahead we were confident of seeing out the game but Fenwick headed in a few minutes later. It was a major mental blow to concede such a poor goal. We were terribly disappointed but it was vital for us to pick ourselves up for the replay.'

Tottenham took on Queens Park Rangers in the replay at Wembley on 27 May 1982. The teams were:

Tottenham Hotspur: Clemence, Hughton, Miller, Price, Hazard (Brooke), Perryman, Roberts, Archibald, Galvin, Hoddle, Crooks.

QPR: Hucker, Fenwick, Gillard, Waddock, Hazell, Neill, Currie, Flanagan, Micklewhite (Burke), Stainrod, Gregory.

Tottenham became the first team to retain the FA Cup since Bill Nicholson's team completed the double in 1961 then retained the cup in 1962. The final was decided by a penalty for the first time since George Mutch won the cup for Preston in 1938. Tottenham won with Hoddle's spot kick but it was a less than convincing performance by the favourites. Allen didn't recover for the replay but Stainrod, John Gregory and Gary Waddock went close for QPR. Most pundits felt Rangers should have had a penalty when Crooks challenged Fenwick and Hughton caught Currie in the area.

Frank McGhee of the *Daily Mirror* praised QPR:

> They brought Tottenham's great goalkeeper Ray Clemence as close to panic as he has ever been in his distinguished career. But somebody up there did not love them last night.

Of Hoddle's winner, David Lacey of *The Guardian* wrote:

> The penalty QPR gave away had an air of inevitability about it and was less to do with the absence of Roeder than the weighty presence of Roberts. The Tottenham player intercepted a pass from Stainrod near the halfway line and sprinted through a gap in the inside-right position. He went on into the penalty area with Currie in pursuit and when the tackle arrived subsided almost gratefully, sensing that the referee's decision was inevitable. Hoddle sent Hucker the wrong way.

Tony recalled: 'As ever it was a great atmosphere under the lights. We went ahead with Glenn's penalty and at half-time were reasonably confident. However, the second half was a different story. QPR dominated the game. They were by far the better team and should have equalised. We were hanging on and could barely get out of our half. It seemed like 45 minutes too far for the team after an arduous season. Our defence, including Ray in goal, were magnificent. We didn't deserve to win but when the final whistle went there was a feeling amongst us all of total relief. Walking round Wembley afterwards felt different to the ecstasy of the previous FA Cup Final replay. However, we had finished what was a wonderful season with a trophy. Winning in consecutive years was something special.'

Tony returned to Wembley in August 1982 but Tottenham this time lost out to Liverpool in the Charity Shield as a goal by Ian Rush separated the teams. After a reasonable start to the 1982/83 league season, the coming months for Tony would be frustrating due to injury, although he was back for the final third of the season when Spurs enjoyed a more consistent run and fourth-placed finish. Everton ended Tottenham's two-year FA Cup defence in the fifth round at Goodison Park.

Tottenham made a poor start to the 1983/84 season, taking until the fifth match to register a 3-0 league win against Leicester City. Their opening home match finished 1-1 against Coventry City on 29 August 1983. It was a match Tony recalls but not for footballing matters, as his wife Julie was due to have their first child. He said: 'Keith blamed me after the game for not getting close enough to a cross which led to their equaliser after Glenn had scored a penalty. An argument ensued but Keith cut it short to tell me to get over to Harlow hospital as Julie was giving birth! Lucy was born in the late evening.'

Tottenham's form picked up before a mid-season dip. It ended in a disappointing eighth-place finish and early exits in both domestic cups, but fans would witness a glorious UEFA Cup campaign!

Chapter 10

Glory, Glory Nights

TOTTENHAM HOTSPUR have a rich history of involvement in European football. The first British club to win the European Cup Winners' Cup in 1961/62, when they famously defeated Atletico Madrid 5-1, UEFA Cup success followed against Wolves in 1971/72 before an infamous defeat in the final two seasons later due to crowd trouble against Feyenoord. Tony played four seasons of European football for Tottenham before a ban on English clubs because of the Heysel Stadium disaster when Liverpool played Juventus in the European Cup Final. His third campaign ended in glory, but it began following their FA Cup success in 1981 when Spurs participated in the European Cup Winners' Cup and faced Dutch giants Ajax in round one. Tottenham won the away leg 3-1, Falco (2) and Villa scoring, before completing a 6-1 aggregate success with strikes from Tony, Falco and Ardiles. The teams for the second leg at White Hart Lane were:

> Tottenham Hotspur: Clemence, Miller, Roberts (Lacy), Hughton, Perryman, Villa, Ardiles, Hoddle, Galvin, Archibald, Falco.

> Ajax: Galge, Wijnberg, Boeve, Molenaar, Ophof, Jansen, Lerby, Schoenaker, Hamberg (Silooy), Vanenburg, Kieft.

The goals came in a devastating spell of attacking football. Alan Thompson of the *Daily Express* wrote:

> There was no warning. In the 68th minute Glenn Hoddle seemed to be strolling quite happily down the left wing like a man on an afternoon walk. Suddenly he darted forward and put over a 50-yard crossfield pass to Mark Falco in the inside position. He controlled the ball and turned it back for Tony Galvin to crack a 15-yard angled shot into the top corner. The Dutch defenders never moved. They were spellbound. Seven minutes later they were again reduced to a set of helpless watchers as Hoddle instigated another brilliant move. From a similar position on the left he put over another perfect pass, this time to Steve Archibald, who beat full-back Jansen before coolly putting his pass across goal for Falco to knock it in from five yards. But if those two goals were the result of brilliant teamwork, the third was a spectacular effort that sent the fans cheering as Galvin squared the ball into the path of Ossie Ardiles for the Argentinian to hit a 20-yard shot into the top corner. In those 15 minutes Ajax might as well have not been on the field.

Keith Burkinshaw spoke to correspondent Peter Blackman about Tony's thunderbolt: 'I haven't seen a finer goal this season. It was tremendous and there was no way any keeper could stop it.' He added: 'If we can put out a club such as Ajax so impressively, then we should look boldly ahead to our next challenge, whoever it may be.' Ajax coach Kurt Linder believed that Galvin would set Europe alight. 'We did not know much about him, but I feel it was his sharp brain that had a lot to do with our defeat,' he said.

The draw was kind to Tottenham as they faced Irish part-timers Dundalk only two rounds before the quarter-final. But the Irish Cup holders pushed Spurs all the way at White Hart Lane as the home side scraped through 2-1 on aggregate. A tougher clash awaited in the third round against Germany's Eintracht Frankfurt. Tottenham took a 2-0 lead into the return, courtesy of second-half goals from Miller and Hazard. But the second leg came days after the League Cup Final defeat against Liverpool and Tottenham named the same XI. Roberts replaced Ardiles with Spurs 2-0 down. Villa came on for Falco with 20 minutes remaining, before Hoddle's 80th-minute goal settled the tie on aggregate.

Tony recalled: 'Going away to any German team is a big task. It was a tough game and we were on our way out until Glenn saved the day with a superbly taken shot from the edge of the box. We were given the runaround most of the game, having dominated the first leg. Clemence had a great game. I didn't contribute much in the game but really shouldn't have played because of my shin injury from the Liverpool game.'

Spurs, going for a third cup final of the season, were drawn against Spanish giants Barcelona, with Dinamo Tbilisi and Standard Liège meeting in the other semi-final. The line-ups for a highly anticipated first leg at The Lane were:

Tottenham Hotspur: Clemence, Miller (Jones), Price, Roberts, Hughton, Perryman, Hazard, Villa, Galvin, Hoddle, Crooks.

Barcelona: Urruti, Ramos, Alexanko, Olmo, Manolo, Gerardo, Estella, Sánchez, Carrasco, Simonsen, Morán (Moratalla).

Barcelona, far from playing free-flowing football, went out to stop the hosts at all costs with a series of blatant fouls. Galvin, Hoddle,

Crooks, Hazard and Perryman were all targeted. 'Animals! The Butchers of Barcelona shake battling Spurs' headlined one newspaper. The visitors' approach left a nasty taste after referee Egbert Mulder dismissed Juan Estella in the 57th minute. Roberts cancelled out a long-range effort by Antonio Olmo that Clemence badly misjudged. The *Daily Mail* noted that Tottenham were 'provoked to the limit by the most cynical Spanish tackling'. The *Daily Telegraph* agreed with the sentiment: 'The second half showed the worst elements of European soccer as football became secondary to numerous off-the-ball incidents, many of which escaped the attention of the referee.'

Tony explained: 'The first leg was one of my most painful nights as a Spurs player. Barcelona were a team with an impeccable pedigree and arguably my biggest challenge against a giant of European football. Here were two teams full of attacking intent. The lads were excited by the challenge. Steve and Ray had been here before, but the rest of us had not. On the night I was shocked. I was told a few years later by an esteemed sports journalist that UEFA wanted Barcelona in the final so they played a team of destroyers in that first leg. Even in my Goole Town days against "Mr Scary", John King, I hadn't faced a more cynical team. Barcelona were a disgrace. They kicked lumps out of us and should have had several players sent off. The referee was weak. Unfortunately, Ray made an error with a hopeful long shot and we were a goal down. Nobody said anything to him on the pitch or in the dressing room. Ray, bless his soul, was a consummate professional who had achieved more than any of us, but mistakes happen. The problem was Barcelona became even more cynical and defensive. Thankfully Graham Roberts rescued the situation with an equalising goal. We would have won the game had the officials adhered to the laws of the game. It was a travesty.'

Barcelona went into the second leg on the back of a 3-1 win against Real Madrid. The teams at the Camp Nou were:

> Barcelona: Urruti, Alexanko, Ramos, Gerardo, Sánchez, Olmo, Moratalla, Manolo, Simonsen (Zuvuria), Quini (Vigo), Carrasco.

> Tottenham Hotspur: Clemence, Roberts, Price (Falco), Hughton, Villa, Perryman, Hazard, Galvin, Archibald, Hoddle, Crooks (Brooke).

Barcelona beat Tottenham on aggregate, with Allan Simonsen scoring the only goal. They duly hosted the final and defeated Standard Liège. The Spanish giants didn't use cynical tactics, although the *Daily Telegraph* wrote: 'Crooks was fouled early on by his marker Ramos. This was a warning of what might befall him if he stepped out of line and he never escaped the attention of his escort.' Barcelona prevailed but were fortunate that Archibald was not awarded a penalty. *The Times* wrote: 'Barcelona's determined performance made one wonder why they had played so disgracefully in the acrimonious first leg at White Hart Lane. They demonstrated that when they concentrate on football they can be formidable indeed.'

Tony recalled: 'It was a must-win game or had to be a high-scoring draw, which was a test of character for us. We lost against a different team. We played well but couldn't get the equalising goal. The game was lost in the first leg. In my anger I destroyed some sound equipment on my way off the pitch. Somebody shouted at me, but I shouted back that they were f***ing cheats. Such is football!'

After retaining the FA Cup, Tottenham looked to go one better in the European Cup Winners' Cup the following season, but their hopes ended in the second round against Bayern Munich. Tony missed both legs because of injury but he had played in

Spurs' opening match of the tournament. In September 1982 he was in action when Tottenham travelled to Northern Ireland to face Coleraine and won with two goals by Crooks and one by Archibald. But he was missing a fortnight later when Spurs won the second leg with goals by Crooks, Mabbutt, Brooke and substitute Terry Gibson, to go through 7-0 on aggregate. Tony was also absent when Bayern drew 1-1 at White Hart Lane before going through 5-2 on aggregate. Aberdeen under Alex Ferguson famously knocked out Bayern and won the trophy against Real Madrid.

Tottenham, Watford, Nottingham Forest and Aston Villa competed for the UEFA Cup in 1983/84. Tony was back in the frame when Spurs thrashed Drogheda United 14-0 on aggregate in the first round. He scored in the first meeting when he visited the Republic of Ireland, by then his country at international level. Spurs won 6-0 before thumping Drogheda 8-0 at White Hart Lane, when they had six different goalscorers. Tottenham then had a tougher tie when they drew Feyenoord. The clash evoked memories for Spurs fans because they had lost out 4-2 on aggregate to the Dutch giants in the UEFA Cup Final in May 1974. The teams were:

Tottenham Hotspur: Clemence, Stevens, Roberts, Hughton, Mabbutt, Perryman, Hoddle, Galvin, Brooke (Crook), Archibald, Falco.

Feyenoord: Hiele, Wijnstekers, Troost, Nielsen, Duut, Cruyff, Jeliazkov, Hoekstra, Gullit (Van Til), Vermeulen, Houtman (Stafleu).

Tottenham took the game to Feyenoord in the opening leg, which, with some symmetry, they won 4-2 at White Hart Lane. Steve Archibald and Tony both scored twice, but correspondent Steve Stammers wrote: 'Two late goals in a Johan Cruyff-inspired revival by Feyenoord makes the second leg in Rotterdam anything but the formality it threatened to be at one stage.' Spurs had produced unforgettable football in the opening half. After Archibald opened the scoring, Tony headed home a Hoddle cross. Archibald struck again and the match appeared to be over by the 40th minute. Stammers noted: 'Hoddle threaded a ball through to Galvin who beat Feyenoord's clumsy attempt at an offside trap to run on and beat the unprotected Joop Hiele.'

Tony was centre stage in Rotterdam on a memorable night for Spurs. Stammers described Hoddle's performance as 'one fit for a king' in Tottenham's 2-0 win. It was written:

> Hughton made a perfectly-timed run to score the opening goal in the 25th minute before Tony Galvin completed the scoring late on. It took 84 minutes for the second goal to arrive and it came as Feyenoord applied a spell of late pressure in an attempt at least to end the match level. Gary Mabbutt created the goal with a well-judged through ball that Galvin picked up, took into the penalty area and shot past Hiele.

Tony recalled: 'Fans have told me that our first-half performance against Feyenoord in the first leg was the best they'd seen from our team. Glenn was on fire that night; we murdered them and went 4-0 up at the break. It was one of those games when everything clicked. They got two goals back, which made things tense, but we were outstanding. Cruyff was coming to the end of his incredible career after starring for Ajax, Barcelona and Holland in his pomp. He still showed glimpses of his genius, but we deserved the win. In the return, again we put in a great performance to advance.'

History then repeated itself in the third round, as Tony added: 'We took on Bayern Munich but I missed the tie because of injury. It was another tight affair, but we played really well. Bayern were a powerful outfit, as they are nowadays. We lost the away game 1-0 but, after Archibald levelled the tie in the return, Falco got a crucial goal that saw us through.'

Tony was in his element on European nights and helped Spurs progress to the final. They overcame Austria Vienna 4-2 on aggregate in the quarter-finals and then defeated Hajduk Split thanks to a crucial away goal from Mark Falco after a titanic battle. The teams for the second leg were:

> Tottenham Hotspur: Parks, Miller, Roberts, Stevens (Mabbutt), Hughton, Thomas, Perryman, Hazard, Galvin, Archibald, Falco.

> Hajduk Split: Simović, Čop, Jerolimov, Miljuš, Rožić, Vulić, Vujović, Šušnjara, Gudelj, Pešić, Prekazi.

Tony recalled: 'The first leg was the most intimidating atmosphere I've played in. I'd not come across a ground where they were allowed to throw fireworks on to a pitch. Hajduk had an outstanding team. I followed up a saved Falco penalty with a pass back to him, which he dispatched into the goal. It would prove crucial. We played well in Split, but succumbed under significant late pressure and conceded two goals. In the return, Tony Parks had come into the side as Ray was injured and made a crucial stop. Micky Hazard grabbed the all-important goal early on that took us into the final on away goals. It was a cracking but tense atmosphere.'

Tottenham's run to the final against Anderlecht was all the more impressive as Hoddle had been sidelined since March with an Achilles tendon problem and Ardiles was also struggling with injury. Anderlecht had beaten Benfica to win the UEFA Cup the previous season, and had controversially reached this year's final after overturning a 2-0 first-leg defeat against Brian Clough's Nottingham Forest to win 3-2 on aggregate. Anderlecht's second goal was a contentious penalty. Erwin Vandenbergh scored two minutes from time, only for Forest to level through Paul Hart, but his goal was inexplicably disallowed. Forest would have advanced on away goals. In 1997 it emerged that Anderlecht had bribed Spanish referee Emilio Guruceta Muro. Forest had been cheated out of a place in the final. Anderlecht were subsequently banned from UEFA competitions for a year.

The teams for the first leg of the final at the Constant Vanden Stock Stadium, Brussels on 9 May 1984 were:

> Anderlecht: Munaron, De Greef, Grün, Czerniatinski (Vercauteren), De Groote, Scifo, Vendereycken (Arnesen), Hofkens, Vandenbergh, Olsen, Larsen.

> Tottenham Hotspur: Parks, Thomas, Hughton, Roberts, Miller, Perryman, Hazard, Archibald, Falco, Stevens (Mabbutt), Galvin.

Correspondent Robert Armstrong observed that Tottenham had made a 'splendid contribution to the proud pantheon of British club performances in Europe' in a 1-1 draw. He wrote:

> Tottenham showed few signs of inhibition in carrying the game to Anderlecht whenever a gap opened in their generally well-organised defence. With Galvin always willing to provide width by breaking down the left flank, the Spurs strikers Archibald and Falco were certainly not left to fight a losing battle against the man-to-man marking of the Anderlecht centre-backs. Spurs' midfield men established some control after the early alarms. Perryman proved a tenacious ball-winner, Stevens showed a subtle sense of weight and angle in passing and Hazard

made timely interceptions and threatening breaks from the centre circle. The hard-working Galvin also operated in a secondary role as a dual left-back.

Tottenham's counter-attack broke the deadlock in the second half. Armstrong observed:

> The goal could hardly have been more simple. Hazard struck an outswinging corner from the right and Miller sprinted through from a deep position to propel a glorious header into the roof of the net from 10 yards.

Anderlecht levelled when a Parks error allowed Morten Olsen to pounce following a corner five minutes from time. Parks was criticised in the press but remembers the equaliser as a deflected shot, so felt hard done by. But Spurs were still in the tie going into the second leg.

Parks reflected in *The Boys from White Hart Lane*: 'When we came off the pitch the feeling was we'd done a really good job – they know we can play and we've held them at their place, now we can finish them off at ours. European nights at White Hart Lane were brilliant – when that Shelf side was packed it was awesome.' And Tottenham had an away goal to take back to The Lane for the second leg.

Tony recalled: 'We were outstanding away from home and, after going a goal up, we should have closed the game out. And we had plenty of chances to win. I remember putting in crosses from which Archie and Mark Falco could have scored. If we'd gone two or three up, then the game would have been over. We outplayed Anderlecht, but they got a fortunate late goal. It was a night when we deserved to win and on a personal level I felt that

I'd had one of my best games in Europe. I was running well with the ball and felt great, but we had to settle for the draw. It was a good result, but it could have been a brilliant win.'

The teams for the second leg on 23 May 1984, were:

Tottenham Hotspur: Parks, Hughton, Miller (Ardiles), Mabbutt (Dick), Thomas, Roberts, Hazard, Archibald, Falco, Stevens, Galvin.

Anderlecht: Munaron, De Greef, Grün, Czerniatinski (Brylle), De Groote, Vercauteren, Scifo, Vendereycken, Hofkens, Olsen, Arnesen (Guðjohnsen).

ITV commentator Brian Moore said it would be a night for 'strong nerves'. He would be proved right! With Hoddle injured, Perryman suspended after a booking in the first leg and Ardiles on the bench, not fully fit, a tough night was anticipated for the hosts. Tottenham brought Hazard into the line-up as playmaker for Hoddle and Mabbutt for Perryman. Spurs went into the clash having never been beaten at home in 39 European matches across ten campaigns. The final was decided by a penalty shoot-out, with an unlikely hero.

The early exchanges saw Tottenham go close through Archibald and Falco. Alex Czerniatinski forced Parks into a save, before Stevens fired over and Mabbutt shot wide. Thomas cleared from under his own bar, Frank Arnesen then failed to beat Parks after a quick break, before Archibald missed a chance set up by Galvin before the interval. The visitors struck on the hour. Olsen found Czerniatinski, who beat Parks to put Anderlecht ahead on aggregate. And the match was almost up when Willem Hofkens shot wide with only Parks to beat. Galvin had opportunities, Roberts headed over, before Ardiles replaced Miller. The Argentine found Archibald, who forced Jacques Munaron into a save on 84 minutes. Galvin then found Falco. The ball fell to

Ardiles, who lashed it against the crossbar. Soon the stadium erupted when Hazard found Roberts, who evaded Hofkens and Olsen to chest the ball down and crash home. Before the final whistle Spurs claimed a penalty in vain when the ball struck Olsen's hand. Enzo Scifo, Archibald, Arnór Guðjohnsen and Olsen were also all off target.

In extra time both teams knew a slip could prove fatal. A Falco header was cleared off the line, and Archibald and Galvin went close amid increased tension. With neither team finding a winner, a penalty shoot-out would decide the victors in front of the Paxton Road end. After Roberts stepped up to score, Parks gave Tottenham the edge when he saved from Olsen. Efforts by Falco, Stevens and Archibald were matched by Brylle, Scifo and Vercauteren, before Thomas missed when his spot kick would have sealed the win. With the scores tied 4-4, Parks had the chance to become the hero as Guðjohnsen stepped up to place the ball on the penalty spot. As a packed crowd held its breath, Parks took his place in goal and duly turned Guðjohnsen's strike around a post with a double-handed save to signal wild celebrations.

Parks recalled the tense moments in *The Boys From White Hart Lane*: 'As soon as the ref blew the whistle for the end of extra time the nerves went. I knew that I could save at least one without a doubt. It didn't faze me, because you're never going to get the blame for letting in a penalty.' Parks described the spot kick as 'the worst penalty in the world': 'It was so predictable. His run up was poor, it was short, he wrapped his foot around it, it was a beautiful height to dive at. I got my hands on it, did a couple of rolls and got up and I was off. I genuinely did not know what to do so I just ran. If that gate in the corner had been open I would've been down at Seven Sisters in seconds. I remember Ray Clemence just clothes-lining me across the throat and I was under a pile of bodies.' Parks added: 'The biggest thing for me in the shoot-out was the two faces of Danny Thomas. The despair when he missed and the absolute ecstasy just seconds later … We didn't have one individual that night who was outstanding; it was a really good team effort.'

The second leg of the final at White Hart Lane was an epic encounter, as Tony reflected: 'Our squad showed its resilience with Glenn out, Steve suspended and Ossie not fully fit. Ray had been injured, but was fit again. However, Burkinshaw decided to stick with Tony Parks. From the kick-off we were tense, a bit like the Hajduk game when we scraped through. You can't help but think you're in touching distance of something big. Mentally that is tough and the tension got to us. Anderlecht handled the occasion better. Maybe because of the first-leg draw at home, subconsciously they felt their best chance had gone, so it helped them to relax. They opened the scoring, which ratcheted up the tension, but then towards the end Graham Roberts equalised. I still felt that we could maybe nick a goal and avoid penalties, but a lot of our lads were struggling physically. I'd also found it tough, but probably played my best football of the leg during extra time. I had a lot of the ball, which acted as a release for the lads. And, bizarrely for the occasion, I didn't feel nervous or on edge. I felt strong, went for it and tried to get crosses in or get in the box. I just kept running with the ball, but it was even-steven with both teams having chances. We knew Tony had a knack of saving penalties and, of course, it worked out. Danny missed, but Tony saved their last effort. That moment has gone down in club folklore. The atmosphere was incredible, the best I knew as a player at The Lane.'

Looking back on the shoot-out, Tony recalled: 'Micky Hazard thought he was next up, but it's still a bit of a blur who it might have been. Luckily it never came to it. I do, though, distinctly remember chatting with Chris Hughton, who thought it might be one of us, but neither of us were particularly keen. We did practise penalties but you can't replicate the pressure of a shoot-out in training. I know for a fact if I'd have had to walk up, I'd have been a nervous wreck because there were not many shoot-outs in our day.

'During the two legs I felt that we were the better team and deserved to win the trophy. What I did not realise until recently, though, was that Anderlecht were UEFA Cup holders. When people say to me, "Oh, you only beat Anderlecht," they don't realise that they were a crack outfit with a team full of international players at that time. We had international experience, but Anderlecht, compared with now, were at a different level because money was on a level playing field. There was no Premier League paying large sums of money to overseas footballers. Top stars invariably stayed in their own country, but if they did move, it was to Italy or Spain. Ruud Gullit, Frank Rijkaard and Marco van Basten graced AC Milan after making their names in Holland.'

The thought of having to take a penalty in the shoot-out wasn't the only test facing Tony. Speaking to the *Sunday People* a few days after the victory, he told the correspondent how tough extra time had been. Tottenham's trainer had never seen such a severe attack of cramp. 'Both my legs went as stiff and hard as planks,' he said. 'It happened when I saw a gap between defenders. I decided to go for it, but then suddenly found my legs wouldn't do as they were told. I just went in a heap. It was weird. I've never experienced anything like it. My legs were locked from top to bottom. I couldn't bend them. When I tried, I got pain that felt like torture. Mike Varney came on and managed to get me a bit mobile again. I had to soldier on to the end because by then both our substitutes were on. I pride myself on fitness, but this was a case of running myself silly. I'd never known a match played at such a pace for so long and I'd never seized up that way before. I had all these long passes knocked in front of me to chase and in the end, it was more than I could stand.'

All these years later Tony recalls a famous achievement: 'I loved European football. We played domestic league and cup matches in midweek, but there was an extra-special atmosphere on a European night at The Lane, which harked back to the days when Tottenham, playing in all-white, provided unforgettable occasions for fans in the early 60s under Bill Nicholson. Unless there was a clash the team didn't wear its traditional white shirts and blue shorts in Europe. It was different and supporters from that generation were among the first British fans to witness what football had to offer in the European Cup, European Cup Winners' Cup and UEFA Cup. Of course, there was a great atmosphere against the top First Division teams and particularly in derby clashes with Arsenal, but in Europe the atmosphere was on another scale.

'The key ingredient on a European night was the crowd. They were louder, noisier, more positive and encouraging than for an average league or cup game. They were our 12th man and psychologically maybe fans felt we had a better chance of winning a trophy. There was less criticism so the whole atmosphere meant that as a player you were more up for it. Tottenham had not won a European trophy since the UEFA Cup in 1972. Supporters really got behind us to succeed. You could sense a different atmosphere from an FA Cup run. It's hard to explain, but the feeling of history seemed to envelop the ground. Tottenham were the first British club to win a European trophy and that history counted. Fans were really proud of that achievement and it came out on European nights. Older supporters have told me many times it felt like the "glory, glory nights" again at The Lane.

'Winning the UEFA Cup in front of our own supporters was the highlight of my Spurs career. I have never experienced so much joy from so many people on that very special evening. Walking round the ground on our lap of honour, after Parks's magnificent penalty save, I said to myself that this was something I could never have envisaged. This was the ultimate. It couldn't get any better than this. There was joy on everyone's faces behind those hideous fences. What a night that was! No, I didn't take a penalty, so a big thank you and respect to those who did. We celebrated with family and friends long into the night. We also acknowledged the thousands of fans celebrating on the high street. It was a magical occasion for everyone.'

Before the final, Keith Burkinshaw announced he would step down, which came as a tremendous shock to the players and fans. He's remembered and respected because of the club's achievements and style of play during his tenure as manager in the late 70s and early 80s.

Tony said: 'It came as a huge blow to find out that Keith was leaving. He did a fantastic job bringing the club back into the big time with promotion from the Second Division. I was so fortunate that he signed me when he did. Great players arrived at the club, which bolstered a squad that already had players with huge talent. Keith gave me my break. He was a typical straight-talking Yorkshireman, just like Bill Nicholson. With Keith you always knew where you stood. He didn't go over the top with praise, but if you played well, he'd tell you. However, if he was not happy about something in your game he'd let you know and you'd take it on the chin because you respected his opinion. Keith was fair with all the lads. He was 'old school' and a great coach. When we heard Keith was resigning, it made us even more determined to win the final against Anderlecht. I'm delighted we delivered.'

Chapter 11

Galvin 'Shuffle' Dazzles Hull

CHRIS GALVIN looked on his £40,000 transfer from Leeds United to Hull City in 1973 as a positive step in his football career. He might have been moving down to the Second Division but he was hopeful of regaining some momentum and getting regular league football.

Hull reached the FA Cup quarter-finals and won the Third Division in style as champions in 1966. The generosity of chairman and benefactor Harold Needler had turned them into a 'moneybags' club intent on progress. But that impetus began to dwindle until Needler moved City manager Cliff Britton sideways to general manager and brought in Arsenal and Northern Ireland defender Terry Neill as player-manager.

Hull were among the promotion challengers in his first season in 1970/71 but failed to build on it. Neill, who captained his country, was still in charge, although he had given up playing, when Chris left Leeds, but the club had started to go backwards. Most significantly City had started to shop for bargain buys. Chris arguably came into that category but he had been a part of the first-team squad at Leeds for several seasons so was clearly a technically gifted player and would have benefitted from training with and being around world-class players.

The background to Chris's move began during the summer of 1973 when articles began to appear in the local press that City were keen on signing him from Leeds. For example, the *Sunday People* ran a story on 22 July that summed up his situation at Elland Road:

> Ambitious Hull, preparing for an all-out drive for promotion, might sign 21-year-old Leeds midfield player Chris Galvin this week. We understand that Hull have offered £40,000 and Leeds are ready to let Galvin go to give him the chance of regular first-team football. Galvin's First Division appearances have been limited because of the wealth of talent at Elland Road, but he has several games in European football to his credit.

Mike Casey of the *Yorkshire Evening Post* wrote a thought-provoking article about the challenges facing young, talented players at Leeds United. The story centred on Chris, Rod Belfitt, Jimmy Greenhoff and Terry Hibbitt. In 1968 Greenhoff and Belfitt had played in the Football League Cup Final win over Arsenal and Hibbitt was one of the Inter-Cities Fairs Cup winners against Ferencváros. All had now departed Elland Road, having failed to break through.

Don Revie was acutely aware of the dilemma facing up-and-coming professionals, with youngsters fighting for too few places. He told Casey: 'It's one of the toughest jobs of managership with a top club – keeping lads such as Chris happy. When you have a first-class scouting system such as ours, covering the whole of Britain and supported by a training staff of the calibre of Les Cocker, Syd Owen, Maurice Lindley and the other backroom boys, you inevitably create problems for yourself. They keep coming up with potential stars such as Frankie Gray, Peter Hampton and John Shaw, but it's obvious not every youngster on the books will eventually clinch a regular first-team place. Some are bound to be disappointed. A big first-team pool – say 17 or 18 players – is a must these days for clubs such as United who are so heavily committed in domestic and European competitions, but there are still only a limited number of opportunities, even allowing for injuries. So, all you can do is make every player feel an important part of the set-up with the prospect of a regular place some time or other. And when a youngster who has worked hard for the club since joining straight from school, comes and says: "I think my prospects will improve with another team," you understand his feelings and wish him good luck.'

Revie also made the point that the Central League wasn't the ideal training ground to stardom: 'Up-and-coming youngsters cut their teeth in reserve football, but the best school is the first team, playing in front of 40,000 to 50,000 crowds. You can't beat playing at such grounds as Old Trafford, Anfield, White Hart Lane. That's where footballers learn by experience, soaking up the atmosphere. The only way to become a top-class player is by competing with and against top-class players.'

Chris explained the background to his own inclusion in Hull's summer intake: 'When I arrived for pre-season training at Leeds, I went to see Don because I was back to square one. It was obvious to me that I'd have to leave the club to get regular first-team football. I'd played just six first-team games since making my debut. Playing so little was no good for me because it was affecting the pace that I did have. It didn't matter how much training I did with the first-team squad, I was not match-fit, so in my mind it was time to move on. Also, I had to move on because none of the lads with whom I'd been an apprentice had broken through on a regular basis. I told the gaffer and he wanted me to stay, but my mind was made up. The squad picture for the season had just been taken when Don called me into his office to tell me Hull City and Wolves had put in bids for me. Hull offered £40,000, which the club had accepted. Don didn't want me to go, but it was my decision.

'Looking back, there is a feeling of what might have been if I'd stayed at Leeds another year because Brian Clough came in after Don had succeeded Sir Alf Ramsey as England manager. At the time when I joined Hull no one knew that Don was going to move on, but I've never been one to look back. You make a decision that you think is correct at the time for the right reasons. Throughout my early days at Leeds I saw progress and thought I'd break through. The Asa Hartford affair when Don told me I'd get a chance and it didn't happen was the cut-off point and in my last six months I realised it would not happen for me at the club.

'Leaving Leeds was tough because my heart was there. Whatever you do, you strive to be at the top and, to this day, I feel that I could have achieved more at Leeds. It was down to me but circumstances didn't help. I'll never accept that players such as Mick Bates were as good a player as myself but Mick fitted what Don wanted and reluctantly I had to accept that situation. Of course, that's a personal opinion, but I never got a sustained spell in the first team to prove myself. It was hard for a young lad to leave a club like Leeds and your attitude changes. It's sad, but it does. All of a sudden it now became more of a job to me.

'You hear footballers say, "I'd play for nothing," because they enjoy it so much at a particular club, but when that's taken away it's only human nature to look at a situation in a different way. All of a sudden you think I can't get to a level that I hoped to achieve. Training and playing gets harder when you play for a team who don't win as regularly. Playing for a side that wins is simpler but I accepted my time at Leeds was now over.'

Chris had to sort out his personal circumstances following the move, as he explained: 'Susan and I had decided to get married and agreed to buy a house in Huddersfield, but Hull and Wolves coming in changed everything, so we pulled out. Wolves were in the First Division, but Don advised me to join Hull, who played in the Second Division, because I'd get straight into their first team. Don said Hull were a good club, one who were going places. They had a good chairman and Neill was an up-and-coming manager, so Don's advice made sense and it seemed a good move. I met Terry in the club car park in front of the ground. He was waiting by his impressive E-Type Jaguar, we chatted and soon agreed terms.'

The close season saw Neill sign centre-half Steve Deere from Scunthorpe United, who bought City's long-serving forward Ken Houghton, one of the heroes of the 1960s, and youngster Stuart Pilling as part of the wheeling and dealing. With a certain amount of symmetry, Deere would become one of Chris's closest friends and Houghton would return as one of his managers at Boothferry Park.

'Moving on from Leeds, although there was a sense Hull represented a step down, I was determined to make things happen. Terry wanted me to play on the left side of midfield, which was ideal. I knew where I'd be playing with a full season in front of me, which I'd not done before. A week into pre-season he told us we were going to play some friendly matches in Northern Ireland at the height of the Troubles. Terry wanted us to go because he would be the first manager to take a team there, despite security challenges, and Hull received a lot of good publicity.'

Chris made his debut in a pre-season friendly against Shamrock Rovers in front of a 2,000 crowd in Milltown on 3 August 1973, when Ken Wagstaff and Roy Greenwood scored in a 2-0 win.

The line-ups were:

> Shamrock Rovers: Dunne, Herrick, Parkes, Fagan, Whelan, McEwan (Davis), O'Neill, Lawlor, Voakes, M. Leech, Daly (R. Leech).

> Hull City: Wealands (McKechnie), Banks, De Vries, Kaye (O'Riley), Deere, Galvin, McGill, Blampey, Pearson, Wagstaff, Greenwood.

Correspondent Mel Moffat welcomed a 'strong and aggressive' performance from Galvin, who 'completely controlled proceedings'. Journalist Noel Dunne wasn't overly impressed with the performance but welcomed one particular summer signing: 'There was one standout player, Chris Galvin, who bossed the midfield and set up a goal for Steve Deere that was ruled out for a foul. Midfielder Galvin was one of their few players to stand out.'

Chris recalled: 'For the first time in my career there was a feeling that I was getting back into football. I played well against Shamrock and really enjoyed it. Most importantly I was contributing to a team's performance and it helped that I got on well with Terry. He believed in me and we spent a lot of time talking about football. After the game, Terry told me that one day he hoped to manage Arsenal and if I did well at Hull, he'd come in for me, and he seemed genuine. I thought that for a manager to say that, then maybe there was a way back for me to the top.'

Hull completed the Irish tour with a 1-0 defeat against Cork Hibernians after a 1-1 draw with Finn Harps. Chris then played in Hull's Watney Cup run, featuring in a group match away to Mansfield Town, the semi-final against Bristol Rovers and the final, which Stoke City won 2-0.

Chris, Greenwood and Jimmy McGill got the goals in a 3-0 win at Mansfield in August 1973. Chris made headlines for his skills, despite being booked. Correspondent Henry Weston's report was headlined 'Galvin's magic opens the floodgates'. He wrote:

> A touch of class and authority bearing the unmistakable stamp of Leeds United steered Hull City through to the semi-finals of the Watney Cup. Chris Galvin, the talented midfield man signed from Leeds for £40,000 this summer, provided that moment of magic in the 48th minute. Moving on to a pass from Ken Wagstaff, Galvin drove a majestic 25-yard shot beyond the reach of Rod Arnold. It was a goal which finally broke the spirit of the adventurous Fourth Division side who had given as good as they got. It also opened the floodgates.

Hull's young midfielder had played a vital part in the Mansfield win to book a semi-final visit to holders Bristol Rovers but he also had the unwanted distinction of being booked in each match since he joined Hull. His fourth booking threatened a two-match ban. Chris had an edge to his game and was adept at winning a 50-50 ball, having trained and played alongside the likes of Bremner, Charlton, Hunter and Giles at Leeds for several years. The art of tackling was a quality Neill recognised as important, having been a quality defender himself and having faced Revie's renowned team on many occasions, but it caused concern among match officials.

Chris, however, had his manager's backing. The *Daily Mail* correspondent Bill Mallinson told readers that Neill would fight the opinions of Irish referees who wanted Galvin branded a 'dirty player'. Neill said: 'The three games in Ireland were all played as friendlies and there was very little physical contact. Chris's offences were rather obscure. He certainly never committed a dangerous tackle nor did he retaliate. If I thought he had gone beyond the bounds, I would not be sympathising with him. His reputation is very important to me. It is quite possible that more will be made out of these bookings than there really is in them. He may be suspended and branded as a dirty player, which he certainly is not. He is a very skilful footballer.'

Chris faced Oxford United in the opening league fixture of 1973/74 but his debut didn't go according to plan in a goalless draw in which he was substituted in the first half. He reflected: 'I ruptured ankle ligaments, which was a real blow because I was raring to go. I had the backing of the boss, and the fans were up for it, but that's football. The bizarre thing that I recall about that game was not so much the injury, which was really frustrating because I wanted to make an early impression, but Howard Galley from Huddersfield, who was a linesman that day. We'd played cricket together years earlier so it was strange seeing him! We had a quick word but, of course, you just get on with the game. Things, however, dragged on in terms of my rehabilitation, so it was the worst possible start and I was out for about two months.'

Hull made an inconsistent start to the campaign, winning three of their opening nine fixtures. When Chris returned to the first team against Orient, Hull enjoyed a reasonable run that included a 4-1 win against Portsmouth, draws with Nottingham Forest and Luton Town, and then a 2-0 win over FA Cup holders Sunderland in front of what would be Hull's biggest league gate at home of the season. More than 17,000 packed the terraces. Chris reflected: 'It was great to finally get a run of matches without thinking that I'd be dropped, although it took time to get match-fit. The atmosphere against Sunderland was fantastic.'

Chris was also involved in Hull's promising Football League Cup run that included draws against Leicester City and then

Liverpool. It provided some impetus. The teams for the first meeting against Liverpool in late November 1973 before a packed Boothferry Park house of 19,748 fans were:

Hull City: Wealands, Banks, McGill, Galvin, Deere, Burnett, Holme, Lord, Pearson, Wagstaff, Greenwood.

Liverpool: Clemence, Smith, Lindsay, Thompson, Lloyd, Hughes, Callaghan, Cormack, Heighway, Keegan, Waddle.

Chris recalled: 'Home fans really got behind us in the League Cup. I got my first important goal for the club in a 3-3 draw at Leicester before we knocked them out 3-2 in the replay. After a comfortable 4-1 victory against Stockport County, we drew a plum fourth-round tie at home to Liverpool. The match took place on a Tuesday afternoon because of the miners' strike, when you could not use floodlights. Liverpool had a full-strength side out. All the stars played, including Emlyn Hughes, Tommy Smith and Kevin Keegan. We battled to a 0-0 draw in a great atmosphere, but lost 3-1 in the replay.'

However, Hull's form in the Second Division remained inconsistent. Following the win against Sunderland, Hull crashed 4-0 at Carlisle United, although reporter Albert Stubbins praised Galvin's efforts in a 'thankless' task in midfield. However, the defeat sparked a mini-revival. It comprised a four-match unbeaten run culminating in a 3-0 win against Crystal Palace. After Deere's fifth-minute goal, Chris set up Greenwood before Wagstaff's late effort sealed the win.

Chris was then out of the first team following a 3-2 defeat at Notts County. The bewildering decision was picked up by journalists in the next two fixtures when Hull drew against Cardiff City and Sheffield Wednesday. One correspondent described Hull's 1-1 draw against the Bluebirds as a 'flop', adding:

Hull are sadly lacking in shooting strength and skipper John Kaye must have tired of providing opportunities, so it was difficult to understand the omission of Galvin, the former Leeds United midfield man who cost Hull about £40,000. Galvin is the type of player who does not restrict his activities to breaking up attacks because he is up and about and ready to become the extra striker.

Another reporter added:

Hull's midfield player Chris Galvin is wanting to know why he is not being picked these days. He is far and away the most stylish player on Hull's books, and one could name at least three players now being regularly selected who are way below Galvin's standard.

Following the Wednesday fixture, the journalist penned:

The consensus of opinion among the Boothferry Park fans was that it was bad team selection to leave out such a progressive player as the former Leeds United man Chris Galvin. Galvin has style and authority which few other Hull players possess and it seems a strange policy for a club to fork out £40,000 which they can ill-afford for a player they leave out although there is no justification for such action.

Chris returned to the first team against Preston North End in the final match of 1973. Hull lost 2-0 and then shared the spoils in a goalless draw at home to Bolton Wanderers, a match that would spell Chris's final league action of the season. He would make two further appearances as Hull travelled to Bristol City for an FA Cup third-round tie. A goalkeeping error handed Hull a replay but they then lost 1-0 in front of little more than 5,000 supporters following the government's introduction of a three-day week. Chris effectively became a scapegoat for a poor performance, as he was dropped from the team.

City struggled in the second half of the 73/74 season without Chris, winning six of 17 league fixtures to finish ninth. Chris had been a cup tie regular, scoring his only three goals for the club to date in those matches, but he started only 14 league games, with one substitute appearance on his return from his early season injury. Initially there had maybe been tell-tale signs of the occasional dichotomy shown towards Chris by Hull's management team of Neill and Wilf Dixon. Gordon Staniforth remembers an ironic incident on the pitch: 'We were playing in a reserve game when Neill was manager and Chris took a corner which went behind. Terry bollocked me for letting him take it in the first place!' And Steve Deere observed: 'Chris didn't score many goals, and at one stage Dixon told him not to try! He told him, "I'm going to fine you if I see you shooting at goal." But Chris's ability was tremendous for all that.'

Chris recalled: 'It was a really frustrating end to the season and knocked my confidence. Middlesbrough, managed by Jack Charlton, won the title ahead of Luton Town and Carlisle United. I played against 'Boro early in the season and you could see what Jack was building in his first managerial post. They ran away with the league and Jack won the prestigious Manager of the Year award, which was noteworthy, as Leeds won the First Division title.

'Of the Leeds lads who went into management, Jack was the most successful. Bobby Murdoch was Jack's first signing and 'Boro's equivalent to Bobby Collins when he came to Leeds in the early 1960s. As footballers they had the same attitude: both were experienced, very aggressive and led by example. Jack had learned from Don but was his own man and built the side around Murdoch and a young Graeme Souness. Leeds had partnered Collins and Bremner, then Bremner and Giles and 'Boro linked up Murdoch and Souness. Like Billy, Souness was always involved and could handle himself on a football field. Middlesbrough, like Leeds, were organised, could mix it and competed against every team. After 'Boro, Jack enjoyed spells with Sheffield Wednesday and Newcastle United then thrived with the Republic of Ireland. Tony played for Tottenham and Ireland when Jack was manager and always seemed impressed with his man-management skills.'

Chris had entered a new football world at Boothferry Park and it had potentially held out some promise for him. Yet it was frustrating for him at times that things hadn't entirely gone to plan in his first season at Hull, albeit in a different way from Leeds. Again he had found that all too often he was going to have to learn to take the rough with the smooth. Something needed to give and, fortunately for Chris, it did soon after he married Susan, whom he had known for about three years, in Huddersfield on 8 June 1974.

Following a full pre-season in 1974/75, Chris finally returned to the first team as a substitute in the fourth league match, a thumping 6-0 defeat at Aston Villa on 28 August, when he replaced Jimmy McGill. Three days later he made his first league start since New Year's Day in a 2-0 defeat at Bristol Rovers and he stayed in the team for a goalless draw at home to Norwich City. Chris's quest for regular league football, which had originally evaded him at Leeds, finally took a turn for the better after a topsy-turvy first season with Hull. It came about following a change of manager at Boothferry Park in September 1974.

'Chris and Tony's parents' wedding day, 1948. Pictured from left are Margaret Cundell, Pat Gallagher, Rose and Peter Galvin, Tommy and Muriel Galvin, Louise and Robert Tucker, Terry Galvin, Eileen Gallagher and one of Muriel's bridesmaids
Chris and Tony Galvin collection

Chris and Tony at their grandparents Rosie and Peter Galvin's home, c.1960
Chris and Tony Galvin collection

Muriel and Tommy Galvin, Chris and Tony with Pat and Michael Barker at a family wedding, c.1963
Chris and Tony Galvin collection

St Joseph's Primary School Junior Cup winners 1960/61. Chris is extreme left, back row *Chris and Tony Galvin collection*

St Joseph's Primary School U11 Huddersfield Schools Section 'A' League and Junior Cup winners, 1967. Tony is holding the football
Chris and Tony Galvin collection

Almondbury Cricket Club, 1966. Chris is extreme right, front row.
Chris and Tony Galvin collection

Hall Bower Cricket Club, 1972/73. Tony is second from right on the back row.
Chris and Tony Galvin collection

All Saints Comprehensive School, Yorkshire finalists English Schools Cup, 1974. Tony is extreme right, back row Chris and Tony Galvin collection

Tony takes a break from his university studies to join Chris for a publicity picture, c.1977 Chris and Tony Galvin collection

Chris in action for Leeds United reserves, c.1968
Chris and Tony Galvin collection

Chris and Leeds United trainer Les Cocker, c.1969
Chris and Tony Galvin collection

Chris helped Leeds United defeat Burnley 2-1 at Elland Road, April 1970

Leeds United 1970/71. Chris is extreme left on the back row

Chris and Johnny Giles congratulate Peter Lorimer on his winning goal against Liverpool, September 1971

Leeds United parade the FA Cup through the city centre, May 1972

Leeds United players applaud the Elland Road faithful after winning the FA Cup. Chris is fifth from right

Chris, centre, joins in a rendition of 'Leeds Leeds Leeds' at Elland Road

Terry Neill left his managerial role at Hull, which was arguably convenient for him because his stock had started to reduce with the fans after only one win in the opening salvo of six league matches. Neill, who graced Arsenal for a decade in his playing days, was in the team that lost to Leeds in the 1968 League Cup Final but was injured when Third Division Swindon Town shocked the Gunners at Wembley 12 months later. Controversially he took charge at north London rivals Tottenham Hotspur. John Kaye, who had not long retired from playing, became his successor after a spell in charge as caretaker. The outcome was that the regular league football Chris had craved finally became a reality.

Chris recalled: 'Terry had told me about his ambition to manage Arsenal soon after I arrived at the club so I was taken aback when he joined their great rivals Tottenham. After a couple of seasons, he did get his chance at Highbury. Unfortunately, Terry didn't come in for me as he had intimated, and enjoyed a lot of success, winning the FA Cup in 1979 during a run of three consecutive finals, but that was for the future.'

The appointment of Kaye, who had already been on City's coaching staff, sparked an improvement in form for Hull, although initially they rued dropped points when they let in late goals in 1-1 home draws against Oldham Athletic and Millwall. Reporters at the match cited Chris as a key player. A correspondent wrote about the Millwall game:

> Unbelievably, except to that dwindling band of diehards still going to Boothferry Park, Hull City had a home win snatched from them for the second time in three days by a goal in the closing minutes. The only difference was that, whereas Oldham's performance at least carried some merit, Millwall's last night was pure smash and grab.

The Tigers bashed and battered at Millwall's white wall and Wagstaff, Grimes and Hawley should have scored. Donaldson kicked off the line, Jones hacked a Galvin drive out of the goalmouth and King saved well from Galvin and Hawley.

Regarding Hull's goal, it was noted:

Immediately after the interval City got their reward for exploiting it with a switch of play from one wing to the other, an accurate centre by Galvin and a close-range volley by Wagstaff, who scored his fifth goal of the season. After that the Tigers should have settled the game.

As for Hull's schemer, they observed:

Largely the spell was inspired by Galvin, who had one of his finest games for the Tigers. Immaculate ball control, tricky dribbling, driving running and accurate passing left Millwall dizzy and ragged.

Hull's form, though, suddenly picked up with 2-1 wins at Cardiff City and Blackpool and a 2-0 home success against Bolton Wanderers thanks to a brace by Wagstaff. A local reporter at the Blackpool clash noted that Kaye valued Chris's return to form: 'Kaye certainly appreciates Galvin's ability and must have joined in the applause when a rocket shot from him nearly split the bar.' The correspondent was of the optimistic opinion that Hull's policy of shooting hard often could result in First Division football.

Chris recalled: 'Kaye had been a great player for West Brom, but there was a lot of pressure on the lads. A change in manager can have an effect and we enjoyed a decent run of form, which included the win at Blackpool when I got the winner. I was contributing to the team and felt settled at the club.'

After a 2-1 defeat to Sheffield Wednesday at Hillsborough, Hull bounced back emphatically with a 3-1 home win against 1973 FA Cup winners Sunderland in front of a delighted home crowd of 15,010. Chris played a key role when he set up the equaliser for John Hawley before a Wagstaff brace sealed a memorable win. Kaye got his tactics spot on but Sunderland manager Bob Stokoe was stunned that his team hadn't taken the points.

Reporter Bill Mallinson, of the *Daily Mail*, wrote:

> It was a day when John Kaye's hunches came off and proved yet again that soccer is full of surprises. Robson put Sunderland in front and Hull must have thought it was not their day. They were unlucky with two first half efforts and referee John Williams took an amazingly lenient view of a double tackle on Chris Galvin in the penalty area. Galvin had his revenge with some superb ball control which set up the equaliser for John Hawley just when Sunderland were in command. The striker left Jim Montgomery helpless with a fine shot. Hull went ahead with 10 minutes left when Dave Watson's mistake let in Ken Wagstaff, who got the goal he had always threatened.

Chris recounted: 'It was a great atmosphere and we deserved the win. The fans were behind us and roared us on. I cut in from the left wing and played Hawley in, he smashed the ball in first time into the top corner. It was a great goal, Montgomery had no chance. We gave Hull supporters a performance to be proud of that afternoon.'

A 5-0 defeat at Notts County, after difficult travelling circumstances, underlined City's inconsistency, but the plaudits continued for Chris and the team in a 2-1 triumph against a Fulham side that included former England heroes Bobby Moore and Alan Mullery. The line-ups were:

Hull City: Wealands, Banks, Croft, Blampey, De Vries, Lord, McGill, Galvin, Staniforth (Fletcher), Hawley, Wagstaff.

Fulham: Mellor, Cutbush, Lacy, Moore, Strong, Slough, Mullery, Lloyd, Busby, Conway, Barrett.

Chris made the first goal for 17-year-old right-winger Gordon Staniforth with 'a brilliant dummy and cross', according to a local journalist, that put City on the victory trail in an entertaining clash. Malcolm Lord scored the second midway through the second half before Hull relaxed, allowing John Cutbush to get a long-range consolation goal almost on the whistle. Another correspondent noted: 'Victory was built on the foundation of Hull's midfield trio, in which Galvin supplied the artistry and McGill and Lord the work and tenacity.'

Chris had sought a transfer at one stage but was now much happier. He even had his trademark step-over named by fans! He reflected: 'My sharpness was returning but I still had a pace issue, so keeping possession was essential. Around this time Hull fans dubbed an old-fashioned body swerve I had in my locker as the "Galvin shuffle". I could go both ways to get a yard on my opponent that sent players the wrong way before getting a cross or pass in and it really helped my game. Staniforth's goal against Fulham was an example. I was aggressive, attacking and helping out in defence.'

Chris had been encouraged to use the 'shuffle' under Neill and his creativity as a player had endeared him to fans. The body swerve, of course, is forever linked with the 'Cruyff turn' that Dutch legend Johan Cruyff performed against Sweden in the 1974 World Cup. But Chris is insistent the manoeuvre was his own invention: 'I made it up myself when I was about 14 or 15 years old at school and found it to be useful. To this day I claim to be the first player to use this trick, even Ronaldo does it! It worked a treat and it's great that Hull fans remember it.'

Bragging rights aside, Chris's return to form under Kaye was picked up in the press. Malcolm Richardson of the *Hull Daily Mail* described the 'Galvin shuffle' as a 'startling party piece' after one match. 'His fancy footwork bamboozled unwary opponents,' he wrote. 'Tigers' opponents were regularly baffled and saw the movement completed on the seat of their shorts.'

When the *Hull Daily Mail* soccer writer Brian Taylor interviewed Chris for a feature on his Hull journey to date in November 1974, he explained that his natural game was to take men on and build an attack. Chris had tried to do that when he joined Hull from Leeds but was dropped with no explanation. Things, however, had changed for the better.

Chris told Taylor: 'All last season John Kaye told me what I ought to be doing and now that he is manager I know clearly what he wants from me. It is the same for me as the rest of the side. We have all got to work and help each other out. It means that I have got to do a lot more work in defence than I used to, but I'm enjoying that and at least I know what's expected of me. And what's more, I know, like the rest of the lads, that I will pay the penalty if I don't do it. That's fair enough. John taking over has made all the difference to me.' Chris, though, wouldn't confirm whether he would ask to come off the transfer list. He said: 'We have had talks about it already and I'm happy enough at the moment. But after what happened last year, I don't want to commit myself, although there is a strong possibility that I might withdraw the request.'

Chris's comments offer a revealing insight into this period of his career. He also bared his soul in a 'club focus' article in a match programme, also in November 1974. Chris disclosed that his favourite subject at school had been mathematics. His other favourites included fish and chips, lager, *Monty Python's Flying Circus*, actor Clint Eastwood and singer Barbra Streisand. And, perhaps typically, he described Brian Clough as his favourite television comedian! Chris said that his biggest football thrill was his Leeds debut against Ferencváros in the European Cup. And he added, tongue in cheek, that the biggest drag for him in soccer was 'running around the track in training and always winning!' Liverpool's Ian Callaghan was his most difficult opponent to date, after facing him in the Football League Cup with Hull the previous season. As for hobbies, there were no surprises when Chris selected cricket. The person he most wanted to meet was Yorkshire and England opener Geoffrey Boycott, again no surprises!

The disclosures gained plenty of publicity as they appeared on the occasion of the visit of promotion-chasing Manchester United on 23 November when City recorded a memorable victory. The teams were:

Hull City: Wealands, Banks, De Vries, Galvin, Croft, Blampey, McGill, Lord, Wood, Wagstaff, Hawley.

Manchester United: Stepney, Forsyth, Houston, Macari, Sidebottom, Buchan, Morgan, McIlroy, J. Greenhoff, McCalliog, Daly.

Chris recalled: 'For Hull fans the campaign was memorable for a number of games, especially two feisty encounters against Manchester United, who had been relegated the previous season when my old team Leeds won the league title for a second time.

There was a sense that Tommy Docherty's team came into the Second Division thinking it was only a matter of time before they'd go up and they eventually did, but their attitude was shocking. They played games as if they had a right to win because they were the biggest club in the league. Of course they were, but thinking opponents would simply roll over and not get stuck in was out of order. That attitude was not going to be the case with the Hull lads. Stuart Pearson had joined United from Hull during the close season, so we went out determined to get stuck into them and won 2-0 in front of our biggest gate of the season, with goals from Wagstaff and Lord. More than 23,000 packed the ground, which was rocking.'

Boosted by the win over the title favourites and eventual champions, Hull backed it up with a victory over Bristol City. But then they endured a five-match league run that yielded three defeats and two draws towards the end of 1974, before a welcome win over Oxford United. The local Saturday night sports headline was 'Chris sinks Oxford at long last', and the *Hull Daily Mail* reporter Brian Taylor wrote:

> Hull City had to work hard for 81 long minutes before they got the goal they deserved against Oxford at Boothferry Park this afternoon. No one was more deserving of getting the goal than Galvin because he had worked as hard as anyone and throughout the match was the player who showed the skill likely to break Oxford's defence.

Buoyed by the win over Oxford, the Tigers endured an inconsistent spell before heading to Old Trafford for the return encounter with the leaders, which proved to be a spirited affair in front of 44,712 fans. This time the line-ups were:

Manchester United: Roche, Forsyth, Houston, B. Greenhoff, James (Davies), Buchan, Young, McIlroy, Pearson, Macari, Martin.

Hull City: Wealands, Banks, Daniel, Galvin, Deere, De Vries, McGill, Lord, Wood, Blampey, Greenwood.

Hull impressed despite going down to a 2-0 defeat, and a correspondent noted:

> Three players were booked, Chris Galvin and Steve Deere of Hull and Sammy McIlroy of United. Referee Ray Tinkler, who tried to separate the men from the bruises when these teams met at Boothferry Park last November, felt his first move with the pencil prevented a repetition. This action cautioned Galvin, but Tinkler allowed him to stay on the field to become man of the match. United gave their supporters a good result, but certainly not a rhapsody.

Chris recalled: 'United and Hull were really up for it in the return at Old Trafford and all sorts went on off the ball. We lost it in the first half. Forsyth scored early on and Pearson got a second on the stroke of half-time. I had a do with Tommy Docherty in the tunnel after one of United's players had a go at me about an incident in the first half. There was a lot of pushing and shoving, but things did calm down. Despite all sorts of incidents, it was great playing in front of a full house. Leeds fans of course recall Tinkler for an appalling decision in a crucial league game a few years earlier against West Brom at Elland Road that ultimately cost them the title. In this game, Tinkler struggled to maintain control and there could have been a couple of dismissals.'

Unfortunately, Hull's form dipped after the defeat. There were turgid affairs, including a goalless draw against Ian St

John's relegation-threatened, financially strapped Portsmouth. Correspondent Keith Macklin, known for his football commentaries on ITV in Yorkshire, described the game as a 'dreary show', although neither team was at full strength. Macklin added:

> Even taking into account the injuries and sickness which ravaged both sides, the game stretched tolerance and charity to breaking-point. To be fair there were some nice touches in midfield from Galvin of Hull and flashes of brilliance from Portsmouth's Marinello. Hull must yearn for the return of their absent goalscorers, while Portsmouth must pray for a financial and footballing miracle.

In the FA Cup third round City faced Fulham and almost knocked them out. Fulham would eventually lose 2-0 to West Ham United in the final at Wembley, but first they had to endure a mighty scare against the Tigers in a tie that went to two replays. The teams for the first meeting at Craven Cottage were:

Fulham: Mellor, Cutbush, Strong, Mullery, Lacy, Moore, John Conway, Jim Conway, Busby, Slough, Barrett. Sub: Mitchell.

Hull City: Wealands, Banks, Daniel, Galvin, Croft, Burnett, Grimes, Lord, Wood, Wagstaff (Deere), Greenwood.

Correspondent Roy Peskett noted:

> Fulham swept majestically to a 10-minute lead and threatened to overwhelm Hull. They might easily have been four up at half-time. Then Hull started to play what

is known as 'typical cup tie football' and from being almost out of it at half-time they changed the game so dramatically that Fulham were perhaps lucky to hang on for a replay. Only Bobby Moore's goalmouth clearance from Alf Wood eight minutes from time kept Fulham in the cup … Through all the panic Chris Galvin stood out for Hull. Three times he cleared over his own bar from almost underneath it. And when Hull manager John Kaye switched the side after Wagstaff's injury, Galvin was sent forward and he crossed the ball for Alf Wood's near winner.

The teams drew 2-2 after extra time in the first replay at Boothferry Park before meeting at Leicester's Filbert Street. Chris recalled: 'Moore was past his best and lacked pace, but it didn't matter because his reading of the game was still superb. You never lose that from your game. All the lads respected him and that also went for Mullery from his Tottenham days. Fulham knocked us out 1-0 in a third-round second replay after a couple of great games.'

Hull finished the season in eighth place after losing only one of their last seven league matches. Kaye had shown faith in Chris, who had started 33 of the 42 matches in the Second Division. There was also a further appearance as a substitute and he made 26 consecutive Second Division starts to mark his second full season in league football.

Chris recalled: 'John was a great bloke and I felt settled, possibly the only time I did in my career. I played my best in the middle of the park and John used a 4-3-3 system, so I had the freedom when attacking to go left or right. I was also enjoying day-to-day life at Hull. Inwardly, coming from Leeds United I still had a feeling that I was playing below where I should be, but we had friends, I was playing some good stuff, so life was great on and off the field.'

Chapter 12

King Billy then Relegation Woes

HULL CITY'S chairman and benefactor Harold Needler died in July 1975 as the club prepared to go on a pre-season tour to Scotland. He was replaced by his son Christopher. The team made a promising start to the 1975/76 season, winning four of their opening six matches, against Blackpool, Bristol City, Orient and Nottingham Forest. But it might have been better because they lost to a last-minute goal away to Oldham Athletic.

The success at home to Blackpool was significant, as the headline in the *Hull Daily Mail* was 'Chris Galvin special gives Tigers points'. Hull should have won comfortably against a poor Blackpool team, but Chris's goal shone like a beacon. It was reported:

> The one goal the Tigers did score was a beauty. Wood, Wagstaff and Grimes steadily built up a promising attack. The ball was switched to Lord on the right and his cross was only partially cleared. The ball went out to Galvin, who was lurking on the left, and he cleverly cut inside to crack a fierce right-foot shot into the top corner of the net. This gave Galvin the opportunity to parade some adroit footwork. The goal boosted City's confidence and in the

second half they were even more able to push the ball around neatly due to the teamwork which was the most heartening facet of their display.

Another journalist wrote:

> Galvin was the one man who managed to rise above the mediocrity which surrounded him and it was fitting that he should score the goal to give Hull their first win of the season. It came after 44 minutes of a mistake-ridden clash with Blackpool that was a constant source of frustration to the small Hull crowd. Galvin, standing on the left of Blackpool's penalty area, gathered a Lord cross before neatly side-stepping a desperate lunge by Alcock. He then fired a rising volley into the top corner of the net.

A wonder goal by Alf Wood with a scissor-kick accounted for Orient at Boothferry Park. A correspondent noted: 'Back-pedalling appeared the order of the day with Hull struggling to find a route to goal.' But he added: 'The only noticeable spark was the confident approach of Hull's midfield anchorman Galvin as he displayed tricky thinking and classy footwork on a day when they scraped home.'

A week later the Tigers travelled to Nottingham Forest, then managed by Brian Clough. The teams were:

Nottingham Forest: Middleton, Anderson, Gunn, Clark, Chapman, Richardson, Curran, McGovern, O'Hare, Bowyer, Robertson. Sub: O'Neill.

Hull City: Wealands, Banks, De Vries, Galvin, Croft, Roberts, Grimes, Lord, Wood, Fletcher, Greenwood. Sub: Deere.

Hull came from behind at half-time to secure a fine 2-1 win. John Robertson had given Forest the lead, stabbing home after Jeff Wealands had blocked his first penalty of the match. Forest dominated the first half but Hull struck twice after the resumption to secure the points. Correspondent Tony Turner described Galvin as 'a tower of strength' in the triumph. Turner wrote:

> Hull snatched an equaliser 60 seconds after the restart, but the Forest defence had to shoulder the blame for the upset. When Chris Galvin stole through, there was very little challenge from the home players as he met a free kick from Vincent Grimes. It was the same story when Roy Greenwood whipped in the winner four minutes from time.

Hull, in fact, then went on a run of seven league matches without a win. Grimes denied Portsmouth a win in a sequence of four draws in a row, but reporter Alisdair Ross was clear that Hull's Galvin was the standout Hull player in a feisty 1-1 draw at Fratton Park. 'His stylish, skilful play kept Hull alive when all seemed lost,' he noted. City then led until shipping a late goal in a 2-2 draw at home to Bolton Wanderers, but they were far from fluent. Correspondent Eric Greenwood wrote:

> The only time that Hull were seriously in contention despite their whole-hearted effort was in the first half when Galvin spurred them on to some powerful raiding. It brought them goals from Lord, whose shot was deflected past Siddall by Allardyce and from the crafty Wagstaff, whose 30-yarder dipped into the net.

There was then a thriller at Oxford when Hull finally returned to winning ways at the start of November. Chris opened the scoring with a 20-yard shot that went in off a post and Wagstaff made it 2-0 just after half-time. McGrogan then hit back for United, but after Grimes had re-established a two-goal lead for Hull, Foley scored a late consolation for Oxford. David Park reported:

> Referee Clive Thomas visited both dressing rooms at the end to enthuse: 'That was the finest Second Division game I have ever handled. You are a credit to the game.' How right he was. Both teams produced their midfield generals. Peter Houseman, ex-Chelsea veteran, belied his years as he displayed all his imaginative skills to inspire United. However, he had his counterpart in Chris Galvin whose shrewd tactical sense kept Hull on the boil.

The inconsistent Tigers then lost three league matches in succession, including a 2-1 home defeat at the hands of promotion favourites Chelsea. The teams were:

> Hull City: Wealands, Banks, De Vries, Galvin, Croft, Haigh, Grimes, Gibson, Stewart, Wagstaff, Greenwood. Sub: Wood.

> Chelsea: Bonetti, Locke, Harris, Stanley, Droy, Dempsey, Britton, Wilkins, Maybank, Hutchinson, Garner. Sub: Hay.

Chelsea, with experienced professionals Peter Bonetti, Ron Harris, John Dempsey and Ian Hutchinson lining up, eventually took control. The *News of the World* correspondent Gilbert Johnson nominated Chris as Hull's star player on the day. Chelsea ultimately ended up in mid-table obscurity.

Hull then had three league wins, followed by four defeats, but equally demoralising was their fourth-round exit from the Football League Cup at Doncaster Rovers, when they failed to take a host of chances.

Chris reflected: 'The season started well. We were playing with confidence and scores reflected it. Of course, it's great hitting the local headlines as I did with the only goal against Blackpool and then scoring against Nottingham Forest. But we struggled to finish teams off and, apart from a couple of short winning bursts, found ourselves hovering just above the relegation area. Our worst period was during Christmas and New Year when bizarrely we completed the double over Forest. Cloughie had taken over, but there was no indication he was about to lead them to domestic and European glory.'

Chris continued to impress reporters but Hull remained frustrating. At the end of January 1976 they let a point slip away against Blackpool at Bloomfield Road in injury time for a 2-2 draw before their record low attendance of 4,966 spectators. A correspondent wrote:

> Substitute Ronson pulled Blackpool out of the doldrums with an injury-time equaliser in a bleak, shivering game before their worst league gate in history. Even Blackpool seemed to have resigned themselves to defeat, which would have been their sixth in as many matches against bogey side Hull. With Galvin controlling everything in midfield, Hull calmly kept the lifeless Blackpool players at bay.

But then a goalless draw against Chelsea at Stamford Bridge sparked an 11-match league run in which Hull lost only once as they improved during the second half of the season. The sequence included a surprise midweek 2-1 win at high-flying Notts County, when John Hawley and Dave Sunley scored for City before Bolton pulled a late goal back for County. However, Chris saw red for the only time in his Hull career between their two goals. He picked up his ninth booking of the season after a clash that left County's full-back Pedro Richards limping and then was deemed to have wasted time at a throw-in and was sent off in the 57th minute.

The Tigers suffered only one defeat in their good run against promotion-chasing Bolton Wanderers at their bogey ground Burnden Park. Despite the loss, Hull, and especially Chris, earned praise for their performance after home supporters had slow-hand-clapped their own team. But Hull followed up the setback with wins against Oxford United and Bristol Rovers. They completed the double over Oxford with a 2-0 success and then won 1-0 at the Eastville stadium. It was written:

> Bristol Rovers were foiled by the brilliant goalkeeping of Wealands as they fought to stave off their fourth home league defeat of the season. The aggressive Galvin, who had been the outstanding midfield player in the first half, floated over a long centre from the left. Eadie was badly positioned and too far off his line. And as the ball sailed over him, Sunley was left with a simple chance to head in from a couple of yards out. The goal brought Hull their fifth away win of the season. They have now taken nine points from their last six games and relegation fears are fast fading.

A run of four draws followed, including a hard-fought 1-1 clash at Plymouth Argyle after the City party had spent the week in the Channel Islands before returning to the West Country. Correspondent George Rogers reported that Hull scored after continuous Plymouth pressure. Hull struggled to contain Plymouth's talented young striker Paul Mariner, who would soon star for Ipswich Town and England. But Rogers felt that City had earned a share of the spoils thanks to a dominant display by one of their midfield players. He pointed out: 'Galvin rallied Hull into midfield action in a fiery second half and his raids down the left posed problems for a defence who had it too easy for too long in a one-sided first half.'

But there was a brief hiccup near the end of the season when Kaye and some of his players, including Chris, were involved in a heated Easter exchange on the way to a goalless draw away to Carlisle United. It was a postscript to a 4-1 home defeat on Easter Saturday against Bob Stokoe's Sunderland, who were on their way to promotion, but it was soon forgotten. As it was, inconsistent Hull ended the campaign with a 1-0 defeat at Wembley-bound Southampton, who faced First Division Manchester United in the FA Cup Final a week later. Saints stunned the Reds at Wembley.

Chris reflected: 'We finally found form in a spell that took us to safety. Southampton had a strong side including great players such as Jim McCalliog, Mick Channon and Peter Osgood. They won the cup with a Bobby Stokes goal, which was a real surprise. We ended the campaign six points off relegation. Of course, it's satisfying when reporters praised my game. I'd received plenty of criticism down the years so it gives you a boost, but you still have to go out and perform in the next games.'

The Tigers had dropped to 14th in the Second Division but Chris had enjoyed another solid season, starting 37 of the 42 league fixtures, coming on as a substitute in one more and starting five out of six cup ties. He also contributed four league goals, and the appearance record might have been even better but for a slight groin problem and a suspension midway through the campaign.

Hull stalwart Ken Wagstaff played his last match for the club during the season. Voted by fans in 2004 as the club's greatest-ever player, Chris enjoyed playing alongside him at the end of his Hull career. He said: 'Ken was good enough to play at a higher standard, but he was happy with the situation. Ken never had to buy a drink when he went out! He is a club legend with players such as Ken Knighton and Ken Houghton. I just missed out on playing alongside them because they both left the club just before I signed, but they are fondly recalled in the club's history.' Chris would though soon come across Houghton as a Hull manager!

The 1976/77 league season began badly for City when they lost 1-0 in a bruising battle at Hereford United and suffered serious injuries to Dave Roberts, Vince Grimes and Alf Wood. Chris also missed the opening day, as manager Kaye again had to put the focus on youth, but he was soon back in the action as Hull impressed in consecutive victories over Luton Town and FA Cup winners Southampton. Both wins made welcome reading in weekend sports editions, with Hull sitting second in the table.

Chris recalled: 'During pre-season I had picked up a knock but came on as a substitute in a 4-0 win at home to Saints, who seemed to be still celebrating their win over Manchester United the previous May, but we weren't complaining, it was a great result.'

Chris then impressed in his first start of the season in a 1-1 draw away to Carlisle United. Correspondent Bill Woodcock wrote:

> Galvin had a glorious time in the 20 minutes after half-time before exhaustion set in. His ball skills and inch-perfect passing cut great gaps through to goal as Carlisle's defence refused to be drawn into ungentlemanly conduct.

Not surprisingly he paved the way to the equaliser with a shot that felled defender Carr, leaving Hawley, who played despite a broken wrist because of Hull's long injury list, to sprint in and push the loose ball home.

After a disappointing midweek loss at Orient in the League Cup, Chris returned to the bench when Bolton Wanderers thumped City 5-1 at Burnden Park, and he observed: 'Bolton were among the promotion favourites and battered us. Sam Allardyce and Peter Reid were regulars in the side. Reid would win trophies with Everton. Both enjoyed managerial success. There was also vast experience in former Manchester United players Willie Morgan and Tony Dunne. Peter Thompson, who starred for Liverpool and England on the wing, was coming towards the end of his playing days. They had a really strong side.'

Kaye had been building a team with several talented youngsters, including full-back Peter Daniel, centre-back Stuart Croft and striker John Hawley, who were among the players to make a mark. But it was clear he needed to give his Hull squad a boost. A bid to sign Arsenal's Alan Ball failed, and the board also baulked at a £45,000 asking price by the Gunners for talented striker Frank Stapleton, who had made his debut the previous season. Hindsight is easy, as Stapleton would enjoy a stellar career.

Undeterred, Kaye responded in spectacular fashion when Billy Bremner joined on a two-year deal from Leeds United for £25,000 at the end of September 1976. Hull's boss had made an inquiry about Bremner following Leeds signing Tony Currie for £240,000 in June 1976, with United's manager Jimmy Armfield rebuilding his team. Kaye's persistence finally paid off, and he was well aware of what Bremner could offer Hull in experience, on and off the pitch.

Kaye had captained West Brom, winning the League Cup and FA Cup in his playing days. In Richard Sutcliffe's book *Bremner: The Complete Biography*, Kaye recalled that it was an era when West Brom had a decent record against Leeds. 'We were not overawed despite Leeds being such a good team,' he said. 'They had tremendous players who weren't afraid to dish it out. Or to their credit, take it too.' When Leeds needed a goal, Revie would send Bremner forward, and his skipper had a knack of scoring important goals. Kaye faced Bremner on many occasions. Of an early encounter, he recalled: 'Soon after moving up front, he whacked me a couple of times and I thought, "I'm not having this." So, I gave him an almighty whack back. As he got off the floor, we just looked at each other and, although neither of us said a word, our faces said, "Right, we can get on with playing now we've both had a crack." And that is how we played the rest of the game, hard, but fair.' A match Kaye didn't discuss with Bremner after signing him for Hull City was West Brom's infamous win against Leeds in April 1971 when referee Ray Tinkler allowed a controversial offside goal by Jeff Astle that cost United the title. Kaye felt Billy would still be 'angry'! The argument is set to rage on.

Bremner's package exceeded the club's pay structure but any concerns disappeared when Kaye explained the situation to his squad shortly after the deal was confirmed. If the team was successful, players would benefit from bonuses. Chris's team-mate, goalkeeper Jeff Wealands, welcomed the impact Bremner made in the dressing room. He told Sutcliffe: 'The great thing with Billy is he didn't arrive with this attitude of "been there, done that", which is something you can get with big-name players. Instead, he was a real down-to-earth lad, who loved hanging around with his team-mates. We respected him because of what he had achieved with Leeds but he never played on that.'

And Chris recalled: 'When John told me he had a chance of getting Billy, I told him to snap him up. It was a real coup, even though Billy was coming towards the end of his career. His instincts might be a shade slower but the lads knew of his standing in the game and realised what he could offer the side in terms of experience. Fans were excited by the move, there was a buzz around the city, it was the biggest story in the sports pages. I couldn't wait to play alongside Billy. At Leeds I'd trained and played alongside him and he was a brilliant footballer. It didn't matter where you were on the pitch with Billy, he'd find you. His vision was amazing and he'd pop up to score his share of goals. His arrival at the club was a real boost.'

Bremner missed the deadline by a few hours for an away trip to Burnley, which finished goalless, but over 16,000 fans packed Boothferry Park for his highly anticipated debut against Brian Clough's Nottingham Forest. You couldn't write a better script. City won and Bremner was credited with the only goal of the match, although there was a question of whether his free kick was deflected into the net. But no journalist present was going to deny Bremner the headlines in the Sunday sports pages.

Chris was injured for the match but watched from the packed stands with the home fans. He reflected: 'Billy was a great player, but didn't have star players around him anymore. He added thousands to the gate because fans were keen to see if he could still make an impact. Of course he could, but he had to adapt to the level. During the game, I recall Billy trying to play a ball blind across his body, as he'd done at Leeds for years, but whereas the likes of Paul Reaney or Paul Madeley would read his pass, none of our lads did and the crowd let him know. "You're not at Leeds now, Bremner, watch where you are passing!" was the message and they were right in a way. The Hull lads were not at the same level technically as the Leeds boys. But credit to Billy, he just got on with it, scored the winner and grabbed the headlines as he had many times before!'

Chris finally played alongside Bremner for the first time since his Leeds years when he scored Hull's goal in a 3-1 defeat at Charlton Athletic. City bounced back with a win and Chris contributed in a 2-0 home triumph against a strong Wolves outfit boasting many players from their First Division days, including former Leeds apprentice Terry Hibbitt's brother Kenny. Hawley scored a brace for Hull in front of the *Match of the Day* cameras. The teams were:

> Hull City: Wealands, Daniel, De Vries, Bremner, Croft, Haigh, Nisbet, Lyall, Hawley, Hemmerman (Sunley), Galvin.
>
> Wolves: Pierce, Palmer, Parkin, Daley, Munro, McAlle, Hibbitt, Carr, Sunderland, Kindon, O'Hara. Sub: Patching.

The victory took Hull into fifth place in the table. A correspondent noted:

> Hull rolled back the Wolves defence with a barrage of machine gun-like passes from their captain and midfield dynamo Bremner. City had chances in the early stages, which with a modicum of luck might have put them ahead. Galvin, a quick-silver raider on the left, forced Wolves 'keeper Pierce into a fine fingertip save.

But it was not going to be long before Chris was out of favour. Following draws at Fulham and Blackpool, then a win against Plymouth Argyle, he was substituted against Bristol Rovers and then dropped. Chris would start only seven league matches alongside Bremner during the campaign. Hull by now were mid-table in the Second Division. After the best part of three seasons as a regular in Hull's first-team line-up, Chris found that his extended honeymoon period was over.

Chris was available for sale at £25,000 but joined Third Division York City on loan towards the end of 1976, a deal that proved beneficial for both parties. Newspaper snippets noted that Chris turned down a move to Carlisle United because he preferred to be situated close to his wastepaper business in West Riding, which he ran with former Leeds team-mate Trevor Cherry and business partner Mike Woodhead. Burnley, Sheffield Wednesday and Sheffield United were rumoured to be considering a bid for him, but nothing materialised.

Chris made his debut for York at Sheffield Wednesday on 27 December 1976, in front of a bigger crowd than Hull fans had experienced that season at Boothferry Park, even allowing for a 16,096 gate in Bremner's debut against Forest. York had won only four league matches and faced a relegation battle. Chris would miss only two of York's next 24 league fixtures.

He recalled: 'I needed regular football and it was obvious to me it would not be at Hull at his point. Former Manchester United manager Wilf McGuinness was in charge at York. Wilf was a great character and made me feel wanted, so I agreed to go. Gordon Staniforth also signed from Hull to give the team a boost. We both went straight into the team against Wednesday, who were the biggest club in the division. Over 22,000 fans packed Hillsborough, which was an amazing attendance for a Third Division match. We lost 3-2 but played well and I really enjoyed the atmosphere of a big crowd.'

Following a 2-2 draw at home to Gillingham, York defeated Crystal Palace and Chesterfield, both matches ending 2-1. They had taken five points out of six after a run of seven matches without a win, which included an FA Cup exit. But there were signs the new arrivals had given the team a timely lift.

Chris had delighted City's fans in the victory over promotion hopefuls Palace, managed by Terry Venables, on 22 January 1977, and duly received praise for his match-winning efforts. Correspondent Peter Snape of the *Yorkshire Post* wrote:

> In the fourth minute Galvin rapped home a header from Cave's immaculate cross, an opening first created by Holmes' beautifully-weighted pass down the right. In the 60th minute Holmes ran on to a pass from Pollard at the edge of the area, dummied to go inside, checked and then went round on the outside before floating a cross over the defence for Galvin again to head home triumphantly. Galvin, in his third game on loan from Hull, was in no doubt whom he had to thank: 'They were both perfect crosses. With the first I might have fouled the defender, but because he was leaning on me, the referee probably let it go. The second I got over the defender and headed it in. It's just a joke that this side are bottom. The effort today was really tremendous.' Ironically for all their effort and not a little skill, victory could not lift York from the bottom yet. Relegation still stares York in the face. But for one glorious afternoon at least they were able to shade their eyes from its gaze.

Another reporter wrote:

> Chris Galvin's second goal, a carbon copy of his first, sent York's success-starved fans wild with delight. Twice

Galvin rose above the Palace defence to clinch a first league win for York in more than two months. Despite the threat of Barry Silkman on the left, promotion-chasing Palace could create only few chances against York's packed defence. York's star man Ian Holmes sent Micky Cave clear on the right in the fourth minute and Galvin nodded home Cave's slide-rule pass. After 55 minutes Rachid Harkouk snatched the equaliser with a low shot from the edge of the penalty box. Seven minutes later York clinched it when Holmes crossed immaculately and Galvin was in the right place to beat Paul Hammond from six yards.

The *Yorkshire Post*'s Snape wrote about Chris's future at Bootham Crescent. Hull had decided to extend his loan period to York for a second month but Chris made it clear that playing in the Fourth Division wasn't his aspiration, but he had found his touch again. He said: 'I am enjoying it at York, they are a great set of lads and far better than their league position, but naturally I want to play Second Division football.' Chris ruled out a permanent move to York, adding, 'It's certainly better playing in the first team here than in Hull reserves.' It was clear that Chris had to bide his time, return to form at York and then sort his Hull future out.

Three days after York's first victory over Palace, Chris hit the winner against Chesterfield. York, playing the same team, moved off the foot of the table, but it was a closer encounter. The coming weeks yielded a thrilling 4-4 draw away to Tranmere Rovers, further wins against Port Vale and Peterborough United and a share of the spoils with Reading, when Chris earned York a point. Only two defeats came in the period as York continued to fight. Chris was on target again when only an own goal by Bobby Bell denied them another victory at home to Graham Taylor's mid-table Lincoln City, who had won the Fourth Division title the previous season. The match ended 2-2.

After the Lincoln encounter, Chris's immediate future remained uncertain. Terry Brindle of the *Yorkshire Post* wrote:

> Chris Galvin, living on borrowed time, which has done much to allay York City's relegation fears, hammered another life-saving goal last night still uncertain whether his immediate future lay at Bootham Crescent or back at Hull City. Hull's manager John Kaye waited until after the match to inform York's Wilf McGuinness whether Galvin's loan period had been extended beyond the two months he has already played for York. While McGuinness and the York fans had waited on tenterhooks for the decision, Galvin again stamped his skill, flair and goalscoring ability on a match which defied rainswept conditions to produce an unlikely spectacle. 'We have agreed that he can play for York, but we have a clause which gives us the right to recall him at 24 hours' notice,' explained Kaye later. York, whose determination to haul themselves out of relegation danger already represents one of the more heroic stories of the season, showed enough character and commitment to succeed where they once seemed certain to fail dismally.

It was then reported in the *Hull Daily Mail* in late March 1977 that York wanted to buy Chris when his third month on loan expired, but they couldn't afford the required fee and Chris wasn't keen on a permanent move. Kaye insisted on a £17,500 transfer fee, the same figure agreed with Carlisle United two months earlier. In the end, Chris extended his stay at York for another month after discussions. York, though, won just two of their last 12 league matches. Chris scored in a 4-2 victory at home against Swindon Town in his penultimate appearance for the club and then lined up for the last time four days later as York drew 0-0 with Walsall on 23 April. York battled away but lost three of their remaining four fixtures to finish bottom of the Third Division.

Chris recalled: 'We were desperately fighting relegation, but Wilf put no pressure on me. I was able to go out, play my game with freedom and knocked in a few goals. We picked up some good results by playing attacking football and I enjoyed my four-month spell. McGuinness wanted me to join York for the new campaign, but I decided against it.'

Chris was on the mark six times in 22 league appearances for the Minstermen to finish third in their goalscoring charts behind Brian Pollard with 12 in 41 matches and Jim Hinch with 7 in 28. But his season wasn't over. He was recalled from York to play in the final four league fixtures of Hull's season due to injury problems, which dragged on to 17 May 1977.

The Tigers completed the campaign in anonymous fashion. Again, they finished 14th and there was also disappointment in cup football. Chris ended with 12 league starts, two substitute appearances and one goal. The signing of Bremner might not have had the desired impact in terms of results but Kaye had no regrets about signing the former Scotland captain, who led his country at the 1974 World Cup. He reflected: 'Billy was terrific. The younger lads learned so much from him in games and training. His enthusiasm rubbed off on everyone.'

As the Tigers tried to make progress, Kaye brought legendary Leeds United midfielder Bobby Collins to Hull following the departure of first-team coach Phil Holme ahead of the 1977/78 season. Kaye had played against Bobby so knew his qualities. Could Collins help spark a renaissance at City? Chris was ready to stake his claim for a first-team spot, with support from two former Leeds legends.

He recalled: 'Things were changing behind the scenes at Hull. When Bobby arrived, I was pleased. He had left Leeds just before I joined the club as an apprentice, but I had heard about his impact on young lads coming through. The likes of Gray, Lorimer, Madeley and Cooper were breaking through and all spoke about his influence. Billy respected Bobby enormously. They went back to his early years in the first team. Bobby's legacy was still felt at the club, without a doubt he was Don Revie's most important signing because he instilled a tremendous work ethic. Bobby was a fiery character. Could he inspire the Hull squad, especially with Billy also offering his experience? I hoped so.'

Kaye boosted his attack for the campaign by reuniting Alan Warboys and Bruce Bannister. Known as 'Smash and Grab' in their pomp, they had a prolific reputation as goalscorers, notably with Bristol Rovers. Bannister had played for Bradford City and wanted a move back to Yorkshire. Tottenham Hotspur had come in for him but he turned the move down for a chance to play in the same team as Bremner. Other members of the squad had a similar motivation.

Aside from the Bremner-factor there were hopeful signs that there was dressing-room harmony and that team spirit was good. In fact, Chris had naturally been at the hub of it much of the time. For example, a group of players had attended a charity dance at Tiffany's nightclub in Hull in aid of the local Kingston General Hospital shortly after Chris began his loan at York. At one point he took to the microphone on the stage and amazed everyone by embarking on an impromptu version of the old folk song 'Early One Morning', which was once equally memorably performed by

Michael Crawford as Frank Spencer in an episode of television sitcom *Some Mothers Do Have 'Em*. Remarkably, Chris went down very well with the audience, although he alienated the bewildered house band, who not surprisingly had little idea about what was going on when they tried in vain to back him!

Then Chris tried to bring people together during pre-season. He played cricket for Almondbury in the Huddersfield League when he could and, after City had drawn a pre-season friendly 1-1 at Scunthorpe, he organised a match at Sewerby, just north of Bridlington, for his team-mates. Chris's Hull City team, augmented by guests such as club secretary Malcolm 'Mac' Stone and his business partner Woodhead, took on Sewerby's village team at their picturesque cliff-top ground. The game was competitive enough, but it also provided an enjoyable day that brought everyone closer together. Unfortunately, though, it was the quiet before the storm as the football season took shape. Bit by bit unrest began to surface as City struggled on the pitch and remained as inconsistent as ever.

On the opening day of the season Chris was named in the starting line-up. Bannister scored as Hull defeated Sunderland 3-0 at home in front of a 16,189 crowd. Defender Dave Roberts contributed two goals. And following a 2-0 defeat at Sheffield United, City drew the plaudits following a 1-0 win away to unbeaten Crystal Palace, who were hoping to build on their recent promotion to the Second Division. The teams were:

Crystal Palace: Burns, Hinshelwood, Sansom, Graham, Cannon, Evans, Hilaire, Chatterton, Perrin, Bourne, Harkouk. Sub: Swindlehurst.

Hull City: Wealands, Nisbet, De Vries, Bremner, Croft, Roberts, Haigh, Lord, Hawley, Bannister, Galvin. Sub: Stewart.

It was written in the *Hull Daily Mail*:

> Amid the thunder and lightning at Selhurst Park on Saturday, Hull City reigned supreme, serving up their own fire and brimstone to crush Crystal Palace with greater emphasis that the scoreline suggests. Cock-a-hoop Palace lost their 100 per cent record as the magnificent Tigers rediscovered all their snap and drive after the midweek defeat by Sheffield United. The quality of their football was not always of the highest standard, but their determination and strength of purpose were undeniable. City gained this first success in London for more than three years because they went out with the will to win. They always looked as if they wanted two points and there can be no better basis than that for a team who are going to be successful.

After the match, Palace's manager, Venables, complained about Hull's uncompromising attitude and also claimed that Bremner had influenced the referee's decisions. He insisted: 'Billy gets the referee on his side and puts him in his pocket.' Venables did, however, acknowledge the quality of Hull's 40th-minute winner as Chris was said to have 'revelled in the muddy conditions and was never subdued'. It was written: 'Galvin and Lord worked the ball down the left for de Vries to send over an immaculate cross. The Palace defence were caught out of position and Hawley stormed in unmarked at the far post to plant a fine header in the corner of the net.'

Hull's performance next time out in a goalless draw at home to a strong Bolton Wanderers earned them praise. It was reported:

It is true that City created few chances for a home match and seldom looked like scoring, but the game as a whole was always fascinating rather than classical. The Tigers at least refused to yield at all in trying circumstances. In Galvin, City had the one player who looked to have the flair to end the deadlock. He maintained his fine opening to the season and was backed up well in midfield by Haigh. The highly-competitive nature of the game boiled over at times and Galvin was booked for upending Morgan after 29 minutes. Nisbet was cautioned a little severely for a foul on Morgan after 49 minutes and three minutes later Reid was booked for bringing down Galvin as he exacted some retribution. The Tigers played again with pride in their performance for the most part although there it might be argued that if there is the same ambition within the club, then it is time to buy in an attempt to capitalise on the promising, but injury-ridden start to the season.

Bolton would go on to win the league. The assertion that Hull needed to strengthen their squad was correct because they then endured a dreadful run of form. Within an hour of a 2-0 home defeat to Mansfield Town in front of just 6,263 fans on 1 October, Kaye was sacked as manager, before chairman Needler disappeared on holiday. Collins was named caretaker manager. Local newspapers speculated whether Collins or Bremner would get the job on a permanent basis. According to Needler there had been some 30 candidates.

After Hull defeated unbeaten Tottenham 2-0 at home, with Warboys bagging both goals, there was a huge collective sigh of relief at the club. A draw with Millwall followed, then victory against Blackpool. Needler interviewed Collins about the job vacancy after the Blackpool win. On his way home by car, Collins saw Bremner travelling to the ground for an interview. By all accounts Collins was more relaxed in his attitude in the interviewing process and was offered the managerial reins, and with City taking five points out of six during his temporary stint as boss, it appeared the logical choice. Andy Davidson remained assistant manager, and former Hull legend Ken Houghton returned as youth-team coach. Within a couple of days of Collins taking the post, Bremner told the *Yorkshire Post* of his intention to retire when his contract finished at the end of the season.

In the midst of Bobby's caretaker tenure, there was an ironic Saturday afternoon on 8 October 1977 when there was an indication that the Galvin brothers' careers might be going in different directions. Chris headed a 70th-minute own goal just inside the upright for Millwall's equaliser in Hull's 1-1 draw at the Den. Around 200 miles north, Tony scored the first goal and made two others when Goole Town beat Selby Town 7-0 at home in the second qualifying round of the FA Cup!

Back on Humberside, despite his obvious disappointment at not getting the player-manager role, Bremner, the true professional, earned a point at Burnley in a 1-1 draw. But the decision to appoint Collins would prove disastrous, with one league victory, 4-1 at home to Cardiff City, coming before the New Year. The win against the Bluebirds on 12 November should have had a positive effect on the team but Collins decided to criticise his players publicly in an attempt to push them on to greater heights. Six defeats in nine matches followed. The dressing-room spirit nosedived and a strained relationship between Collins and Bremner worsened. To complicate matters there were changes at boardroom level, with Bob Chapman becoming chairman.

With uncertainty on and off the pitch, Chris and John Hawley put in transfer requests after being left out of the first team for several matches. The story broke in the *Hull Daily Mail* on the eve of a trip to Cardiff's Ninian Park on 16 December 1977. Hull had gone four matches without a win. Collins told the paper: 'Chris says that he feels that this is the third time he has been messed around by a manager since he has been at the club. I am drawing up a list of players to be put on offer and he might be on it. I have told John to put his request in writing, but he hasn't done so. He says he thinks he ought to be back in the first team, but I don't think he is fully fit yet.'

Chris told the paper he was settled in Hull but maybe it was now time to move on. He remembers a chaotic period at Hull City: 'Billy and Bobby told me about their plans after Kaye was sacked. Billy would be manager and Bobby his assistant. Billy saw Hull as an opportunity to get into management. I'd be playing and was part of their plans. You play your best football when you are wanted and can see a future. Bobby was a great coach, he mixed things up in training and got on with the lads. But when Billy found out Bobby had been appointed, the atmosphere between the two was dreadful. Billy was the senior professional at the club and it must have been tough on him. Their relationship was seriously affected. I felt really sorry for Billy, but there was a reaction. We beat Tottenham, who had the likes of Steve Perryman, Glenn Hoddle, John Pratt and Peter Taylor in the side. It was a terrific performance against a side who were among the favourites for promotion.

'After we defeated Blackpool, the board appointed Bobby manager. Credit to Billy, despite his obvious disappointment he was a professional and earned us a draw at Burnley. Billy then scored our second as we beat Oldham Athletic in a League Cup replay to set up a trip to Arsenal at Highbury. Not long after we comfortably beat Cardiff but for some reason Bobby slammed us in the press. The dressing-room atmosphere was shocking afterwards. Everything kicked off. Billy and Bobby did not see eye to eye, which was a real problem because I was friendly with both. Bobby pulled me aside one day after training and asked if I was aware of any problems. Of course I was but there was no way I wanted to get mixed up in a spat between the two of them. It was a nightmare situation. I was dropped after the next game against Fulham but came back for the Arsenal clash when we were thumped 5-1. Bobby was out of his depth as a manager. He had brought in Syd Owen as assistant manager, which badly affected team morale. The situation on and off the pitch could not continue like this for long.'

Bringing in Owen after just two months was a huge error of judgement by Collins as Wealands also recollected: 'Syd basically became Bobby's henchman and no one liked him. He had a superior attitude about him, making sure we all knew that he considered Hull to be a big step down from Leeds. Syd lost the players almost straight away. He seemed to expect Bobby Charlton or Peter Lorimer to be playing for Hull City, ignoring the fact we were in the Second Division.'

Hawley and Galvin came back into the team for a festive trip to Notts County that brought a 2-1 defeat. Further setbacks followed against Sheffield United and Sunderland before Bremner scored in a 1-0 home win over Crystal Palace. Chris missed the encounter and then picked up an injury against Brighton in a 1-1 draw at home on 4 February. By the end of the week, Collins and Owen had been sacked. Collins led the team for just over four months, the shortest-reigning manager in Hull City's history at the time. Hull won three times in his 18 league and cup matches in charge.

Chris recalled: 'The board had seen enough, which was no surprise. Bobby had respect as a coach with the lads but lost the dressing room as manager. Bringing in Owen was a disaster. The board should have appointed Billy player-manager because he was an inspirational leader. Billy went on to enjoy promotion at Doncaster Rovers and almost did the same as Leeds United's boss.'

Bannister and Wealands concurred with Galvin about Collins. Bannister said: 'You need to be a bit more subtle as manager, use psychology to get the best out of players. But that was not Bobby. Unfortunately, the board made the wrong decision in sacking John and then compounded it by not giving the job to Billy. The club ended up paying the price.'

Wealands added: 'Confidence was rock bottom; the players were unhappy and it simply wasn't working out. Even in the short space of time he had been in the job, we had three or four crisis meetings when the gloves were really off. Syd Owen really copped it!'

Houghton was soon appointed manager. Ironically, Collins had contemplated upgrading Houghton when he was looking for an assistant, but opted for Owen. However, Chris's season at Hull was virtually over. He recalled: 'I just wanted to get away. I'd been playing the best football of my career before Bobby and Billy had issues. I was getting great reviews up and down the country, but things went downhill fast.'

Chris made two more appearances in a doomed season for City. In his final match, against Burnley, he picked up a season-ending injury as the Tigers went down to a 3-1 defeat, when the highlight was a stunning strike by Hawley. Hull won only one of their last ten matches. Ultimately, they lost the last five to finish at the bottom of the table. Chris started 21 league matches and was a substitute in two others.

He recalled: 'Houghton was a popular choice among fans, but it's rare ex-players at a former club make a go of it as manager, and we continued to struggle. He made it clear I was not a part of his plans. If your face doesn't fit, you have to move on.'

Bremner retired at the end of the season. Bannister summed up his impact on and off the pitch at Hull: 'Billy read the game superbly; there was no one quicker over the first five yards and that is because he saw things before anyone else. Off the field, Billy was a great influence as well. He knew the importance of taking the pressure off because players can be swept away with the hype before a game. Billy had played in so many big games that it was second nature to him. But I always found it fascinating to watch him in the dressing room before we went out, calming everyone down, and in particular the young lads. He was a great captain.'

The final word on Bremner's spell at Hull goes to Chris: 'Playing alongside Billy was brilliant. He was the best player in our team by far, on top of being a great influence off the park. He loved the banter with the lads and was a regular in the card school on the team bus, although the lads told me he was not the best bluffer when he had a good hand! Being a part of the first team with Billy, I felt more of an equal with him and I'd like to think he thought I was a better player than he saw at Leeds. Billy is one of the greats. I was very fortunate to see him at close quarters more than any other player in my career.'

Chapter 13

Big Jack and the Boys in Green

TONY GALVIN never set out to play international football for the Republic of Ireland. Born and bred in Huddersfield, he had an ultimate dream of representing England. And Tottenham Hotspur's Keith Burkinshaw had been championing his belief that England manager Ron Greenwood should call up the left-winger to his squad. But with no move in the offing Tony was aware of his Irish connection and, as with numerous players from his generation, such as Tottenham team-mate Chris Hughton, Brighton and Hove Albion's Michael Robinson, Liverpool's Mark Lawrenson and Bolton Wanderers' Jim McDonagh, it would enable him to test his talents on the international stage.

The first step came when Tony happened to mention his Irish ancestry to Hughton before Tottenham embarked on a European Cup Winners' Cup campaign against Dundalk. Word reached Ireland's manager Eoin Hand, who ordered a background check into Tony's eligibility. Tony's international journey gathered momentum after Greenwood told him not to make a hasty decision about Ireland. He wasn't in an England B line-up for a match at Maine Road nor as an over-age player for the under-23 team and he missed an opportunity for a first full cap in a World Cup qualifier against Hungary on 18 November 1981.

Tony recalled: 'Playing international football is something you hope to achieve when you play the game professionally, but it wasn't until I was a Tottenham regular that my name started to appear in the press as a possibility at this level. I'd played for England School under-18s, but that didn't stop you from representing another nation or playing at full level for one if you qualified because of your family. I was fortunate because my grandparents on Mum's side meant that I qualified to play for Ireland or Scotland. I never knew either because they passed away young, but my grandad, Robert Tucker, came over from Limerick when times were really tough and happened to settle in Huddersfield.

'I remember chatting to Ray Clemence, who kept goal in more than 60 matches, about my prospects of breaking into the England side. Ray spoke with England's assistant manager Don Howe, who told me they'd select me for a B international to see me play at a higher level. It was a route to a full cap, but talking to a number of lads, these were seen as Mickey Mouse games. There was also Watford's John Barnes, West Ham's Alan Devonshire and Arsenal's Graham Rix ahead of me in my position so I decided to go down the Republic of Ireland route. There was little chance of breaking through on a regular basis and you have only to look at England B line-ups to see how many lads made it. Time has proved my decision correct. I'd have probably been a one-cap wonder.

'Scotland boosted their squad with English-based players in the First Division for many years, but the Republic of Ireland searched further down the leagues. In his Leeds days Johnny Giles got the ball rolling in terms of finding players for Ireland, and then Eoin took this to another level. Ireland had a number of top players, including Ronnie Whelan, Frank Stapleton, David O'Leary and Liam Brady. It was a stroke of good fortune on my part that Ireland needed a left-sided attacking midfielder. I was young in playing terms and determined to capitalise on an opportunity.

'Brady was a wonderfully talented footballer and one of my favourite players, which is awkward to admit as a former Spurs player! Tottenham fans hated Liam because he played for Arsenal, but they should respect his talent. Of course, I didn't want him to perform in derby matches but, lining up with him for Ireland, I was delighted he was on my side because he made us a dangerous team. Incredibly skilful, Liam had wonderful vision and the ability not only to go past players but accelerate away from them, which made him special. Liam also had a great shot and first touch. He was world class and the best player I played alongside in international football.

'Representing Ireland came about after a chat with Chris Hughton, who was in the Irish side. Chris spoke to Eoin, who got in touch. The crucial thing was to have proof of my grandad's birthplace, Limerick. I supplied his birth certificate, but it still seemed to take ages before everything was in place. When Eoin eventually selected me, I could sense there was a belief in the team that they could do something special on the international stage because there were so many top-flight players. Eoin really pushed hard to recruit players who weren't born in Ireland, and faced some obstructions from various sections of Irish society, but you have to credit his perseverance. The painstaking dithering by the FAI [Football Association of Ireland] cost me three or four caps. Opting to represent Ireland was an easy decision. I was told to get an Irish passport, which I did, but I kept dual nationality.'

Ireland had been denied a place in the 1982 World Cup finals on goal difference to France in the qualifying campaign. Hand's team was in a 'group of death' with Belgium, France, Netherlands and Cyprus. A 1-0 defeat to Belgium in Brussels ultimately proved crucial. The match included a hotly disputed disallowed goal by Stapleton. The hosts grabbed the winner late on when a draw would have taken Ireland to the finals in Spain. Belgium and France qualified. Until Thierry Henry's handball incident in a World Cup play-off in 2009, the Belgium clash was the most contentious in Irish history.

Ireland faced Spain, Netherlands, Iceland and Malta in the UEFA European Championships qualifying campaign to reach the finals in France in 1984. News of Tony's first international call-up hit the newspapers 24 hours after he had scored twice for Tottenham in a 6-0 win against Southampton in September 1982. The squad to face Netherlands was:

Peyton (Fulham), Bonner (Celtic), McDonagh (Bolton), O'Leary (Arsenal), Devine (Arsenal), Lawrenson (Liverpool), Whelan (Liverpool), Moran (Manchester United), Grimes (Manchester United), Stapleton (Manchester United), Hughton (Spurs), Galvin (Spurs), Martin (Newcastle United), Waddock (QPR), Walsh (Everton), Walsh (FC Porto), O'Callaghan (Ipswich Town), Daly (Coventry City), Langan (Birmingham), Grealish (Brighton), Brady (Sampdoria), Robinson (Brighton).

Tony made his debut in a Group 7 qualifier in the De Kuip stadium, Rotterdam, on 22 September 1982. The line-ups were:

Netherlands: Van Breukelen, Spelbos, Stevens, Van de Korpet, Wijnstekers, Gullit, Metgod (R. van der Kerkhof), Schoenaker, Vanenburg (Van Kooten), W. van der Kerkhof, Van der Gijp.

Republic of Ireland: McDonagh, Hughton, Lawrenson, O'Leary, Brady, Daly (Walsh), Galvin (Waddock), Grealish, Martin, Robinson, Stapleton.

Ireland lost 2-1. Tony limped off in the second half, and recalled: 'They had a great team, which included Ruud Gullit and Willy van der Kerkhof. On the night they took a 2-0 lead before Gerry Daly got a late goal back. The game was close but they were too good for us. I was chuffed to make my debut and it was a proud moment, although I picked up a knock, which was disappointing. I wasn't sure how bad my injury was until reporting for treatment at Tottenham on the Thursday. When Keith Burkinshaw walked into the physio's room, he slaughtered me when the two of us were alone. Keith felt that Ireland was an amateurish set-up and wasn't happy that I returned from my international debut with an injury. I proceeded, much to his annoyance, to miss a few games as a consequence of the injury. Keith told me I'd rushed into playing for Ireland and should have waited for an England call-up, but I was not having it. It was important Keith knew how much I wanted to play international football for Ireland. I'd qualified through my grandparents, felt honoured, thought it would develop me as a footballer and I was determined to take my chance. Whilst I respected Keith's view, he was wrong. I was happy with my decision, even though getting injured wasn't the greatest of starts to my international career. It was a bad start between us when it came to the club versus country battle, but it was the only time we had a blazing row in my Tottenham career. I actually picked up a stress fracture and was out for four weeks.'

Tony was selected for the Ireland squad to take on Iceland in the next round of matches at Lansdowne Road, Dublin, the following month. But he had to pull out because of injury and wait until March 1983 for another international call-up, when he played for an hour in Ireland's 1-0 win over Malta in Valletta in a European Championship qualifier. Substitute appearances came in a 3-2 home defeat to Netherlands and 3-0 defeat away to Israel in April 1984. After a goalless draw with Mexico at Dublin's Dalymount Park, Tony was involved in World Cup qualifiers in a tough group with Switzerland, Norway, the USSR and Denmark. The opening match was at Lansdowne Road against the USSR on 12 September 1984. It was Tony's World Cup debut. Playing the Soviets was football on a different level. The teams were:

> Republic of Ireland: McDonagh, Devine, Hughton, Lawrenson, O'Leary, Brady, Whelan, Grealish, Galvin, Walsh (O'Keefe), Robinson.

> USSR: Dasaev, Sulakvelidze, Chivadze, Demianendo, Baltacha, Oganesian (Gotsmanov), Litovchenko, Bessonov (Zygmantovich), Aleinikov, Rodinov, Blokhin.

Ireland won 1-0 in the Group 6 qualifier, with a Michael Walsh goal on 65 minutes. But it was a close call. Bill George of the *Cork Examiner* hailed Ireland's unexpected 'night of pride':

> The hoped-for goal of qualification for Mexico is still a long way away and the Soviet Union showed just how tortuous the route is going to be. But it is enough now to thrill to the courage of a brave Irish side, to salute an achievement of substantial proportions. It is true Ireland enjoyed their moments of good luck. It is true Ireland were so sorely-pressed in a dramatic closing quarter that the tendency to kick the ball dead to kill the momentum of the game to win respite was irresistible. But they earned their good fortune.

George praised the Irish team and especially Ireland's young winger from Tottenham, who was winning his sixth cap. He wrote:

> Galvin was particularly exciting, linking marvellously with the fluid and sophisticated Liam Brady and punching

holes in the Soviet defence. His ability to strike accurate crosses with both feet made him altogether too good for an opponent – even for such a full-back as Sulakvelidze. Brady, acknowledging his impact, sought him often.

Charlie Stuart of the *Irish Press* wrote:

> All right, we had a little bit of luck, especially that disallowed goal for the Soviets in the 57th minute. Then there were those heart-stopping moments when first Rodionov and then Litovchenko hit the woodwork in the 88th minute as the USSR threw everything forward in an attempt for an equaliser. And what a glorious 65th-minute goal by Mickey Walsh to send the Soviets home pointless, only their third defeat in 39 games … At the final whistle the Irish were heroes to a man. How well they deserved the adulation of the deliriously-happy 28,000 crowd. Make no mistake – this result will make headlines throughout the world because the Soviets are currently reckoned to be virtually on a par with European champions France.

Stuart noted that Galvin added strength to the Irish attack and was always a thorn to the Soviet defence.

Tony recalled: 'The atmosphere was incredible throughout the game, but it did get tense towards the end. It was a fantastic experience and I had a good game. The USSR did feel disappointed because they had a goal disallowed before we scored, hit the bar twice in one attack and on another day Oleg Blokhin would have got a penalty late on. But we battled away and got a great result. We had a number of chances in the game, but defensively we were awesome. O'Leary and Lawrenson were outstanding and McDonagh rose to the occasion and pulled off some unbelievable saves.'

Tony started World Cup qualifying defeats in Norway and Denmark before correspondent John Carter interviewed him for an article in January 1985. Tony spoke about playing for Ireland as a Yorkshireman. He said: 'Of course I get some stick. I have to defend both Yorkshire and the Irish, but I enjoy it. I suppose it is the kind of situation that appeals to both the Yorkshiremen and the Irish!' Tony added: 'I love playing for Ireland. The atmosphere is tremendous, the dressing room spirit is great.'

Home friendlies followed against Italy and Spain, with another World Cup qualifier, a goalless draw against Norway in Dublin, sandwiched in between on 1 May 1985. Ireland failed to qualify after finishing fourth in their group. Hand's contract wasn't renewed. International teams faced criticism in the media and Ireland were no different. Hand had a running feud with outspoken pundit and journalist Eamon Dunphy, who also clashed with Jack Charlton during his time as manager. Dunphy wasn't a fan of Charlton's style of international football. Matters came to a head at the 1990 World Cup in Italy after Ireland had drawn with England and Egypt. Charlton reacted to Dunphy's criticism by telling him he wasn't a proper journalist. Following Charlton's death in 2020, Dunphy praised him for his leadership and acknowledged that Ireland had enjoyed a glorious decade while he was manager.

Before Charlton's appointment, the FAI executive committee placed adverts in the British and Irish press. It was also in UEFA's official bulletin. Numerous candidates were considered, including Johnny Giles, Billy McNeill and Bob Paisley. Permission to interview Brian Clough was refused by Nottingham Forest, and

Irish youth team manager Liam Tuohy had been in the shake-up. Paisley had stepped down from the Anfield hot seat and was keen on a new challenge. He appeared favourite to land the job but the FAI 18-man selection committee chose Charlton by ten votes to eight.

Big Jack had enjoyed success at Middlesbrough and later managed and resigned as manager of Sheffield Wednesday and Newcastle. Outspoken and a regular as a TV pundit and on the after-dinner circuit, he had impressed the FAI. The choice of Hand's successor brought the Galvins' football wheel full circle in one sense. Tony would get the opportunity to work at close quarters with England's 1966 World Cup winner Charlton, who had been one of Chris's team-mates during his years at Leeds United.

Tony recalled: 'Eoin did a great job laying a foundation for a higher-profile manager, and following the appointment of Jack, we went to another level. I've always been grateful to Eoin for my international break, but when I first met the squad I was surprised how amateurish it appeared to be in some ways. We gathered on a Sunday and a number of Irish lads would disappear to see family. At the hotel there were cliques in the camp as the Liverpool, Manchester United and London lads stuck together. It was not good for team bonding. The training ground was a public playing field adjacent to the hotel; it was awful compared to back home. Eoin fought hard with the FAI to improve both the training facilities and training kit. It was an uphill battle but I suppose a shortage of funds was the issue.

'At the time of Jack's appointment, it was ironic that Chris had been at Leeds with him and now he was my manager. I'd heard plenty of tales about Big Jack, but now I'd see at first hand his managerial style. Jack played for Don Revie and Sir Alf Ramsey so they must have influenced his managerial style. It's no secret that

Leeds United could look after themselves. As for England, they had world-class players such as Gordon Banks, Ray Wilson, Bobby Moore and Bobby Charlton, and a superb man-marker in Nobby Stiles, but they also earned the right to play with the non-stop running of Alan Ball. Jack would confide in me at the training camp in Malta prior to the 1990 World Cup that a manager should always resign before getting sacked, as it was a way of preserving your reputation. I had to laugh. Typical Jack!'

Charlton wanted to bolster his squad so circulated football clubs to discover whether any non-international players had an Irish mother or father, or grandmother. He recalled in a book on his Ireland tenure, *The Team that Jack Built*, meeting John Aldridge after he scored a hat-trick for Oxford United against Ipswich Town in November 1985. Aldridge was on board. His team-mate Ray Houghton's father was from Donegal. Charlton now had a strike partner for Stapleton and a right-sided midfielder in Houghton to balance Kevin Sheedy or Galvin on the left flank. Both made their debuts in Charlton's first match as manager. Maurice Setters joined Charlton as assistant manager to find even more talent.

Charlton was quick to end the practice of the Dublin-born lads visiting family during get-togethers. He imposed on the squad disciplines learned from Revie. He said: 'When you go to prepare for the football match, nothing else counts, you're preparing for the football match.' Charlton told the players, 'Look, when you come in to play for us, you're here to represent Ireland to play and win an international match, you're here to prepare for two days for that game and we're going to do it properly.' Charlton's actions quickly developed a greater togetherness and improved team spirit.

Big Jack was his own man. When he selected an 18-man squad for a three-nation tournament with Iceland and Czechoslovakia to celebrate the 200th anniversary of the founding of Reykjavik in May 1986, Mark Lawrenson, Ronnie Whelan and Jim Beglin withdrew due to a club trip to Spain. David O'Leary turned down a chance to join the squad because of a family holiday. It would be nearly three years before O'Leary got another call-up. The tour cemented Mick McCarthy and Kevin Moran as first-choice centre-backs. Charlton wanted to set a pattern of play for his squad, so instructed his full-backs to play the ball behind the opposing full-backs in both matches then close them down to see whether they could play out from the back. He also wanted his team to get the ball into the opponents' penalty area quickly. Iceland couldn't cope, and Ireland won 2-1. The Czechs were then beaten 1-0. After just a handful of matches, Charlton had a style of play for his Irish team.

Charlton observed in *The Team that Jack Built*: 'The Icelanders didn't know what hit them. They never got out of their half. The Czechoslovakians in the next game couldn't get out of their half. They couldn't understand what was going on. And it caused so much chaos. Just one simple ball played in behind and instead of just one guy chasing it, everybody chasing it.'

Tony played in both matches, and observed: 'Jack's philosophy at international level came from his experiences playing under Ramsey. He recounted a story to us why Ramsey selected him for the 66 World Cup side. Ramsey wanted England to defend in a certain way. Jack would be the first to admit he was not the best defender in his day but alongside Bobby Moore gave England the balance Ramsey wanted. Ramsey picked Jack for a certain role. He was not the best centre-half available, but Jack performed a role and it worked. Jack was upfront with us from the start about playing a certain way. He asked you to do a job and picked players to perform that role. From that first international Jack made me feel ten feet tall every time I went out to play. It was great being in his side because you always felt you'd perform.'

After the Reykjavik trip, Charlton went to the World Cup finals in Mexico. The tournament confirmed his thinking on how Ireland would play in the upcoming Euro 88 qualifying campaign.

Tony recalled a midweek tactical get-together at Lilleshall, which used to be the English Football Association coaching centre: 'Jack was a one-off. We went to the lecture theatre for a tactical talk, but instead of talking about Belgium, Bulgaria or Scotland, who we were due to play, Jack showed us footage of a World Cup game from the 86 finals. He pointed out the playmaker and paused the footage. "Everything goes through him, the No. 10," he said. "Every European team plays the same way. Teams flood midfield. That's where the problems come. Don't give the ball away in our half." That was it. In some ways it was hilarious but Jack just wanted to make a basic point. We then went to the training field for set pieces with Maurice Setters but Jack wasn't there. One of the lads shouted, "Look over there!" Jack had his back to us and was hitting golf balls on an adjoining pitch. Hilarious, but that was Jack. He wasn't even looking at our training. He had brought us together to make that single point. A few of the lads questioned why he wanted the get-together. They were going spare and thought it was a waste of time. Jack didn't hold back, he made it clear that if anyone didn't like it, they could lump it and not come back. Jack told us how we played in terms of tactics, set plays and so on. No one complained again when he wanted us for an ad hoc get-together!

'Jack was unpredictable but he really knew how to motivate players. Sometimes he'd turn up to a training session dressed in his shirt, trousers and brown shoes, make a point then walk off. He might have given the impression of not enjoying turning up every day for sessions but he was terrific coming into something for a short period and getting a message across. Jack might be swinging his golf club away from the training but he was always on the ball. He'd turn around, point his club where someone should be standing then carry on practising his swing! It was bizarre behaviour, but that's how he was at times. Yet on other occasions he'd run a whole session. Jack was an unforgettable character.'

Charlton was a man of method and Tony discovered that his management philosophy was tailored to his individual needs. He explained: 'Ireland under Jack played in a particular style. We were dogged and hard-working, which suited my game. I was in the right place at the right time when my international opportunity came and felt I'd make an impact on the side. Even towards the end of my international career I was still a part of what he was trying to achieve. We did not have a pretty way of playing, because we were direct but very organised. Jack said: "Tony, this is your role in the team," which was not a problem for me. But he didn't just say that to me, he said it to everybody, even Brady, who could unlock any defence with his talent. We all knew what Liam was capable of, but he had his role. Jack was not worried about challenging players. It was a case of "do it my way or you're not in the team".

'Jack was the boss and he didn't care about reputations. Jack was upfront, honest and stuck to his word. He had a clear view of how he wanted his team to play and expected the players to be on board. Jack had a problem initially with some of the Liverpool and Manchester United players buying into his system of play. He also didn't see eye to eye with Liam. Jack didn't want him dropping back to pick balls up from defenders. Liam played a deeper role, linking play, in Italy but Jack wanted him to play higher up the pitch. There was no middle ground with Jack. There would be no passing across the box at the back. We pressed the opposition.

Jack told the creative lads to express themselves in the final third with one-twos, taking players on and crossing from wide positions.

'A great example of Jack's philosophy was Mick McCarthy, who was like Jack in many ways as a player. Mick was an uncompromising footballer and not fussed about the style of football so long as we got the result. He was Jack's lieutenant on the field and kept things simple. Like Jack, if he had to boot a ball away from danger, then he did, or would pass to one of the creative lads. Paul McGrath, though, was different on the field. Rather than being the most vocal, he led by example. Paul was a very talented individual who could play at the back or in midfield. Jack believed that Paul's all-round ability meant he was much better suited to a midfield role.'

Ireland turned their attention to qualifying for the 1988 European Championships in West Germany. These were the days before the fall of the Berlin Wall. It would be a first major finals if the Irish succeeded. Group 7 included Belgium, Scotland, Bulgaria and Luxembourg, and Tony was an integral part of Charlton's plans, starting with a 2-2 draw in Brussels when Ireland fought back twice against Belgium. It was an impressive start to the campaign. After a disappointing goalless draw at home to Scotland, Charlton surprised his critics when Ireland went to Hampden Park by selecting McGrath at right-back, Whelan at left-back and Lawrenson in midfield. Lawrenson scored the winner. Whelan has spoken of the support Tony gave him on the left flank on the night.

Charlton had triumphed tactically and silenced his detractors. Ireland lost away to Bulgaria but won the return at home. Bulgaria needed a draw against Scotland to make the finals but the Scots pulled off a 1-0 win, with a goal from substitute Gary Mackay on his debut three minutes from time, to signal a huge party in

Ireland. The FAI sent a crate of champagne in appreciation to the Scottish FA! Tony played in seven of the qualifiers. Ireland won four of them and qualified for the finals as group winners by one point from Bulgaria. Tony also scored his only international goal in a 2-0 win in Luxembourg on 28 May 1987.

But there was a concern as to whether Tony would make the Irish squad for the finals because he was getting so little game time at Sheffield Wednesday, following his transfer from Tottenham Hotspur earlier in the season. Eight nations would contest the finals – Denmark, England, Netherlands, Italy, Republic of Ireland, Soviet Union, Spain and West Germany. Ireland would face England in their opening match, followed by the Soviet Union and finally Netherlands, with the top two teams in the group advancing to the semi-finals.

Many of the world's leading stars would participate, including Denmark's Peter Schmeichel and Michael Laudrup; England's Peter Shilton, Bryan Robson, Glenn Hoddle and Gary Lineker; Italy's Giuseppe Bergomi, Franco Baresi, Paolo Maldini and Gianluca Vialli; Netherlands' Frank Rijkaard, Ronald Koeman, Marco van Basten and Ruud Gullit; the Soviet Union's Anatoliy Demyanenko and Igor Belanov; Spain's Jose Camacho and Emilio Butragueno; and West Germany's Lothar Matthäus, Jürgen Klinsmann and Rudi Völler.

Tony, for his part, did make Charlton's Republic of Ireland 20-man squad for the finals in Germany, which comprised: Bonner, Peyton, Morris, McCarthy, Moran, Whelan, Hughton, Anderson, McGrath, Houghton, Sheridan, Sheedy, Galvin, O'Brien, Stapleton, Aldridge, Kelly, Byrne, Cascarino, Quinn.

Tony recalled: 'When Euro 88 came around, Jack said, "Don't worry. Make sure you play a few games before the season ends so you're match-fit." Jack didn't care who I was playing against, he just wanted me to be sharp, which gave me a huge boost. For our supporters and country, this tournament was the start of something massive. We'd never qualified for a major tournament, but finally we were there and they were determined to enjoy the occasion. Our fans were fanatical followers. They were popular wherever they travelled for games; there was never any trouble. The Ireland fans gave us magnificent support.'

Tony played in friendlies at home to Romania and Poland and then a goalless draw against Norway in Oslo just 11 days before the first match of the tournament, as the build-up to the finals gained momentum. The two big talking points in the Irish media before the meeting with England in Stuttgart on 12 June 1988 surrounded who would lead the attack and which player would line up on the left wing. John Aldridge and Frank Stapleton played in Oslo, despite their recent poor form for Ireland, and so did Tony on the wing, but it had been expected that Sheedy would face England provided he was fit. In the end Charlton picked Aldridge, Stapleton and Tony.

A front-page headline in the Saturday night edition of the *Sheffield Star Green 'Un* read 'England test for Galvin'. Charlton explained: 'I have gone for my most experienced side and Tony knows exactly what he is expected to do. Kevin has not played that many games for us and he is not as good as Tony at the type of game that we like to play.' Asked whether his team were good enough to qualify for the semi-finals, he said: 'We are here to enjoy the competition and we'll see how we are placed after tomorrow.'

Charlton recalled in his official life story, *Jack Charlton: The Autobiography*, that most of the England squad had taken part at the 86 World Cup finals so were used to a major tournament. However, England boss Bobby Robson was under pressure from the press before a ball was kicked and Charlton knew this. It was all new for Ireland so he kept the atmosphere relaxed for his squad. Tactically, Charlton was concerned about wingers Chris Waddle and John Barnes. They could be a major threat so he told his team to press the defence but not too hard so they would pass the ball along the back line, which would slow down the game and play to Ireland's strengths. Waddle and Barnes would have to come back to get the ball. The tactic worked. Only late on did England chase the game. Ireland enjoyed a stunning 1-0 win. The teams for the Group 2 meeting were:

> England: Shilton, Stevens, Adams, Wright, Sansom, Waddle, Robson, Webb (Hoddle, 60), Barnes, Lineker, Beardsley (Hateley, 83).

> Republic of Ireland: Bonner, Morris, Hughton, McCarthy, Moran, Whelan, McGrath, Houghton, Galvin (Sheedy, 77), Aldridge, Stapleton (Quinn, 63).

The *Irish Independent* produced a four-page special edition 24 hours later to celebrate the landmark result. Correspondent Noel Dunne exclaimed:

> Unbelievable! Well, not really. These Republic of Ireland players believed in themselves at the Neckarstadion in Stuttgart yesterday. And the boys in green just keep on making history with this glorious – the superlatives could be an Irish-mile long – triumph over England. All sparked off after only six minutes with a never-to-be-forgotten goal by Ray Houghton. A long ball – we saw a lot of these from both sides in the course of the afternoon – carried to Tony Galvin, his centre ended in Kenny Sansom fluffing his clearance and John Aldridge seized the opportunity to knock the ball on to Houghton who headed with such

precision that not even Peter Shilton, who was earning his 99th cap, had a hope of stopping the ball. And surely this display will now at last relegate our other victory over the old enemy, back in 1949, to second place in the record books.

Renowned correspondent Brian Glanville offered his view in the Irish publication: 'The magnitude of Ireland's achievement in Stuttgart yesterday can scarcely be exaggerated.' Tony told Glanville that the fact Glenn Hoddle wouldn't be starting the match was a 'bonus for Ireland'.

A relaxed Charlton quipped in the interview room, 'I think we got away with a lot of things today ... someone likes us up there! The weather certainly impacted on Ireland's hustling style of play. It made it doubly hard for us. When we took a 1-0 lead, it was difficult for the rest of the game because the climate did not suit the type of performance we give. We like to hustle and we have a high work rate. After such an early goal we then had to sit it out and we had a few things to worry about at the end. We were a bit lucky. I expected England to try to win the game in the last 20 minutes, but Packie Bonner made terrific saves.'

Charlton refrained from singling out any players for special praise, but was well aware what the result would mean to the travelling Irish supporters. 'They'll drink the place dry tonight, but I guarantee they won't fight,' he beamed. 'The Irish are the best in the world for parties.'

England manager Bobby Robson was magnanimous in defeat: 'It's a marvellous win for the Irish. Their fighting spirit saw them through all afternoon. After the goal they were very inspired.'

The aftermath of the result left the Irish counting the cost of several injuries. Charlton was tight-lipped about McGrath's chances of making the Soviet Union match because of a knee injury sustained in the England win. Other players nursing minor injuries included Hughton, Houghton and Stapleton. Tony was among numerous players who were dehydrated. It emerged the next day that it took him 12 bottles of water and over two hours to give a urine sample for the random dope test.

Soviet Union had edged past Netherlands 1-0 in the other group match, so whoever won their clash with Ireland in Hanover would be all but guaranteed a semi-final place. The line-ups for the match on 15 June were:

> Republic of Ireland: Bonner, Morris, Hughton, McCarthy, Moran, Whelan, Houghton, Aldridge, Stapleton (Cascarino, 80), Galvin, Sheedy.

> Soviet Union: Dasaev (Chanov, 67), Khidiatullin, Kuznetsov (Gotsmanov, 45), Demyanenko, Rats, Alienikov, Zavarov, Protasov, Belanov, Sulakvelidze, Mikhailichenko.

It was a match in which Ireland led through a brilliant Whelan strike before Tony took centre stage after being blatantly upended in the penalty box by Soviet keeper Dasaev. After Irish penalty appeals had been ignored, Ireland had to settle for a draw, following Oleg Protasov's late equaliser. Not awarding the penalty was pivotal, as it might have sealed the most famous win in Ireland's history. Renowned correspondent Peter Byrne of the *Irish Times* described the incident as 'a moment that will live in our lives for years'. Byrne also wrote:

> Jack Charlton scanned the horizons of the impossible yet again and 15,000 Irish supporters, who turned this superbly-appointed stadium into a bowl of song, ensured that the response off the pitch matched the heroics on it

… A banner in the crowd called on 'the leprechauns of the world' to unite and for much of the 90 minutes it looked as if the 'little men' were about to achieve a win which would reverberate all the way to the Kremlin … By the time it was all over, the Irishmen, no less than their opponents, were almost out on their feet and no wonder. This, I have no hesitation in saying, was the bravest display I have seen from any Irish team, and I am not excluding that success over England last Sunday. On that occasion the Irish were often surviving by their bootlaces in the closing stages, but this was different. Taking their courage in their hands, they ran at the opposition with conviction and overall created the majority of the scoring chances.

At full time Charlton was adamant that the Spanish referee had denied his team a penalty. He told the *Irish Times*: 'When a player is flattened in the penalty area, there is only one award – a penalty – and he did not get it. Had the incident taken place outside the area, I am certain that the referee would have blown the whistle. I feel that he was more concerned with the Russian player's injury than in noting what happened exactly and, after watching the incident on television, I am certain that I am right.'

He added: 'Once more I was proud of the way the lads played and, on the night, I think we deserved the extra point. Everybody worked extremely hard and I think we succeeded in making the Russians look less than brilliant. Given the time and the room, the Soviets can be exciting, but on this occasion we closed them down so effectively that they only rarely threatened us.' As for the upcoming Netherlands clash, Charlton said: 'It ought to be a good match. We have both beaten England, we are both in line for qualification and it's everything to play for.'

In his autobiography, Charlton recalled the Soviet manager's 'down-in-the-mouth expression' when they shook hands. Ireland had done everything but win. It was a superb performance.

Karl MacGinty's 'player-by-player' ratings were complimentary about Tony: 'This man has turned the clock right back in the finals. Galvin terrorised the Soviet defence with several swirling, arching crosses and actually got on the end – albeit unsuccessfully – of a couple of chances himself. Charlton's faith in him has been well-placed.'

The final game against the Netherlands in Gelsenkirchen ended in heartbreak for Ireland when substitute Wim Kieft headed the winning goal from a mishit cross by Koeman on 82 minutes. But the goal should have been ruled out because Van Basten was in an offside position when Kieft struck. Nevertheless, it had been a stupendous campaign as the Irish squad captured the hearts of a nation and put their country on the footballing map.

Noel Dunne of the *Irish Independent* wrote:

> So near and yet so far. But for a cruel stroke of misfortune the Republic of Ireland's great soccer adventure would be all set for another chapter in Hamburg tomorrow. Instead of sitting at home still dreaming, no doubt, of what might have been, Jack Charlton and his Irish heroes might so easily have been taking on West Germany in the semi-finals of the European Championship. What a thought! Alas, it was not to be. The luck of the Irish … You must be joking!

… Charlton and his players left Germany with bundles of messages of congratulations to soften their sadness at having failed to make the semi-finals … The players and the fans can be proud of themselves, although it has to be admitted that the Republic of Ireland would have defied all football logic, if there is such a thing, had they gained that precious point. It was a cruel end for the Irish after they had defiantly repelled everything the talented Dutch side could throw at them.

Charlton told the paper: 'I just wish it had been a good goal and then we would have said, "Yes, the Dutch were the better side and they finally managed to score." This has been a great experience. I have had a lot of pleasure and satisfaction from the players, who have behaved impeccably on and off the field, and I have made a few mistakes, which I won't make again. We know where we are now – there to be shot at, but that's what we want. We have lost only once in 12 matches and we want to be up there with the best.'

After going out, Charlton mused in his autobiography: 'Of all the ways to lose a game! We had competed like Spartans for three games, played well enough to have won all three, and yet we were out of the championship – all because of the biggest fluke of the year.' The question remained whether Ireland would have done better had Brady and Lawrenson been available. Charlton observed that his team weren't a 'million miles' from winning the trophy. It had been some effort. An estimated 200,000 fans 'roared their appreciation', recalled Charlton on their return.

Looking back on the tournament, Tony recalled: 'Most pundits didn't give us a chance against England but they underestimated us. It was a huge game and we knew how historical our victory was to supporters and the country. The celebrations went on into the early hours. We then played really well against a good Soviet team and should have won the game. Before equalising they were frustrated because they expected to beat us. The turning point was the penalty incident. It was a blatant foul by Dasaev but the referee was influenced by his antics. There were times when we played that referees always seemed to give the benefit of doubt to the bigger teams. At 2-0, the game would have been over. In my Irish career this was our best-ever performance.

'In our final game a draw against the Netherlands would have taken us through. They'd lost to the Soviets and beaten England so had to beat us to qualify. We hung on as they hammered away at us until ten minutes from the end when they scored a deflected goal that sent Bonner the wrong way. We'd stuck at it and could not argue the better team won, but it was a huge disappointment after battling away for so long. The lads were gutted because we'd done well in the first two games. The Netherlands defeated the Soviets in the final, which showed that we were in the stronger group. They had world-class players in Gullit, Van Basten, Koeman and Rijkaard. Van Basten's goal in the final was unbelievable. It's a struggle to think of a better one in the Euros or World Cup since. It was a great Dutch team.'

Ireland had surprised the football world, and the squad returned home on a plane named St Jack, but they couldn't have anticipated the heroes' welcome they would receive from fans at Dublin airport. Their arrival was accorded arrangements only reserved for state visits. The squad took their place on a specially constructed ramp to hear Taoiseach Charles Haughey declare Charlton an honorary Irishman. Some 200,000 fans took to the streets of Dublin as the squad lapped up an unforgettable open-top bus journey from the airport. Garda reinforcements were brought in to help the bus make it through the packed crowds. Ticker-tape streamed down from office buildings. Whitehall was impassable, motorists blew horns, fire engines and ambulances set their sirens off, drivers abandoned buses. The civic centre was full of mayhem, but the squad eventually made it to the

Municipal Gallery at Parnell Square for an official welcome-home ceremony.

The Republic of Ireland's escapades at Euro 88 have stood the test of time and gone down in Irish folklore. Charlton told the *Irish Times* in 2018: 'That was our best chance of hitting the jackpot and I'll tell you why. We were new to that level of football, and opposing teams simply didn't know how to deal with us. On top of that we had a core of good players who were just coming to their prime when we set down in Germany.'

Tony later played in one World Cup qualifier, a 2-0 defeat away to Spain in November 1988, before earning his final international cap in a friendly against West Germany. It took place at Lansdowne Road on 6 September 1989 and finished in a 1-1 draw. But then hamstring and back injuries ultimately interfered with his hopes of playing in the 1990 World Cup. It meant that, in the end, Tony won 29 caps for the Republic of Ireland between 1983 and 1989. His impact for the national team was recognised when the *Irish Independent* published *The Legends* magazine, listing Tony 36th of the top 50 Irish soccer players of all time.

Recalling the end of his international career, Tony reflected: 'Following the Euro championships Ireland went straight into their World Cup qualifying campaign with Spain, Hungary, Northern Ireland and Malta in Group 6. Jack kept me in the squad for experience, but I'd be on the bench because he was going to play Sheedy on the left-hand side. Jack told me that if we qualified for the 1990 finals in Italy, I'd be involved and, true to his word, that is what happened. I made two further appearances for Ireland – versus Spain when we lost 2-0 in a qualifier in Seville and then against Germany in Dublin in September 1989.

'Jack told Stapleton, Brady and myself that, if we did okay against West Germany, we'd go to the World Cup. There were a lot of players on the periphery, but Jack knew what he wanted in his squad. Liam was coming to the end of his career and, after 30 minutes, Jack took him off. At half-time, initially there was no team talk. Liam was fuming but Jack stood his ground. Jack explained it was tactical but Liam was not having it and announced his retirement after the game, which was a sad way to end his Ireland career. Before we went out for the second half, Jack told us we had to play better. I got more involved, and after we had secured a 1-1 draw, Jack came up to me and told me I would be going to Italy. There was no "Well done!" Jack said: "Stay fit and don't get injured." I was in the squad. Typical Jack!'

Of the Brady incident, Charlton recalled in his autobiography that when a German player 'waltzed past' Brady and Dorfner equalised, then Brady was being 'run all over the place', he decided to substitute him before half-time. Brady felt Charlton should have waited until half-time, but Charlton told him: 'My job is to save this game, not to pander to your pride.' Brady wouldn't play again for Ireland under Charlton.

Recalling the 1990 World Cup, Tony said: 'I was now at Swindon with Ossie Ardiles as manager, having signed on a free from Wednesday, and unfortunately picked up a back injury that needed an operation, so Bernie Slaven took my place. I was not fit enough to play in the finals but Jack wanted me to join up with the squad as a guest. Ireland famously met Pope John Paul II at the Vatican and had an incredible World Cup, when they reached the quarter-finals, but I had returned home before they were knocked out by Italy. The World Cup experience was bizarre because I was not doing anything in reality. I sat in a suit next to Chris Hughton on the substitutes' bench as a guest for the first game against England, which ended in a 1-1 draw. Before the next match, though, out of the blue I heard about financial irregularities being investigated at Swindon so got permission from Jack to return home and offer Ossie moral support. Ireland's travel organisers kindly arranged for me to fly home straight after the England game.

'Germany went on to win the World Cup, although many writers felt it was the worst final of all time against Argentina. Of course, England should have beaten Germany in the semi-final, but lost in a penalty shoot-out. When people ask who my last international game was against, they don't always realise it was against the world champions-elect.'

Jack Charlton led the tributes to Tony regarding his international career in his official testimonial programme against West Ham United just after he left Tottenham Hotspur in 1987. Charlton said: 'He knows what I want from him. That is, to pick up and balance in midfield. I ask him to be direct, to run at defenders and get his crosses in. He has done everything I've asked of him and I am delighted by his attitude. He always turns up and he's not caused a moment's trouble.'

Eoin Hand recalled: 'If you wished to stretch a defence then Tony was the man to do it. Not only that, he gave the width to midfield and could also stop the opposing right-back from overlapping at will, by funnelling back. I felt he gave an Irish team additional options.'

Several of Tony's Irish team-mates also paid tribute. Chris Hughton said: 'The lads with the Irish squad enjoy having him with us, though he is often teased that he only got his qualification because his great-great-grandfather once took a day trip to Ireland! I room with him on international trips, the Cockney Paddy and the Yorkshire Paddy! My own nickname for him is "Mr Grumpy" because he is terrible first thing in the morning.'

Pat Bonner recalled: 'As I've got to know Tony better, as a fellow member of the Irish international squad, I've found him to be a quiet, serious fellow and he's a very good professional. I'm glad he decided to make himself available to play for Ireland, when there was talk of him possibly being selected for England. He's been a great help for us.'

Liam Brady observed: 'Tony is the type of player who does his own job, drops back to help others, and comes off the field shattered!'

Ray Houghton reflected: 'His strength is running at people, getting to the back line and whipping over crosses. He has done that so well for so long, nowadays, they are centring from deep. I've always felt Tony must have powerful lungs because he "works" all along the flank. It amazes me too that he can go to within an inch of the white back line, probably end up on the deck behind – but still put over his cross!'

And Ronnie Whelan said: 'People on the terraces don't see the amount of work he puts in. His game is not glamorous. We all know of him as the winger who goes at defences and whips the crosses in. I valued this help an awful lot when, as a makeshift full-back for Ireland in Scotland [during the European Championship qualifiers], he did so much running to keep the tricky Pat Nevin off me. I'd say professionals appreciate the role Tony plays more so than supporters.'

Charlton recalled what his left-winger brought to the team in his autobiography: 'Tony was an aggressive runner, a lad who took on full-backs and went for the back line. He was a one-off as far as Ireland was concerned for, in my time, he was the only one who did that job perfectly.'

The last word on his Irish adventure under Charlton goes to Tony: 'Jack did an amazing job for Ireland and I was really impressed with him as an international manager. He had a group of lads who were loyal and respected him. Jack knew what he wanted, trusted the lads selected to do a specific job and, if they didn't, then they didn't play for him. We had plenty of critics who accused us of winning ugly but I never felt that. Jack wanted us playing to our strengths. Winning was a good habit, not losing was a good habit. I was honoured to represent Ireland, and have no regrets. It was fortuitous the team had a number of really talented players, but I had a positive attitude, was single-minded and got the maximum out of my body and ability. I was also very proud of the fact that I was part of a team that laid the foundations for a decade of great achievements by the Irish team.'

Chapter 14

Slow Boat to China

HULL CITY manager Ken Houghton transfer-listed Chris Galvin, who attracted interest from Chesterfield before the start of the 1978/79 season. But he then became a pay rebel as the ramifications of players' new freedom facility began to set in. Chris, goalkeeper Eddie Blackburn and Welsh international team-mate Dave Roberts trained on their own to keep fit. Chris had support from Lincoln City, where former Leeds United full-back Willie Bell was manager, but by early September 78 he and Blackburn had ended their pay dispute. Roberts joined Cardiff City.

Chris recalled: 'I'd known Willie since my earliest Leeds days. He was great with the apprentices and always found time to give us the benefit of his experience as a top-flight footballer. I really appreciated Willie asking me to train at Lincoln as it helped me stay fit. I had no regrets about making a stand at Hull but, of course, you miss the training, banter and playing. The Saturday afternoons were the worst because I was so used to travelling to games for a match. In the end the matter was resolved.'

Chris eventually began his sixth season at Hull back in the Third Division that he had experienced during his loan spell at York. John Hawley, Billy Bremner and Peter Daniel were among players to depart during the close season, but Hull were among the favourites for promotion and made a positive start, winning four of the opening six matches. But then they went nine league matches without success when the winter months kicked in. Chris made a handful of starts in this run of poor form before being dropped.

Chris rejected a £15,000 transfer to Scunthorpe United and put in a transfer request, which was granted. Manager Houghton said: 'He is upset at being left out. I've had a long talk with Chris about it and we have come to an agreement that we circulate all Third and Fourth Division clubs that he is on offer. He's a good lad who doesn't cause any trouble, but at the same time he wants first-team football. He doesn't see any chance of commanding a first-team place with us and I can understand how frustrating it can become for a player.'

Another handful of appearances followed. Chris made an impact in City's 3-0 Boxing Day success at home to Mansfield Town and then scored both goals in a morale-boosting 2-1 victory at relegation-threatened Walsall at a snowy Fellows Park on 6 January 1979.

'Galvin turns the tide for Hull', read one newspaper headline. Correspondent Peter Gill reported:

> Two goals by Chris Galvin gave Hull their first away win since early September. And manager Ken Houghton, who did not feel the match should have started on the snow-covered pitch, must have been delighted by the way his side recovered from being a goal down at half-time. The football served up by both sides confirmed that Lincoln referee Peter Richardson was correct in deciding the game should be played.

Of Chris's brace of goals Gill wrote:

> In the 71st minute Hull were level, Galvin meeting a cross from Edwards with a firm downward header although Kearns was at fault in allowing the ball to slip through his hands and bounce over the line. Walsall bounced back and tried desperately to regain the lead, but it was to be Hull's day. With only two minutes left de Vries slipped away down the left, his cross caused panic in the Walsall penalty box and, as the ball broke free, Galvin blasted it into the roof of the net.

But Chris's frustrations began to mount, even though he scored twice more in a 2-1 win at Chesterfield and 1-1 home draw against Sheffield Wednesday. The season dragged on, with six fixtures taking place in May 1979 after a severe winter, but Chris wasn't involved in the final nine matches. His last appearance for the Tigers would be a goalless draw against Blackpool at Boothferry Park on 16 April 1979. Hull ended the campaign in eighth place. Chris began 15 league matches, appeared as a substitute in four more and scored four goals.

He reflected: 'The club were expected to challenge for promotion, but it's never that easy after relegation and we soon hit a poor set of results. Houghton brought me back for a few games and I could still make an impact on a match. I showed that with the winner against Walsall and Chesterfield but I was in and out of the first team.'

A troublesome knee problem was a major part of Chris's inconsistent form. Time was no longer on his side. The onset of the problem coincided with Hull's relegation to the Third Division. He pointed out: 'Retirement was by now a serious consideration.

Running with a limp must have looked comical in games but, as with most footballers, you soldier on. However, I had to be realistic as to the impact I could have in a match.'

Chris realised it was time for him to move on. In all he began 132 league matches for Hull, appeared in 11 more as a substitute and scored 11 times. In addition, he was on the mark once in nine FA Cup ties. He also scored once in the Football League Cup – on his club debut in the competition at Leicester City – in 11 starts plus one substitute appearance. It had often been a roller-coaster ride, but Chris reflected: 'Overall I enjoyed my time at Hull, who had some great professionals during my days at the club, but I was ready for a new start.'

Throughout it all Chris was a popular figure in the dressing room, even though he insisted in a programme profile that one of his hobbies was arguing with team-mate Steve Deere! It was a factor that became a lively feature among Hull's players. Deere, a generally mild-mannered and easy-going figure, was often the butt of Chris's comments, but took it all in good spirit. He said: 'Chris was a wind-up guy with a good sense of humour. He could talk about any subject, so always got the banter going. We'd have political discussions after training and end up disagreeing because he'd wind me up! Chris was always deadpan, but funny and witty, and there was nothing nasty about his joking. When Chris first came to Hull we roomed together for away trips, so became good pals. He was a good lad to have around, but got up to antics because he didn't want to go to bed at the deadline. We'd find him wandering round the hotels at all hours!'

Deere recalled a pre-season tour to Scotland when Terry Neill was manager and the players had an 11pm deadline: 'The hotel was out in the wilds, some of us drifted off and walked down the road for some fresh air. When I got back to the room, there was no sign of my bed. I eventually found it in a lounge at the bottom of the corridor, so slept there. Eventually I wheeled it back to the room. Chris had been fast asleep but I was sure he was responsible, though of course he denied it!'

Gordon Staniforth added: 'Chris was very funny in the dressing room and would play a lot of practical jokes. But I don't know why he picked on Steve as his victim so often because he was a few inches bigger than Chris! But he'd wind Steve up. There was never a dull moment with Chris about. But above all I remember his broad smile. Chris had a nice way of going about life and was a breath of fresh air when he came. You wondered why Leeds United let him go.'

In addition, Peter Fletcher and Chris became close pals. Fletcher was part of a player-exchange deal that took future England striker Stuart Pearson to Manchester United early in the summer of 1974. Fletcher, who later had success at Chris's hometown club Huddersfield Town, recalled: 'I had a great time at Hull. Chris was a bit of a character with a dry sense of humour that appealed to me and we soon hit it off together. We became good pals because we were in the same area. We and our wives, Margaret and Susan, often went out. You did everything together in those days and bounced off each other. There was not much money about and it was all more or less on a level, so you saw everyone socially. The joking and camaraderie drew you in.'

Chris's ability was respected by his Hull team-mates on the pitch. Deere, who played alongside Kevin Keegan and George Best during his league career, reflected: 'Chris as a midfield player had such talent. He was at Leeds when they were in their heyday. He used to tell me how they included him as a young player when they'd take squads into Europe to give him the experience of going away on trips and being part of the team. The fact that he made his Leeds debut in a European game when they were one of the finest teams around was a testimony to his quality.'

Fletcher added: 'Chris was an old-style inside-forward. He wasn't the quickest, but had a football brain and was a good player.' And Staniforth agreed: 'Chris was extremely skilful as a footballer. He had tremendous ability on the ball. I wouldn't say he was so good with his defending but he had this double trick with his step-over and not many people had seen that before.'

Aside from Chris's team-mates off the field, his public acclaim would last long after his departure from Boothferry Park. The story goes that a staunch supporter in the best West Stand seats had a catchphrase every time Chris was on the substitutes' bench and City went behind or began to struggle. This character would repeatedly yell, 'Bring Galvin on!' at the top of his voice for all around him to hear. Because he was close to the press box, for years it became a regular occurrence for a member of the journalistic corps to shout, 'Bring Galvin on!' whenever the Tigers found the going tough!

On the pitch, as Hull saw the 1978/79 season out, Chris was carefully weighing up his future when out of the blue he was given the opportunity to play football on the other side of the world – in Australia! The prospect thrilled him, but things didn't work out well. It was effectively the quiet before the storm.

Chris explained: 'Hull offered me a payoff through the club's insurance because of my knee and I was considering it when Australian side South Melbourne Hellas put in a £15,000 transfer bid for me from nowhere. Hull accepted the offer but I was not match-fit. Melbourne's manager knew about the injury but still wanted to sign me. We negotiated a contract and I was excited by the prospect of playing in Australia. Susan also thought it was a great opportunity, so I signed my contract and we put our house on the market. I'd fly out and Susan would follow with the kids.

'I'd got to a stage when nothing surprised me in football, but I was stunned when Melbourne sacked their manager a few days after Hull had released me from my contract. A ticket had been organised and I was waiting for a visa, but felt uneasy as the days passed without any contact. After a few days Hull contacted the club secretary to find out what was happening. The news was not good because the chairman had dismissed the manager and he had no knowledge of my transfer. They would cover my expenses if I cancelled the contract. There was no point in flying to the other side of the world when you are not welcome, so I agreed. Hull were really unhappy because they had missed out on a transfer fee, but suddenly I was a free agent. Hull asked me to re-sign, but I wanted to see what offers might be out there, so I refused. A football club had power over a player's registration in my era; players were treated terribly at times, so for the first time I wanted to decide my own future. When I got home to tell Susan we weren't going, she already knew. It's amazing how news travels in the football world!'

Chris had a new opportunity to consider in time for the final days of the season, but it meant stepping down a division. It brought him into contact with former England winger and Manchester City legend Mike Summerbee.

Chris said: 'Mike was player-manager of Stockport County, who played in the Fourth Division, and had left a message with Susan to call him, which I did. Mike had heard that I was a free agent and asked me to drive over to their ground to discuss signing for the club. I explained about my knee but he still hoped I'd meet chairman Freddie Pye. In the game, Freddie was a larger-than-life character, and when I arrived at the club he was sitting in his office wearing a long cashmere coat, which made me feel at ease. Susan and I were thinking about moving back to Huddersfield, so the move made sense. Playing for Stockport would be an experience. Freddie had plans to take the club forward and they felt I could help. The club had been in touch with the Football League about my registration, Freddie made me an offer and it didn't take long to agree terms. I signed a two-year deal.

'Stockport were a typical illustration of a lower-league club trying to progress, because they had Summerbee and George Armstrong on their books. Both were legends in their heyday. Summerbee had won every domestic honour for Manchester City and Armstrong was a double winner with Arsenal. But they were not the only top First Division players to continue playing. There were loads of lads, including some from my old club Leeds, still playing before hanging up their boots. Apart from Big Jack, Paul Madeley and Mick Jones, who retired because of injury, I came up against Leeds lads at various clubs, including Bradford City and Barnsley. The only sponsorship was a small amount of boot money from Adidas. It's laughable when you think about it now, but that's how it was in the 70s.

'Because I'd signed after the transfer deadline, I was only allowed to train and travel with the first team, not play, but it did give me a chance to meet the lads. During one match Armstrong asked me at half-time what I thought of his performance. When I told him it was shocking, he was almost crying. I couldn't believe his reaction, but his legs had gone. In his day George was a top player, but it was embarrassing to watch. As a player you never like to think the end's going to come, but it does. The crazy thing is, Summerbee played worse, yet was full of it! Mike was a real personality.'

As things transpired, the Football League gave Chris permission to play in Stockport's last match of the season on 14

May 1979 because there was nothing riding on the result. And it was in familiar surroundings, at York City's Bootham Crescent. Chris explained: 'We lost 1-0 but I'd now played throughout the Football League pyramid, which is something I'm pleased about all these years later.' County finished 17th in the league.

At the start of the close season Chris received a request to play for a Super Leeds XI against a Leeds United XI in Eddie Gray's testimonial match on 28 May. A crowd of 19,079 attended for the nostalgic get-together of Don Revie's aces, who ran out 4-1 winners. Peter Lorimer scored twice, with Rod Belfitt and Johnny Giles scoring the other goals for Super Leeds. Byran Stevenson slotted in a consolation penalty for the opposition. The teams were:

> Leeds United: Lukic, Hird, Stevenson, Flynn, Hart, Cherry, Harris, Hankin, Hawley, Currie, Graham.

> Super Leeds: Harvey, F. Gray, Cooper, Bremner, Charlton, Hunter, Lorimer, Galvin (Collins), Belfitt, Giles, E. Gray.

Chris recalled: 'I was delighted to be asked, and enjoyed the occasion. Of course, it was only a friendly, but the lads were still able to show off their skills. Everyone knows what a great player Eddie was and he would carry on playing for a few more years.'

There was a welcome surprise for Chris for the 1979/80 campaign as he was made skipper. Summerbee's team got off to a dreadful start, winning once in the opening ten league matches. County's boss offered his resignation and Jimmy McGuigan was appointed manager. Chris was injured for a period but came back towards the end of the season. County ended a troubled campaign in positive fashion, defeating Halifax Town home and away during their final three fixtures to finish 16th. Chris made 25 league appearances.

Journalist Ian Rushworth covered the final away match of the season on 22 April 1980, which Stockport won 3-1: 'With both sides clear of the bottom four and fighting for re-election to the Football League, the clash had a "let's-get-the-season-over" feeling.' Teenager David Booth scored his first league goal and Tommy Sword slotted home a penalty, before the hosts almost went down to ten players. Rushworth noted: 'County skipper Chris Galvin, who masterminded many of their attacks, was booked for a tackle from behind on David Evans on 39 minutes. And he was lucky to stay on the field later when fouling Mick Kennedy.' Steve Uzelac scored a controversial third to settle the win.

Stockport made a positive start to 1980/81, going on an unbeaten seven-match run that included 2-1 wins over Wimbledon and Port Vale. During this run of form, County enjoyed their most significant cup win as a club. It came in a memorable League Cup second-round clash when they knocked out top-flight Sunderland over two legs on aggregate. Stockport's 1-1 draw in the opening leg at home with a goal from Dave Sunley was a great result, but a 2-1 away victory on 3 September 1980 was a stunning shock before 17,000 fans, by far the biggest crowd of the season for the team. Galvin was involved in the build-up for Sunley to strike, before Sword slotted home a penalty a minute from time for a famous win and place in the third round.

But County stumbled in the league, losing five and winning only one of their next seven encounters, before 2-1 victories over Torquay United and Bournemouth put them in the promotion pack. Although inconsistent, County illustrated their positive football in a 2-0 home defeat against Hartlepool United at Edgeley Park on 27 October 1980. A correspondent wrote:

> There is not a great deal wrong with soccer when two teams from the Football League's bargain basement can provide the sort of entertainment served up by Stockport

County and Hartlepool last night. The ankle-deep slime and driving rain should have cancelled out the game as a spectacle. In fact, all 22 players deserve a pat on the back for proving again how only British players can make the best out of the worst. To their credit, County, desperately short of height and weight up front, never at any stage threw in the towel. The jinking Chris Galvin smacked one shot against the upright and Tony Coyle was desperately unlucky with a near-post header from Galvin's corner, which produced a brilliant save from keeper Martin Burleigh. The Edgeley Park boys needn't be too despondent by this setback. They played their part in a game which proved that, whatever the legislators may say, English soccer is alive and well.

During this period, Chris, somewhat surprisingly, was a regular in the first team, but life was beginning to change off the pitch. He had pulled out of his joint wastepaper business because of financial reasons after eight years. He was then working on a project to run a family coffee bar in Dewsbury. Chris and Susan had sought planning permission for the premises and were due to go ahead with renovating them. With his match fitness an issue, Chris was aware that the end of his Stockport career would almost certainly be the end of his league career in England.

He said: 'My approach to football had changed. I enjoyed the responsibility and the lads did well. I sat back in defence, picked the ball up where I could control possession, then picked a pass and it worked a treat. I enjoyed playing, but my knee was getting worse. I was struggling to train, so I'd play on a Saturday or in midweek and then it would take me two days to get going again. Amazingly I missed only six league and cup games all season.'

Stockport ended the league campaign with six home wins to finish just above the re-election places, which was a relief to the club. During the run-in Chris got the winner against Tranmere, which turned out to be his final goal in English football. He scored three goals in 68 league appearances for Stockport, staying with them until the end of the season, by the end of which he was still only 30. But it was clear to him that he wouldn't be fit enough for another Fourth Division season, so he thought about retiring. Fate, though, took a timely hand – and from an unexpected quarter. Again, it was long-distance information but in this instance everything fell into place to take Chris abroad successfully and prolong his football career.

He explained: 'My knee had got worse and worse at Stockport, so I more or less called it a day when I finished there. But about a week after I'd left Stockport, I was asleep when the phone rang early one morning and a voice said: "This is Willie Wong from Hong Kong." He explained that he ran a team called Tsuen Wan, but I thought: "Someone's taking the Mick big time," so I told him to ring back in an hour and put the phone down. An hour later Willy rang back and was being serious. He was for real and wanted me to play in a newly formed league in Hong Kong. Willy offered me a two-year deal. I'd be earning double my top salary in England. To say I was stunned was an understatement. I explained that I was packing in because of my knee, but Willy was fine with the situation, even if I'd be limping around the football field! Willy wanted me to fly out for a month to see how it went. He was sure that I'd be okay because the standard was lower than the Football League. I discussed it with Susan and she said: "What have we got to lose?" I was earning more than I'd ever been on and it was a chance to see a place that I'd heard a lot about, so I agreed.'

Tsuen Wan FC had been promoted to the First Division of the local league in readiness for the 1981/82 season and Chris was seen as a marquee signing for them in view of his background. Clubs in the league included Eastern, See Bee, Bulova, Happy Valley, Seiko and Tung Sing.

Chris observed: 'Flying out was about an 18-hour flight and we stopped twice, so I was shattered by the time we touched down. It was 80 to 90 degrees with 100 per cent humidity when a club representative met me. The last thing I needed to hear was that they had arranged a friendly game in the afternoon so club officials and local press could see me in action. It was a struggle with the humidity and I must have looked shell-shocked, but got through 25 minutes and showed enough for them to think they had a good signing. Tsuen Wan was near the border with China and the club were financed by the local council. Massive companies such as Seiko sponsored teams based in Hong Kong, so they had a number of ex-internationals playing out their careers.'

As Chris started to take in football on another continent, a family tragedy at home almost ended his China experience before it began. He said: 'After signing, Dad suddenly died, which was a huge shock to us all. I told the club I'd rather not stay, but Tsuen Wan were brilliant. They gave me a return ticket and told me to come back when I felt ready. At first, I didn't think I'd go back, but it was a challenge and too good an opportunity not to experience.

'Tsuen Wan struggled to be competitive on the pitch, but I enjoyed the campaign. Every side had to have seven Chinese players and the game was played at a really slow pace. Fixtures were spread out, which gave my knee a chance to settle. It would seize up after a match for a couple of days and I could barely walk. But I got through and was pretty fit overall. After a few games Susan flew out with our daughters, Laura and Leanne; the club paid our kids' school fees and accommodation, which was great, and we quickly loved the lifestyle.'

The football and culture were different from what Chris knew. On the pitch he didn't settle for a quiet life far away from home. When he received a four-match ban following a sending off against South China AA after a scuffle with former Danish international Flemming Nielsen, the club's appeal to the Hong Kong FA made headline news. Chris was also in the headlines when an audacious move to bring his brother Tony across for a short spell during the English close season failed in June 1981. Chris recalled: 'It was a great shame. Tony was keen to play a couple of games. I'd never played with Tony before and it would have been an enjoyable experience for us both.'

Chris had discovered a new lease of life to his career. There was even an opportunity for representative football and a chance to play against one of the game's greats. Chris recalled: 'I was able to hold my own even with a dodgy knee and played for a Hong Kong XI against foreign teams in friendly matches. It was during one of these games that I came up against George Best one final time. Bestie was the most gifted footballer of his generation at Manchester United and was right up there with Pelé and Eusébio as the greatest of the era. George, Bobby Charlton and Denis Law were unstoppable on their day as a strike force. Bestie had a few short spells at clubs after retiring from United, including Fulham, which is when I'd played against him for Hull at Craven Cottage in October 1976. Rodney Marsh and Bobby Moore were also in the side. Bestie was no longer the player he had been, but he showed touches of brilliance and it was a privilege to play against him. But when George flew to Hong Kong for an exhibition game, it was embarrassing. They took him off at half-time because he was drunk and put him on the first plane home. It's dreadful how things turned out for him, and his battle with alcoholism has been well-documented.

'The Hong Kong experience with George was sad to witness at close quarters but I prefer to remember Bestie for his football skills. George in his prime was unplayable, especially during the mid to late 60s in the First Division and Europe. The Portuguese press gave him the nickname "El Beatle" after he destroyed Benfica in a European Cup tie and, of course, the image of him wheeling way after scoring in the 1968 final at Wembley against Eusébio's Benfica is iconic. Thankfully Bestie has never lost his status as a true legend of the game.'

The Chinese New Year saw an annual four-way tournament in January 1982. Chris was named in a Hong Kong XI to face favourites Austria Vienna, Seiko and Hallelujah. Vienna won 2-1 in front of 19,000 fans at the Hong Kong Stadium. As a result, Hong Kong played Seiko in a third-place play-off match. Hong Kong lost 5-3 in a penalty shoot-out after a 1-1 draw. All things considered, the China experience was positive, but Chris soon had a dilemma, as he explained: 'Tsuen Wan informed me they were folding because of financial constraints. They could not compete with bigger clubs. It was disappointing but I told them "fair enough" and we arranged to return home. It had been a great experience and I thought that was it. But before I'd had a chance to decide my next step, another team in the league contacted me. I was a free agent and they would improve my contract. Despite my knee problems it did not take me long to agree. But when I flew back to meet my new team-mates, Tsuen Wan had re-formed and held my registration. When I got in touch with the club to explain I'd signed for another team, amazingly they matched the offer.'

By the opening match of the season Chris was part of the coaching set-up with his former Hull City team-mate Dave

Roberts. Chris had recruited Roberts to play for Tseun Wan during the previous season on a trip home, after Roberts left Cardiff City and was looking to continue his playing career. Both found an approach to football they had previously not been accustomed to. Coaching was challenging, as most of the squad were part-time, but a British influence on footballing matters from the coaching duo was increasingly pronounced.

Roberts takes up the story: 'Chris proved to be a great mate. I was so grateful for what he did because I was at a loose end. If it hadn't been for Chris, I'd never have extended my career. Hong Kong was not my favourite place, but it added to life's rich pattern. We trained hard, played hard and took the games seriously. Chris and I were quite vocal, so we more or less ran the on-field matters. Sammy Yu was the official coach and Chris was good pals with him. We organised pre-season training for the second season. The Hong Kong boys had a surprise because they were not keen on work! I know that Chris was the first true professional to play for Tsuen Wan. He'd played for Leeds United and had all their good and bad virtues instilled in him. I think that's why we got on, because I wanted to do it properly. Chris had a great work ethic and he no doubt got it from his days at Leeds.

'Chris was a joker in the dressing room, but he was a real professional when it came to training and playing. I played at Fulham with Johnny Haynes and at Hull with Billy Bremner, who were two proper professionals. They were not athletes, but they always wanted to win in training and Chris had a bit of that in him. Chris was never a shrinking violet and once caused a riot in Hong Kong when starting a free-for-all in a relegation battle, which resulted in our ten men being lucky to get off the pitch with a 1-0 win! He was never quiet, but was sensible in terms of decisions on and off the field.'

Football in the Far East engendered a full gamut of emotions and situations for Chris. But he embraced the various aspects of the game and its pervading culture in Hong Kong. This spell of his career gave him a thoroughly positive attitude on the overall experience: 'The team struggled but I really enjoyed getting involved with the training. It was such an enjoyable period of my career on and off the pitch, topped off by the birth of our youngest daughter, Sara. This time, though, it was finally time to retire from the game.'

When the football was all over, Chris went into business during the summer of 1983, running Woodhead Sports, a shop in Wakefield Road, Huddersfield. The venture and other openings were effectively a legacy of his time in the Far East. He said: 'I earned more than double my salary in England by playing in Hong Kong, which might sound crazy, but it's true. At the time I had a place at Huddersfield University for a certificate of education teacher training course but I couldn't turn that type of money down. Playing in Hong Kong enabled me to invest in a sports shop, which I ran for ten years. At the same time, I arranged exhibition games in Hong Kong and China. Chelsea, Norwich City, Crystal Palace and Manchester City all went out to play a Hong Kong XI. I tried to take out Manchester United and Arsenal, but the money involved was ridiculous. Then I started importing merchandising products for English clubs in the 1990s, thanks to contacts in Hong Kong. The business was interesting. We supplied top clubs with shirts, scarves and all sorts, but eventually it was not financially viable, so we moved on to a number of businesses.

'I was one of the first agents to take players into China, but getting a fee was impossible at times. Clubs wanted young lads struggling to make it in the UK. The Professional Footballers' Association had a list of players available on free transfers. This was an opportunity to extend their careers and contribute to pensions, but a number of lads let themselves down and missed out on lucrative deals. A few went on to play in the North American Soccer League but never earned a fortune. I sensed something would happen in China, but not to the level it has done. Players are earning a fortune in the Chinese Super League. Money turns heads, despite what anyone says. My two seasons in Hong Kong gave me opportunities. I've always believed that in life you make decisions and move on. My football career took me on a journey I could never have imagined.'

Chapter 15

Sojourn to Civvy Street

PETER SHREEVE, Keith Burkinshaw's assistant, took over a Tottenham Hotspur team full of self-belief following their 1984 UEFA Cup success. New players arriving at the club included million-pound partners Clive Allen and John Chiedozie. Both slotted into the team, while Steve Archibald left for Barcelona.

Tottenham opened 1984/85 with six victories in their opening ten league matches, including an opening-day 4-1 win at Everton. Tony for his part was on target in a 3-1 victory at home to Norwich City and then there were two goal-fests – 5-0 against QPR and 4-2 against Luton Town. The run also included a home victory over defending champions Liverpool, courtesy of a Garth Crooks goal.

Tony offered fans a view of life at The Lane in a players' monthly column for *Spurs News* in September 1984 after their fine start, which had made them into early pacesetters: 'The mood in the dressing room is one of confidence. But as I keep telling everyone, they are early days yet and we know the only way we can stay there is to keep on winning.'

Spurs matched the same set of results during another ten-match spell. Suddenly talk of a title challenge was all over the media. Among numerous impressive performances was a 2-1 win at Nottingham Forest. Micky Hazard opened the scoring with a spectacular goal, only for Peter Davenport to strike back. Tony sealed the points, as Tottenham battled away with Everton, Manchester United, Arsenal and Liverpool.

The Forest win came just over a week after Tony and Julie had their second child, as Tony recalled: 'I was fortunate enough to be present at both births. Thomas was born on 2 November, the day before a home game versus West Brom. We were booed off the field after a 3-2 defeat! This was not an uncommon occurrence in those days as Spurs supporters were keen to let us know if our performances fell below their expectations. But we bounced back with a great away win against Forest, then defeated a strong Ipswich Town side 3-0 at Portman Road.'

The *Football Post* correspondent Duncan Hamilton noted under the headline 'Forest are galvanised!' how Tony had secured the points in an outstanding performance:

> After absorbing Forest's pressure, Spurs went on the counter-attack and got back in front through Galvin in 73 minutes. The winger controlled a long, high ball, which Mills failed to cut out. Galvin's shot flew across Sutton and crept inside the far post.

Tottenham led the table at Christmas and on New Year's Day for the first time in over 20 years, when they played Arsenal, who were four points adrift. Spurs' 2-1 victory at Highbury is listed in a top ten of derby clashes in the *Evening Standard* and the *Daily Telegraph* from November 2017. The teams for the 1 January meeting were:

Arsenal: Lukic, Anderson, Adams, Talbot, Caton, O'Leary, Robson, Nicholas (Williams), Mariner, Woodcock, Allinson.

> Tottenham Hotspur: Clemence, Stevens, Mabbutt, Roberts, Miller, Perryman, Chiedozie, Falco, Galvin, Hoddle (Allen), Crooks.

Arsenal dominated the first half, going close through Paul Mariner and Tony Woodcock, who opened the scoring with a backheel on 43 minutes. In the second half Glenn Hoddle took centre stage, setting up Crooks for an equaliser. Graham Roberts made the Sunday headlines with a sneaky V-sign to Arsenal fans during the celebrations and there was further joy when Galvin fed Falco to seal the win on 73 minutes.

Following a 2-2 draw at QPR, Tottenham were due to play Everton at White Hart Lane. The Everton match in the end was postponed and Tottenham were no longer leading the way by the rescheduled fixture in mid-March. They remained undefeated away for the rest of the season but inconsistent home form was affecting their momentum.

Spurs were going well in the UEFA Cup, having eliminated Club Brugge and Bohemians Prague after Sporting Braga, and now faced Real Madrid in the quarter-finals. Meanwhile, the league season ultimately fell apart during March 1985, although they did become the first Spurs team to defeat Liverpool at Anfield since 1912. Crooks scored the only goal of the match to complete a historic double over the reigning champions.

Tony recalled the heartache of this period: 'We played well against Madrid. There was an electrifying atmosphere. I had a goal disallowed for a ridiculous offside decision. I received a clever Micky Hazard pass and then rounded the keeper to slot in. I was not offside but the linesman possibly flagged for Garth, who was not interfering with play. An own goal by Steve Perryman proved costly. We had every confidence we'd overturn the first-leg score, but Real held out for a fortunate aggregate win. Falco had a headed goal disallowed – another dubious decision – in the second leg. It left us feeling incredibly deflated. Perryman was sent off for a fairly brutal assault on the Argentina international Jorge Valdano. The referee had no option but to issue the red card, with Steve walking off before he had put his hand in his pocket.

'Defeats against Aston Villa and Everton before the run-in ended our title challenge and we never recovered. We should have beaten Villa, but the Everton defeat killed us and ended our hopes. One win followed in the next five games, then a late spurt, winning four of our final five games. After beating Coventry and Newcastle, Watford hammered us 5-1. We let the fans down that day and they let us know what they thought of the performance.

'It was a huge disappointment because we'd not won the league since the double team. Although the league title was beyond us, a highlight was the Anfield victory a couple of weeks before the Villa game. Being a part of a title-winning side would have been phenomenal but it was not to be. Everton finished top, while Liverpool edged us into third place. In the last game we defeated Nottingham Forest but it was an incredibly disappointing end to what had been a great season for the most part. Some might say, "Typical Spurs," and some might be right. We hadn't delivered and we were all mightily disappointed.'

In 1985/86 Tottenham were unpredictable in the First Division despite some team strengthening. Tony was in and out of the team because of injury. He explained: 'Having gone so close and enjoyed so much success, we struggled to get going at the start of our campaign. Shreeve made two superb signings in Chris Waddle and Clive Allen. Clive's dad, Les, was a member of the double team, so there was history with the Allen family, especially with Paul Allen later joining from West Ham. It's often tough for a top player's son to make it, but Clive was an exception. He'd made his name at Queens Park Rangers and would come into his own the following season.'

Tottenham's home fixture list was interrupted during October 1985 due to the Broadwater Farm riots in the local community. Amid national media coverage of the riots, the club endured an inconsistent campaign, going out of both domestic cup competitions early, although they ended the league season with a seven-match unbeaten run, including five wins. Tony featured in every match of that run, but Spurs still finished tenth.

One of those victories came in March 1986, in front of a poor home crowd, when Tony took the plaudits after a spell out through injury. A newspaper reported:

> Only 10,841 paid to see a 5-0 win over miserable West Brom – the lowest at White Hart Lane for a league match since World War 2. But a more significant point was the return of winger-cum-midfielder Tony Galvin, who can be as important to Spurs as Bryan Robson is to England and Manchester United. Without him they have slipped out of the race for Europe and the FA Cup, but he was back with a goal against Albion and the scoreline said the rest.

The First Division programme finished on 5 May, when Tony scored a hat-trick in an eight-goal bonanza at home to Southampton in Spurs' late flourish. Four days earlier the club had honoured Ossie Ardiles with a testimonial match against Inter Milan in front of a 30,536 crowd at White Hart Lane. Spurs won 2-1 but the match is remembered for the star turn, Diego Maradona, just a month before the Mexico World Cup. The line-up was:

Tottenham Hotspur: Clemence (Jennings), Roberts (Thomas), Hughton, Mabbutt, Miller, Galvin (Samways), Ardiles (Waddle), Falco, Allen, Maradona, Hoddle.

Tony recalled: 'Ossie's testimonial was a feisty affair with lovely skills and delightful football from both teams. Maradona flew in from a warm-up game with Argentina against Norway and wore Hoddle's number 10 shirt. But he had forgotten his boots so wore a pair of Clive Allen's! He was the biggest name in the game and got some reception. He'd joined Napoli, where he'd lead them to the Serie A title. Ossie was his hero and mentor. Maradona looked up to him and it was a very special evening. There was a hush in the dressing room beforehand when Diego walked in. The lads were in awe of him and went over for autographs, which was the only time I saw that as a player. To line up alongside Maradona was some experience, even though it was a testimonial. He was in his heyday, super-fit and a global star. During the game he was unbelievable, even though it was a friendly. We had some team out that night.

'Maradona was an exceptional talent. He was so strong on the ball, you could not get it off him. He had an amazing first touch, instant change of pace and a left foot you would not believe. A few weeks later Diego led Argentina to their World Cup win. He was magnificent throughout the tournament, though England fans recall him for the "Hand of God" goal in the quarter-finals, but he also scored arguably the greatest-ever World Cup finals goal in the same match. Steve Hodge famously swapped shirts with him and sold it for over £7m at an auction in 2022.

'Sadly, Maradona passed away in 2020 and the world rightly mourned a superstar of the game. Their was a similar global reaction to Pelé's death shortly after the 2022 World Cup that illustrated *his* impact on the game. The master of footballing tricks burst on to the scene at the 1958 World Cup and is arguably football's greatest-ever player. For me he stands just ahead of Maradona, Messi, Cruyff and Best.'

Tottenham's last three league matches summed up the team, because they defeated Queens Park Rangers 5-2, Aston Villa 4-2 and then Southampton 5-3. The match programme for the final game, against Saints, offered a historical note in that Tottenham hadn't lost a final home match for nine seasons. Southampton hadn't won at White Hart Lane in nine visits. The *Daily Mirror* headline was 'Galvin grabs three'. Correspondent Harry Miller wrote:

> Galvin grabbed a glorious hat-trick as Spurs ended a disappointing season in storming style. He piled on the agony for slithering Saints, who had also been savaged 6-1 at Everton on Saturday.

Tony recalled: 'I was delighted to get the only hat-trick of my professional career. Southampton were forced to play a rookie keeper, Keith Granger, when Peter Shilton pulled out with a hamstring injury; however, you have to take advantage of such situations. We could sense Granger was nervous from the start and I still have the ball somewhere!'

During the close season, David Pleat, who had enjoyed an eight-year spell at Luton Town, replaced Shreeve. Changes were afoot at White Hart Lane and Tony would start just 20 league matches in 1986/87. With Tony playing a bit-part role, Spurs finished third and enjoyed an exciting League Cup run.

They made a poor start to the season, picking up wins against only Aston Villa and Manchester City in their opening six matches. Following a 3-1 home defeat to Chelsea, Tony lost his place in the starting line-up. He recalled: 'I was really disappointed when Spurs sacked Peter because he had been my coach from the start. Things quickly went downhill for me when Peter was sacked. I had a huge row with the assistant manager after the Chelsea loss because he thought I was not fit enough to play. Pleat dropped me. The lads defeated Leicester City and then won a League Cup tie against Barnsley. I was recalled for a great win against Everton but the writing was on the wall, even after another memorable win at Anfield. Clive Allen scored the only goal of the match.

'There's an old saying that "lightning doesn't strike twice", but it did against Liverpool. After not enjoying a victory there for decades, suddenly we'd won twice in three seasons. Greavsie was right when he used to quip "football is a funny old game"! That was a great day for the travelling supporters but I picked up an injury during the match and was substituted. Apart from a brief run in December, I was more a substitute than starter. I had a knee problem but being on the bench was not ideal. However, I did make contributions to a season where we fell short in terms of trophies.

'Every manager wants to put his stamp on a side, so Steve Hodge and Nico Claesen came in. We switched from two strikers to playing one up front, which was an interesting tactical change. Clive Allen led the line in front of a five-man midfield and was unbelievable. Clive could not stop scoring; he hit 49 goals in all competitions. It was incredible. Pleat wanted me to play a different role. Midfielders on the right and left joined the attack. It took me time to adapt because I'd been playing mainly on the left-hand side. Suddenly this fluid formation had players coming inside and joining in. Sometimes I played, other times I came on from the bench.'

Tony enjoyed a memorable moment during a difficult campaign when he scored a spectacular goal as a substitute for Hodge at

Charlton Athletic on New Year's Day. Tottenham moved into a share of fourth place alongside Nottingham Forest and Norwich City, as Arsenal led the table, ten points clear of Everton and Liverpool. A correspondent wrote:

> With two minutes of a lively New Year derby remaining Galvin collected a pass on the edge of the box and hammered the ball right-footed fiercely into the top of the Charlton net. This goal brought a sigh of relief from the large Tottenham contingent among Charlton's biggest crowd of the season, nearly 20,000. They knew there now was no further danger of Spurs allowing victory to slip through their fingers.

With Hodge sidelined through injury, Tony played in a home defeat to Arsenal after the Charlton win but was omitted from Spurs' FA Cup squad against Scunthorpe United in a third-round match. He was then on the bench as Hodge scored twice in a 3-0 win against his former club, Aston Villa. Spurs then played West Ham in a League Cup fifth-round tie at Upton Park on 27 January. With Hodge cup-tied, Tony was in the line-up. It would be his last start in the competition for the club. The match ended 1-1.

Tony recounted: 'Going into the West Ham game I knew I'd reached a turning point. We murdered them but could not score a winner. I had one of my best games under Pleat and afterwards he made a point of telling me that that was what he wanted. Against Crystal Palace in an FA Cup fourth-round match [31 January] we won 4-0 but I picked up a dead leg. It was one of those injuries when it was more painful afterwards. We were due to play West Ham in the League Cup replay a few days later and naturally I wanted to stay in the side because we were playing well. I had a fitness test, but Pleat felt I was not running properly, so rested me. I thought we'd win and, sure enough, we thumped them 5-0 at The Lane. From that point, I struggled to get back in the team. Pleat preferred Hodge, Claesen and Waddle in midfield, and they were on a run, so I couldn't blame him, but from my perspective I was not given a fair crack at the new system of play.'

Speculation about Tony followed in the media. Correspondent Steve Stammers noted that Derby County and Sheffield Wednesday had expressed interest in Tottenham's £100,000-rated winger. And reporter Steve Tongue penned a revealing *London Daily News* article entitled 'Galvin flies in the face of the greedy 80s' in February 1987. Tongue noted that the first name former manager Keith Burkinshaw selected on Tottenham's team sheet was T. Galvin. Now it was opposite the number 12. He observed:

> Once or twice it has appeared among the young shavers of the reserve side, where the cherubic faces and modish hairstyles contrast with his 30 years and early-Beatles look. There above all he is reminded that time moves on and begins to wonder whether after nine years he should move on, too. The signing of Hodge for £650,000 has made it a thoughtful time in the Galvin household. When the new manager pays that sort of money for someone six years younger who plays in your position for England, you can be forgiven for thinking about a new workplace.

Tony was a substitute against Arsenal in the League Cup semi-final. The tie went to three matches, the last of which would be the toughest night of Tony's Tottenham career, as he recalled: 'We won 1-0 at Highbury before losing 2-1 at White Hart Lane. Away goals did not count as in Europe and there were no penalties. A third game took place at The Lane. We led 1-0 when I came on for Chiedozie to help run down the clock, but Arsenal scored two late goals. I barely touched the ball. Ian Allinson ended up an unlikely hero with the winner. Our fans were stunned. Of course, to lose against Arsenal in a semi-final made it even tougher to take. The dressing room was the worst atmosphere I experienced as a player. It was a real kick in the teeth. But at least Luton Town caused a shock in the final by winning at Wembley!

'When I was the odd man out in our 14-player matchday squad for the FA Cup semi-final win over Watford at Villa Park it was clear I'd not feature in the final against Coventry City, who in the other semi-final defeated Leeds United, now playing in the Second Division under Billy Bremner. You gave your all when selected, but I picked up a cartilage injury in a defeat against Nottingham Forest. It was my final game for the club. Looking back, it's bizarre it should be Forest after I'd turned down speaking to Cloughie a decade earlier.

'After seeing a specialist, he suggested I have it cleaned out, but Pleat was not keen. I thought about it and decided to have the procedure, but first I asked Pleat if he could tell me whether I'd be one of the substitutes at Wembley and then I'd reconsider. As anticipated, Pleat told me I'd probably not be, so I told him I'd have the operation because I wanted to get fit for an upcoming European qualifying game for Ireland versus Luxembourg. Pleat might not want me in the side, but my country did. I wanted to give myself every chance. If I did nothing, I'd have to have the operation at a later date and I did not want to leave it until the summer. I wasn't involved in the FA Cup Final build-up so I trained on my own to get match-fit.

'During my rehabilitation work at the training ground, Pleat asked what I would do if the club offered me wages below what I was currently earning. I found this conversation odd but said I would reject the offer, fully aware that, if this did happen, then I would be eligible for a free transfer, which would make me a more attractive proposition for a club, because no transfer fee would be involved. Pleat thanked me for being honest. Whatever differences we had, I desperately wanted the lads to lift the cup. I sat on the bench at Wembley, and when Clive opened the scoring early against Coventry I really fancied us to win. But Coventry were on a mission and showed amazing spirit in the game. They eventually won 3-2 as a consequence of a freak Gary Mabbutt own goal. As you can imagine, the after-match dinner at White Hart Lane in a huge marquee on the pitch turned out to be a massive anti-climax.

'A couple of weeks after the final I scored my only international goal for Ireland, against Luxembourg in a 2-0 win. I was worried that not being in the Tottenham first team might affect my international career, so it was important that I played in that game. There was no doubt in my mind that it was absolutely the right decision to have had the operation. To me there was no alternative. Ireland and Spurs meant everything to me, but I had been forced into a corner. I had to look after my own well-being with my contract coming up for renewal. These were pre-Bosman days, so there was no freedom of contract. Getting an improved deal was tough at Tottenham. It seemed to take ages to get anything and the club would argue about £1,000 here and there, which seems crazy in the modern era. Now it's a case of £100,000 here and there! Agents were just coming in, so a friend of mine who was a solicitor organised my last contract. I'd spent my first six months at

Tottenham as a part-time player and went full time in August 78, so there were discussions if I'd done a proper ten years. Technically I hadn't. I felt stitched up.

'Although I could have hung around, I couldn't see a future at Spurs. Pleat wanted to build his own side, which I respected, but by the new season he had broken up a successful team. Falco, Miller and Roberts and Hoddle, who had all won major honours, had departed. I was next in the frame. That is life for an ageing footballer at a top club. However, I was really upset and angry how I was effectively being pushed out of the club I'd given everything to. In the end I was offered similar terms, which was a surprise. I played against Bournemouth and Exeter during pre-season games but my days at Tottenham were numbered. I didn't want to be stuck in the reserves when Ireland had a chance of qualifying for the European Championship finals.

'A couple of clubs, including Sheffield Wednesday, came in and I was allowed to speak to them. Pleat felt Wednesday would offer better terms and, after speaking with manager Howard Wilkinson, I was very impressed and signed in August 87. Howard wanted to start playing a more expansive game by bringing footballing-type players in. A fresh start seemed sensible. But I didn't really have a choice. At times in life you have to be honest and also have some self-esteem, so I joined.

'My departure from Tottenham after a near decade of service left me feeling let down. What rankled most during negotiations was I'd be guaranteed a testimonial only if I left. I was really uncomfortable about having a testimonial match when I was not at the club. In the end, Howard contacted a few managers and Celtic agreed to play Tottenham, which would be an attractive game, but the police blocked the match because of potential crowd trouble. West Ham agreed to play, which I appreciated.

Leeds United 1972/73. Chris is second from left in the middle row

Chris at Hull City, 1973/74 season

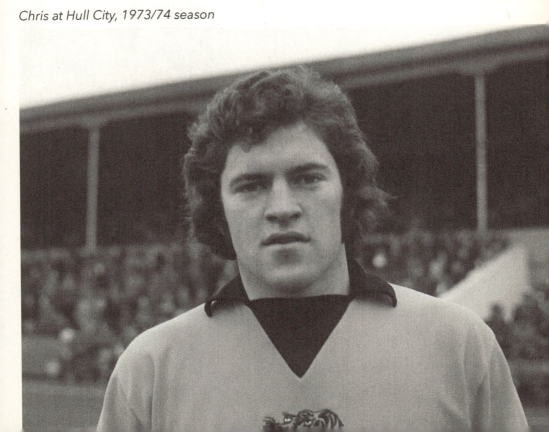

Chris, fourth from left, helps defend a Fulham free kick at Craven Cottage, December 1973

Chris in action for Hull City at Charlton Athletic, October 1976

Tony in action during the 1981 FA Cup Final

Tottenham celebrate winning the 1981 FA Cup, Tony is fourth from left on the back row

Tony and Tony Currie battle for possession in the 1982 FA Cup Final

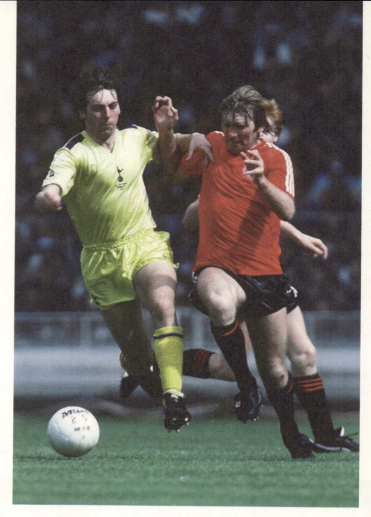

Tottenham celebrate winning the 1982 FA Cup. Tony is fourth from left on the front row

Tony takes on the Barcelona defence. European Cup Winners' Cup semi-final at White Hart Lane, April 1982

Tony gets away from West Ham's Alvin Martin, August 1984

Tottenham celebrate winning the 1984 UEFA Cup against Anderlecht. Tony is extreme left on the front row

Tony in action against Watford, August 1985

Tony with Dave Peacock and Chas Hodges, aka Chas & Dave, at his testimonial dinner, October 1987
Chris and Tony collection

The Republic of Ireland team that faced England at Euro 88: Tony is on the back row, extreme right

Tony in action at Euro 88

Tony heads clear from USSR's Igor Belanov at Euro 88

Tony wins possession against Holland, Euro 88. Frank Stapleton, Holland's Ronald Koeman, Paul McGrath, Ronnie Whelan and Mick McCarthy watch on

Life after hanging up the boots! Top left, Tony and Ossie Ardiles at Newcastle United, 1991. Top right, Tony with his children Thomas and Lucy, 2023. Chris and Susan with daughters Leanne, Laura and Sara, 2013. Bottom left, Chris and Tony, 2023. Bottom right, Chris and Susan, Val and Tony, 2023

Chris and Tony Galvin collection **apart from top left**

'Pleat left soon after me, for reasons that are well-documented, but when I was approached by a leading Sunday newspaper to do the dirty on him for a not-inconsiderable sum, I rejected the idea. That would have been cheap and it is never nice to knock a person when he or she is at a low ebb. As things transpired, Pleat's vision didn't work. I felt little sympathy because he made my final months at the club really tough. Leaving a club after so many years is not easy, but aside from Pleat's tenure, I loved my time at Tottenham. Interestingly, I met Terry Venables, Pleat's successor, soon after joining Wednesday and he asked me why I had left Spurs, because he was confident I could have continued to do a job for the club. I briefly explained the situation and he fully understood, but still believed I should have stood my ground. Hindsight is a wonderful thing!'

Sheffield Wednesday endured a dreadful start to the 1987/88 campaign. Tony made his debut in a 3-0 defeat to Coventry at Hillsborough on 31 August, when his new club were bottom of the table after five matches. Without a win, draws followed at Southampton and Derby County, then Wednesday won their first match of the season at the tenth attempt in league and cup when Charlton Athletic were defeated 2-0 at the end of September 87. Then five weeks after his move to South Yorkshire, Tony faced Tottenham at White Hart Lane, which proved to be his final appearance against his former club. The match took place on 3 October 1987, and the line-ups were:

> Tottenham Hotspur: Clemence, Stevens, Thomas, Samways, Fairclough, Mabbutt, C. Allen (Close), P. Allen, Ardiles, Hodge, Claesen.
>
> Sheffield Wednesday: Hodge, Sterland, Worthington, Madden, May, Proctor, Marwood, Megson, Chapman, West, Galvin (Bradshaw).

Tottenham defeated Wednesday 2-0, and Tony was taken off with an injury at half-time. A couple of weeks later, on 20 October, he pulled on the famous white shirt of Spurs one last time for his testimonial match against the Hammers, which ended in a 2-2 draw. The line-up was:

> Tottenham Hotspur: Parks, Stevens (Polston, Hodge, Close), Hughton, P. Allen (Ardiles), Ruddock, Mabbutt, C. Allen, Archibald (Gray), Villa, Samways (Moncur), Galvin.

Ricky Villa and Steve Archibald made guest appearances on a night when torrential rain hit the attendance. Paul Allen and Clive Allen gave Tottenham a 2-0 lead before Alan Brazil and Eamonn Dolan levelled the scores.

In the official Tottenham Hotspur programme for the match against the Hammers, Bill Nicholson recalled his never-ending drive to Buxton in the Peak District the night he discovered Tony: 'The weather was horrible and my wife offered to go with me. It was raining when we set out, then it turned into sleet and subsequently snow. Road signs warned of floods in the Derbyshire hills and with the sleet and snow turning to slush, the roads were very hazardous. It crossed my mind that perhaps we would be better advised to go back to London, but we stuck it out hoping that the match would still be on. By the time we arrived at the Buxton ground, the pitch was covered by an inch of snow. We sat with a handful of spectators huddled at the back three rows of the grandstand, away from the driving sleet. To my surprise, the game went ahead and Tony played well enough to suggest he had the potential for us to work on if we signed him.'

Keith Burkinshaw recounted a phone call from a friend in Scunthorpe informing him that Goole Town had a promising outside-right: 'Bill Nick checked the information on a dark, wet and windy night in Buxton, gave me the thumbs-up and Tony was on his way to becoming a Spurs player. What a bargain and what satisfaction he gave me as a manager.'

Peter Shreeve added: 'His work rate on the left-back side of the field, and his ability to get crosses in when all appeared lost was a very special quality. His native Yorkshire upbringing gave him a tough edge and as a boy he was a pleasure to deal with. Yes, the "Russian" had a bit about him!'

Tony's former team-mates offered anecdotes. Skipper Steve Perryman led the accolades: 'A test of a player is always what the opposition think of him. Up and down the country, coaches and management always bring up Tony's name as a player to watch. When coming up against Spurs they would always see if Tony was in the side, before the big names, to keep a close eye on him. They always emphasised his strong running ability and incredible stamina. It was an honour for me to play in the same team as Tony.'

Strikers Steve Archibald and Garth Crooks benefitted from Tony's wing play down the years. Archibald said: 'Tony contributed in so many ways to many famous victories. I may have credit for the goals I scored, but a lot of them can be attributed to Tony's hard work down the flanks.' Crooks agreed: 'There was a game, I can't remember who we were playing, when to be quite honest, we had a somewhat unimpressive first half – all of us except Tony, who was not only murdering the right-back, but was continually trying to gee-up the rest of us. We came into the dressing room at half-time, rather sheepishly, and Shreevesy ignored all of us except Tony, who he slaughtered for "lack of effort". Peter and Keith then went out into the treatment room, and TG went into a blinding rage, and the air was blue! Peter returned just as we were about to go out for the second half and I noticed him wink at Stevie P. and the skipper wink back. It worked. Tony had an even better second half, scored, and we won the match that we hardly deserved! ... He's an unsung hero, but players more gifted than him have always appreciated him with his legs and lungs.'

Playmakers Glenn Hoddle and Ossie Ardiles were in the TG fan club. Hoddle said: 'Tony is a great player to have in your side. He and I, I felt, we were on the same wavelength. He would make instinctive off-the-ball runs, anticipating exactly where I was going to hit a long pass. He was probably better at doing this than anyone else I've ever played with, and so I think we were able to complement each other. He's a truly good professional.' Ardiles recalled: 'In training he used to kick us and claim that it was part of our education process! When he got in to the first team, he showed what a strong competitor he was. He's a smashing lad, very honest, and you can always count on him being there.'

And Micky Hazard noted: 'In my opinion he was a vital cog in our side. Without him our team of world-class players didn't function. He was a great "getter", particularly for Glenn, though he got his own fair share of goals.'

Tottenham's goalkeeper and defence joined the chorus of praise. Ray Clemence observed: 'Without Tony in the side we lacked balance. He was vital to us on our left side. He's a player of immense strength, whether in attack or at left-back. He was certainly very helpful to me, as he would give his goalkeeper options, as well as cover when we were under pressure.' Chris Hughton recalled his Irish international team-mate was an 'automatic selection' at Spurs. Paul Miller noted: 'I remember his first game for the reserves, he got stuck into their full-back. I mean, really, us defenders are supposed to kick wingers, not the other way around! But seriously, Tony is a great professional ... He always gives a side balance on the left and he's so unselfish.'

And Graham Roberts reflected: 'Tony was a great player to have in your team. He was probably the fittest I ever played with, and could run all day.' Danny Thomas added: 'So many incidents make me smile, but none more so than some of our five-a-side training games. If things were not going well for him, he might just suddenly let out a yell and boot the ball right out of the ground, literally! The funny thing is that we came to expect it, so nobody was surprised!'

Tony recalled: 'We had a number of events that were well-supported, including a dinner at the Bull's Head Restaurant in Turnford, when Steve Perryman, who was Brentford manager at the time, was among the speakers. We also had a charity cricket match at St Margaretsbury Cricket Club when an Argentina shirt signed by Diego Maradona was among the raffle prizes. Unfortunately, only a few overs were bowled because the rains came and the match was abandoned. This was a shame for everyone concerned, including the cricket club, who were hoping to generate some money from what was expected to be a sizeable crowd. The weather seemed to hang around for a few days, because on the day of the West Ham game it poured down, which had an impact on the attendance. I was grateful to all the brave supporters who turned out, along with my special guests, Labour leader Neil Kinnock and his wife Glenys, and Derek Jameson, who I used to regularly listen to on the BBC Radio 2 breakfast show.'

Away from friendly action, Tony helped Wednesday defeat Norwich City and then Portsmouth. Victories followed at West Ham in the league and Aston Villa in the League Cup. But an injury at Villa Park resulted in Tony having a lengthy spell out. Apart from several substitute appearances, he would make only one further start, in a 3-0 win at Luton Town in April 1988, as Wednesday ended the campaign comfortably in mid-table.

After appearing at the European Championships, Tony returned to his club, and Wednesday got off to a flyer when the 1988/89 season kicked off, with an opening-day win against Luton Town. But he was dropped after four league matches, following a disagreement with his manager when Wednesday lost 2-0 at QPR. Tony recalled: 'It wasn't surprising because we had a major row after he substituted me following a vociferous disagreement with the referee, who failed to award me a penalty. I was blatantly brought down by David Seaman. Howard made his point that I'd risked getting sent off and should have handled the situation better, but it's not that easy in the heat of the moment. However, I understood his viewpoint. He resigned soon after, having received an offer he couldn't turn down from Leeds.'

When Wilkinson took the helm at Leeds United in October 1988, Peter Eustace, a former legend at Wednesday, accepted the post, but he only lasted three months during a dismal run of form that brought just one league win. Tony made two substitute appearances under Eustace, at Coventry City in a 5-0 defeat and at home to Liverpool in a hard-fought 2-2 draw. With Wednesday battling relegation, Ron Atkinson took the managerial hot seat in February 1989. Tony hadn't started a match since the 2-0 defeat at QPR in September 88, a bizarre situation as he was still an international footballer. However, Atkinson recalled him against Southampton after five months on the sidelines, and he played his part in a 1-1 draw, supplying a last-minute cross for Mark Proctor to equalise.

Tony had endured 18 months during which he wasn't a first-team regular with Wednesday, yet Jack Charlton continued to select him for international football. Now Atkinson picked him to play at Wimbledon, following his impact against the Saints. Before the match, journalist John Donoghue evaluated a bizarre situation in the *Daily Express*, in which Tony told the paper that Charlton had kept him going. He said: 'I thought very seriously about packing it in. Going to work had become quite painful. A lot of people thought that in the circumstances I wouldn't go on being selected for Ireland. But Jack took the view that I had been in every one of his squads and hadn't let him down. That was something I appreciated.'

Following a 1-0 defeat at Wimbledon, Tony scored against Charlton Athletic in a 3-1 win and then featured at Everton as Wednesday's relegation battle continued. To boost his match fitness Tony played several reserve matches, including a midweek one against Leeds United at Elland Road, where he witnessed the impact that Wilkinson was beginning to make at his new club: 'Both teams included a number of first-team players, so it was going to be competitive. As we were getting ready to kick off I recognised a number of the Leeds players but also noticed that they only had ten men. Literally, just as the referee was about to blow his whistle this very familiar figure ran out of the tunnel and across the pitch to line up opposite me. It was Gordon Strachan, recently signed by Howard from Manchester United. I asked him what on earth he was doing here. Gordon said he was on the golf course when Howard rang and told him to get his skates on and get down for the reserve game! Gordon made it with seconds to spare. For me this had the Brian Clough mark all over it. Howard was making the point that Strachan might be a very important player to the club but always remember who is in charge! He was keeping Gordon's feet on the ground. Strachan was a crucial signing for Howard because he set an example of what it took to be a top professional. And Gordon was outstanding at Leeds. He led the side to the 1989/90 Second Division title and old First Division in 1991/92. The best managers always ensure they are in charge. No player is bigger than the club or country. Think Sir Alex Ferguson, Cloughie and Big Jack in this regard. Howard was in that bracket during the early 90s.'

Tony was in Atkinson's matchday squad during the relegation run-in. And in the key penultimate match, he came on in a 1-0 victory at Hillsborough that ensured safety and relegated Middlesbrough. Tony made his final First Division appearance a few days later against Norwich City in a rearranged fixture on 17 May. The match finished 2-2.

He reflected: 'The Wednesday move didn't work out, but it wasn't for the want of trying. I liked Howard and loved the idea of moving to a Yorkshire club. Fortunately, Ron arrived and was a larger-than-life character in the game who brought belief back into the squad. I featured in most of the remaining games as a starter or substitute and came off the bench against Middlesbrough when a Steve Whitton goal ensured First Division survival. Wednesday are a great club with incredibly loyal supporters. I was very much in and out of the side, more out than in, but did enjoy my time there and loved living in Sheffield. I was incredibly disappointed for the club and their supporters that they were relegated the season after I left, but delighted that Big Ron brought them straight back up to their rightful place in the First Division.'

During the 1989 close season Ossie Ardiles contacted his former team-mate out of the blue to join him in his first managerial post at Swindon Town. Tony recalled: 'Ossie wanted staff around him he could confide in to help the team to progress. I signed in August 1989 and played a few games, including one against Leeds at Elland Road. Chris came to the match as I was in the squad, which I appreciated. We got battered 4-0. I came off the bench when we were 2-0 down. Strachan had scored twice, Bobby Davison made it three within a couple of minutes and I got a lot of abuse from the Leeds fans, particularly when I clattered into Mel Sterland. David Batty scored in the last minute. I was soon behind the scenes, which was good for my career because I was keen to be on the coaching side. But it was a chaotic time. I went in as a player, did some coaching, then scouting, and before long I was "unofficial" assistant manager.

'Leeds, Sheffield United and Newcastle United battled it out for the title. Swindon kept in play-off contention. We knocked out Blackburn Rovers and I was in the matchday squad when they beat Sunderland in the final at Wembley. It was an amazing experience. There is no better way to get promotion. We had a good team, played lovely football and looked forward to the new campaign. But an investigation into "financial irregularities" was about to hit the club, although I had no idea about this when I jetted off to the 1990 World Cup finals in Italy with the Republic of Ireland. Before the second match, I heard about the investigations at Swindon so returned to offer Ossie moral support. It was disastrous for Swindon, who were relegated to the Third Division. On appeal they were reinstated to the Second Division but the following season Ossie had to balance the books and sold some of his best players. It proved to be a difficult season but, in January 1991, Newcastle United approached Ossie, after Jim Smith resigned, to become their manager. He asked me to join him as assistant manager in the March. What an experience that turned out to be!'

Tony recalled his time at Newcastle as a 'chaotic opportunity': 'We had no money to invest in players so struggled on the park. Youngsters had talent, but they were too inexperienced. We needed an influx of senior lads to help bed the kids in. Ossie did introduce young players to the first team, including Lee Clark, Robbie Elliott, Steve Howey and Steve Watson, who went on to have great careers. Ossie did a great job at Newcastle but I told him the writing was on the wall after an FA Cup defeat to Bournemouth, and was proved right.'

The manner in which Tony was sacked left him slightly disillusioned with the game: 'I was scouting a Bury striker with my brother Chris the evening before I was dismissed. I was surprised and thought it was odd to see the Newcastle chief scout sat behind us because I didn't know he would be there and Ossie hadn't mentioned anything. The next morning at Newcastle's Durham training ground I was waiting for the kit to arrive, along with the other coaches in our dressing room, for around an hour. There was no sign of the kit and there seemed to be an uneasy silence as there was no sign of Ossie either. I was then summoned to Ossie's office to take a phone call. Ossie told me we'd both been sacked, which came as a huge shock. I later discovered that one of the coaches also knew that Kevin Keegan was the new manager. I wish that particular person could have taken me to one side and explained what was happening, but no such luck. I wasn't allowed back to the ground to receive my formal notice. It was delivered by the newly appointed Newcastle United chief executive in the Scottish & Newcastle Brewery offices opposite the ground. I was told my kit would be passed on to me at a later date.

'I can't say I was surprised by how Newcastle handled matters; sadly, that's football. John Hall had taken over as chairman and was looking to bring in a manager of his own choice. Hall, of course, appointed Kevin Keegan and provided him with the funds to strengthen the squad, which then ensured there was a better blend of experience and youth in the team. I still maintain that Ossie can be proud of what he achieved in a limited time.'

The Newcastle job signalled an end to Tony's management partnership with Ardiles. He recalled: 'When Ossie took the West

Brom job, it came as a complete surprise. I found out when Chris rang to tell me he'd seen a newspaper story about Ossie taking the job. He also warned me there was a rumour Ossie was appointing Keith Burkinshaw as assistant manager. I felt really let down as I was available and we'd worked together for a couple of years. When I rang Ossie, he eventually came on the phone and it was a difficult conversation. After the dust had settled, I realised that Ossie avoided confrontation if he could. At Newcastle he didn't like losing his temper with the players; maybe he didn't know how to handle a difficult situation. There were times when he felt I dived in and lost my temper with players after they'd done something stupid, whereas he wanted to look at the positives. As a manager Ossie had a mantra of positivity. Young players can respond to that philosophy, but when a young player makes bad choices he needs to be told. Our paths didn't cross for some time, but we patched things up, because life is too short.

'Ossie did what was right for West Brom and went on to manage Tottenham briefly. He then worked in a number of countries. Glenn, of course, enjoyed success at Chelsea and took England to the 1998 World Cup, but has not been given an opportunity since. But he seems more than happy with his television work as a pundit. He's one of the best around. Steve Perryman went to Japan as Ossie's assistant and then was a manager around 2002 when they hosted the World Cup. Both enjoyed trophy success in Japan. A few of the Spurs lads also tried their hand at club management, some went into the corporate hospitality circuit, doing question-and-answer events and other type of work. If you can get on the managerial merry-go-round, especially now, you can do very well financially, but you need a very thick skin.

'It was time to move on. Looking back, it was so important Keith Burkinshaw insisted I complete my Postgraduate Certificate of Education when I signed for the club. I didn't fancy going into the school system, but I had options. Whilst in football I'd taken advantage of Professional Footballers' Association educational funding to complete a number of courses, which enabled me to be in a position to apply for the role of a further education lecturer in leisure and sport at Hertford Regional College. Having a vocational skill with my degree was important because my students were 16 to 19 years old, seeking a vocational career. They reminded me in some way of those apprentices at football clubs who were obsessed with becoming footballers. As a PFA representative I used to talk to them about gaining qualifications whilst in football, as there were no guarantees they would make it. Not many of them listened, unfortunately, but some did and hopefully benefitted at a later date.

'Sadly, not enough footballers from my era, and even to this day, prepare properly for a life outside football. Often when I meet supporters they seem surprised that I had a career outside football and this even applies to ex-footballers who I've met over the years. Yes, it's nice to work as a hospitality host at the occasional game at Tottenham but I firmly believe the best thing for ex- or current players' mental health is to have something outside football to focus on. This could be a career, running a business or volunteering. I always believed as a footballer you have a duty to engage with the community and I always tried to do this both in and outside football by attending grassroots football awards, coaching children's teams or volunteering in schools or other organisations.

'Some time after taking up the FE post, a community development role came up at Tottenham and I did have a chat with the club, but it wasn't for me. As well as continuing to coach children I also coached adult teams at amateur level for a number of years at Royston, Buntingford and Potton, with some success at each of the clubs. Although sometimes challenging, I found it enjoyable and rewarding to work with players who were keen to improve but basically just loved playing the game. I enjoyed my years as a lecturer and it was during this period that, after separating from Julie, I got together with Val. We married in 2003 and have 13 grandchildren between us, so life is constantly busy!'

Chapter 16

A Final Word …

IT IS barely surprising that Chris Galvin looks back on his career in football with mixed feelings. There were pluses and there were minuses. There were significant decisions that might not have worked out as well as had been anticipated, but that is often the case with the benefit of hindsight. Chris endured some testing times from his father, Tommy, and it would probably always be open to debate as to what effects they would ultimately have on his development. And yet he retains a sense of objectivity, which means that he will always remain very much aware of the benefits of being part of a strong family unit.

Chris recalled: 'I did have problems with Dad following my career and, as a result, our relationship suffered. From playing in the Red Triangle League as a kid and during my Leeds career, I'd lived at home and for whatever reason we argued about my performances. Dad continued to watch me at Hull City, York City and Stockport County. The atmosphere was trying at times. Dad and I argued and I've never known why. It was frustrating. Susan could not believe it and Tony hid upstairs because he didn't want to get involved. Once Tony's career kicked in, Dad wasn't so critical, maybe he'd realised it was better to leave well alone. Looking back, I'd have been better off not getting Dad tickets

A FINAL WORD ...

for games, which is a shame to say, but the arguments were not worth it.'

For all the issues at home, Chris still had his highs. He was a popular figure in dressing rooms and fulfilled his main ambition as a youngster. He reflected: 'Playing football was all I wanted to do from four or five years of age. And I played until my early 30s, professionally for 15 years, not at the top level apart from 20-odd games at Leeds, but it was a standard not many kids reach. I didn't win major honours, which was disappointing, but that's the case for most players. The modern era sees squad members receive mementos when a team wins trophies, which is important. If that had been in place during my playing days I'd have a tangible reward from my Leeds days from the FA Cup and Fairs Cup, which would have been nice for my family. But it was not to be then.

'The modern game serves squad players far better, which is a great development. We were only allowed one substitute, so after making the first-team squad I was sat in the stands with Joe Jordan, Terry Yorath or other members of the matchday squad for three seasons. I would not have left Leeds if more substitutes were allowed. I could fill in across the midfield, so would have had game time, and my match fitness would not have been an issue.

'Fans often ask me whether the Leeds team of yesteryear would be at the top nowadays. Of course they would, and they could have won more honours with the strength of our squad. Don assembled a team that competed on every level across the park. We had as many world-class players as the top teams of today do, such as Manchester City and Liverpool. Leeds would have been in the Champions League year after year. Only the First Division champions participated then. Now it's the top four and Europa League winners. It was a different era and I'm pleased the game has moved on.

'As a squad member at Leeds, fans associate me with their glory years, which is strangely welcome because I didn't contribute to the successes, but I was training and travelled with the legends, which gave me a special insight. However, as a player you want to do it on the pitch. My sole regret was Don didn't give me a chance to play at the highest level for a sustained spell to prove I could cut it and show the fans what I could do. Being involved in events celebrating the Revie era and the way fans respect the part I played as a squad member means a lot to me. I am now able to look back on that period of my life with a more positive perspective.

'Perhaps I lacked a killer instinct, but my attitude changed mentally after Leeds. There were no sports psychologists around then, but I felt I'd blown my chance at the top level and had to accept playing at a lower-league club. Maybe confidence was a problem, but there were days when I ran out on to a field and felt that things would go right no matter who we were playing. There were spells when I did turn it on and journalists were often complimentary, wondering why I was not playing at a higher level, but the seasons rolled by.'

Chris's association with Leeds United during their glory days is something to be savoured. But his career might have been much more noteworthy if he had gone down different football paths from the one he ultimately chose.

He admitted: 'I could have joined Bolton Wanderers, but didn't. Then at Leeds I could have stayed on a little longer. You never know, I might have got a break after Don had left under Brian Clough or Jimmy Armfield during the 1974/75 campaign when they reached the European Cup Final. But when I did leave Leeds, I could have insisted on speaking to Wolves, who were a First Division side. There were other times when I could have

A FINAL WORD ...

asked lads if a manager was looking to strengthen in my position. But it was not to be.

'My experience is a lesson to starry-eyed kids flattered by Premier League clubs. You can be the best youth player around, there are the odd exceptions but the big boys mainly prefer experience. It might be tougher starting at a smaller club and then moving up the leagues, but it can be done all the way to top-flight football. You need look no further than Jamie Vardy, who started out at Halifax Town, played for Fleetwood Town and then got his opportunity with Leicester City. No one expected Leicester to win the Premier League in 2016, but they stunned the footballing world, and have since won the FA Cup. Vardy is still scoring regularly and has played for England numerous times. Of course, a major aspect is the vast amount of money a club nowadays throws at youngsters who often take a view that they can set themselves up financially for life. If things don't work out, they can try elsewhere. It's a gamble, but a calculated one, and who can blame a young player with talent?

'While I was really ambitious to be a professional footballer, Tony wasn't as interested when he was growing up, yet he enjoyed success at the highest level and seeing him achieve that was tough. Now it's easy to say how proud I am of his achievements, but at the time I was frustrated and jealous, not because he won major honours and played international football, but I was annoyed with myself for making some bad decisions. By the end of my career Tony had broken into the Tottenham side and was preparing for the FA Cup Final, which showed how far apart our careers had gone. We were also at opposite sides of the country so we didn't speak that often, but his success did get to me. One of my lowest points was when Tony made the first team at Tottenham, because I could see my brother doing exactly what I wanted to do. But

Tony had the one thing that I struggled with and that was a burst of pace, which is a massive bonus. There was envy, but I soon accepted it and got on with my life.

'As Tony's career progressed, Dad eased off and stopped being so critical all the time. But all these things make you grow up as a footballer and a man. You learn what is important in life and I've been lucky because I had a strong family behind me. During my career the one constant was my wife Susan and daughters, Laura, Leanne and Sara. Susan received all the brunt of my problems during challenging times but hopefully the good times as well.

'I'm close with Tony and we talk about our careers along with the modern game. I now look back retrospectively and laugh about things more than I did. At every club there were issues … from Leeds United to Tsuen Wan. From being a young kid my personal performance was the key, second to team performance. At the time, obviously, this was not apparent to me but now it is. I enjoyed outstanding games for all the clubs I joined, but there were often periods of not being involved. I don't blame individual managers – too many ex-players do this.

'Putting the team second was not a blatant reaction but at times it upset managers. For me, the key to a game was to entertain the paying fans. The first time this was questioned was at the end of my career at Stockport by manager Jimmy McGuigan. I had reached the point where my knee had become critical and it greatly affected my style of football. Jimmy's plan was to play me as a holding midfielder, meaning less running and using my ability to control and pass the ball. I was reluctant to play this position but Jimmy persuaded me to give it a go as it would extend my playing career. It worked and, for the first time in my career, I focused on the team. When my knee forced me to finish playing in the Football League I was able to play this role in China for two seasons. Within a couple of years of finishing playing I had several operations, including attempts to realign my left leg and later two new knee joints.

'I didn't win major honours but did play alongside some of the greatest players to represent Leeds and then not-so-famous clubs such as Hull, but they were just as important to loyal supporters. My life in football was not all doom and gloom. I had a long professional football career and travelled all over the world. Above all, I did the thing that I dreamt of as a young boy, played the game I loved and finished with plenty of tales to tell.'

Tony Galvin didn't scale the heights in professional football at league and international level by the most common route. He didn't learn his trade as an apprentice at a club as soon as he left school. Instead, his initial priority became his academic studies, and football took a back seat until he came into the game late, making up for the lost time in dramatic fashion. Then he grabbed his opportunities with both hands and duly reached the top.

Tony looks back on how the development process for young players has changed: 'When I got my chance at Spurs, Ossie and Ricky Villa were the first big-money signings in English football. In the late 70s there were only a handful of foreign players throughout the old First Division. Clubs had smaller budgets so consequently carried smaller squads, so if you were playing well consistently in the reserves at a top club such as Spurs there was a chance you would get an opportunity to break into the first team. Also, many Football Combination games were competitive, particularly if you came up against Arsenal, Chelsea or West Ham. I recall one game versus QPR when we were thumped 5-1 and our team included a number of first-team players, including Ricky. These encounters helped to prepare you for the physical battle awaiting you in the first team. Contrast this to the highly technical and almost anodyne football you now experience when watching a Premier League academy game. Good technique is important for a footballer but equally important, if you are to cut it at the highest level, are the physical elements such as tackling, closing down and running, even when you are extremely tired.

'Parents today are arguably better sending a child to play for clubs such as Milton Keynes, Peterborough United or Exeter City that have a better track record of bringing players through to the first team. Those players may then, having played a number of first-team games, get the opportunity to sign for Championship or Premier League clubs. Generally, it is important that players at these clubs are in the first team by their early 20s to allow them the opportunity to impress clubs at a higher level. Of course, it is not impossible for players to break through when they are older. Jamie Vardy would be such an example, who first started out as a semi-professional at Stocksbridge Park Steels FC and finished up winning the Premier League, FA Cup and representing England. He would be described as a late developer and I suppose that term could be applied to yours truly.

'The chances of a youngster at eight or nine years of age procuring a professional contract at a Premier academy is a long shot. And for those that do, the vast majority fail to make the first team. They are let go, loaned out or sold to clubs playing at a lower level or abroad. Parents should consider the track record of a club in bringing young players through to the first team, but as important, what is in the best interests of a youngster? Their education is paramount and what are the options if they don't make it? Of course, there are successes with clubs developing young players, such as Marcus Rashford, Phil Foden, Mason Mount, Bukayo Saka and Jude Bellingham. Gareth Southgate should be

A FINAL WORD ...

praised for introducing young players to the international stage and sticking with them when the going gets tough. Here is an England manager who had a vision, which encouraged managers in the top division to play their best young talent in the first team. England have done well at the last three major tournaments and will be one of the favourites for Euro 2024 in Germany.

'Sometimes the right decision might be not to sign for a particular club and hold off. It might be better to allow the child to mature as a person and as a footballer. This may be achieved by the child enjoying football playing with friends. Of course, it is always important for a young player who has footballing ambitions to continue to train, practise and seek improvement. This brings us full circle to Dad persisting on our techniques and focusing on us being able to kick with both feet during kickabouts in fields close to our home. Both of us were two-footed. It was natural for us to go inside and outside a player on the right or left wing. There is no right or wrong way to determine a child's footballing future but a family must seriously consider the pros and cons of any decision and ultimately do what's best for a child.

'I've never regretted the path I took getting into football, because I probably appreciated the rewards more than lads who were involved from being apprentices. I owe Alan Turner a great deal as he gave me my opportunity to play at a higher level with Goole Town. I was very saddened to hear of his passing in 2022 and will always be grateful for his support. Playing for Tottenham was the highlight, even though it came out of the blue in the first place. I could not have got much more out of my professional career. It was tough at first because you have to get used to full-time training, which is hard, physically and mentally. It's not just the rigours and routine of training, but trying to get a starting place alongside higher-calibre players, including full internationals. I was fortunate to be at Tottenham at that particular time because, being two-footed, I could play in a position nobody else wanted. All those hours kicking about with Chris and Dad paid off, because when the opportunity came to play on the left, even though I was naturally right-footed, I didn't flinch. I knew that I could do that for Tottenham.

'Fans remember the big games such as the cup finals and European nights, and they are great memories, but there were also bad days such as the League Cup Final against Liverpool when, after being injured, I wondered how on earth I stayed on. It's an occupational hazard when you pick up injuries, but you do play when not fully fit at times, although it takes its toll. I was a willing player, so if the team needed me, I was prepared to play. When I look back, I was lucky enough to play seven matches at Wembley. Above all, though, because I was at Tottenham, I played with and against world-class players for club and country.'

The overall outcome was coated with irony, because Tony's brother Chris, his senior by almost five years, had established himself in league football way before he belatedly made his mark. In addition, their journeys had taken different courses. Chris had started with a big club, but Tony had worked his passage to play for one.

Tony added: 'By the time I broke through at Tottenham, Chris had played much of his career and, when you have an elder brother in the game, it has to have an impact on you psychologically. Chris was strong-minded as a 15-year-old, so when Leeds United came calling, it was hard to resist. He joined one of the top clubs in the country but that meant he rarely got a chance. In the modern era he would have got more game time because of the squad sizes, but just look at the number of kids struggling to get opportunities at top clubs. It takes its toll on a player mentally.

'I'm sure that if Chris had gone to a lower-level club, he'd have received more chances and might have had a bigger move further down the line. If you start off at the right club, things can be different. I'd enjoyed success as a youth but was not desperate to be an apprentice at a football club. I looked at football from a different mindset because I had a back-up career. Starting at Goole was the right choice for my career.

'As brothers we'd always been close, but when I signed for Tottenham, Chris was at Hull City and then joined Stockport, so we were miles apart. I went home now and again but we didn't really discuss our careers while we were both playing. At Tottenham it was rare that I got home during the season, so I didn't get to see Chris that often. Maybe there was something under the surface with Chris about my career compared with his, but we never discussed it. We were two footballers in different parts of the country, but then he went to Hong Kong, which was the right thing to do at the time. It was only when I was at Wednesday that Chris came to a few games at Hillsborough because he'd finished as a player, and our relationship quickly went back to what it was as kids.'

Tony achieved everything he wanted domestically and in European competition, although a league title would have been the ultimate. But he was in the right place to enjoy an international career with the Republic of Ireland: 'I was so fortunate that Eoin Hand picked me for Ireland and then, of course, Jack Charlton took the post when I was in the squad. I fitted his game plan so got to experience an unforgettable Euro 88 tournament. Beating England has obviously elevated that squad but, more importantly, we gave fans belief that Ireland could compete on the highest stage, and other squads have gone on to emulate our success, which is fantastic. There were so many highs but the welcome we received on our return from the Euros is something I'll never forget. All in all, I thoroughly enjoyed my life in football and appreciate how lucky I was to experience so many highs. I could not have asked for more out of my years in the game.'

Appendix 1: Chris Galvin's Playing Career

	League Apps	League Subs	League Goals	FA Cup Apps	FA Cup Subs	FA Cup Goals	League Cup Apps	League Cup Subs	League Cup Goals	Europe Apps	Europe Subs	Europe Goals	Other Apps	Other Subs	Other Goals	Total Apps	Subs	Goals
LEEDS UNITED																		
1969/70	3															3	1	0
1970/71											1					0	2	0
1971/72	2	1			1		2		1		1					5	2	1
1972/73	1			1	1		1			1		1				3	0	0
TOTAL	**6**	**1**		**1**	**2**		**3**		**1**	**1**	**2**	**1**				**11**	**5**	**1**
HULL CITY																		
1973/74	14	1		2		1	5		1	3					1	24	1	3
1974/75	33	1	2	3		1										36	1	2
1975/76	37	1	4	3			2			1						43	1	4
1976/77	12	2	1		1			1		3						15	3	1
1977/78	21	2					4			1						26	2	0
1978/79	15	4	4	1												16	4	4
TOTAL	**132**	**11**	**11**	**9**	**1**	**1**	**11**	**1**	**1**	**8**					**1**	**160**	**12**	**14**

Chris played for Hull City in the Watney Cup in 1973/74 & Anglo-Scottish Cup in 1975/76, 1976/77, 1977/78

	League Apps	League Subs	League Goals	FA Cup Apps	FA Cup Subs	FA Cup Goals	League Cup Apps	League Cup Subs	League Cup Goals	Europe Apps	Europe Subs	Europe Goals	Other Apps	Other Subs	Other Goals	Total Apps	Subs	Goals
YORK CITY																		
1975/76	22		6													22	0	6
TOTAL	**22**		**6**													**22**	**0**	**6**
STOCKPORT COUNTY																		
1978/79	1															1	0	0
1979/80	25	1		1			2									28	1	0
1980/81	41		3		1		5	1								46	1	3
TOTAL	**67**	**1**	**3**	**1**	**1**		**7**	**1**								**75**	**2**	**3**
TSEUN WAN																		
1981/82	18															18	0	0
1982/83	18															18	0	0
TOTAL	**36**															**36**	**0**	**0**
CAREER TOTAL	**263**	**13**	**20**	**10**	**3**	**1**	**19**	**1**	**1**	**9**	**2**	**1**		**0**	**1**	**304**	**19**	**24**

313

Appendix 2: Tony Galvin's Playing Career

	League			FA Cup			League Cup			Europe			Other			Total		
	Apps	Subs	Goals	Apps	Subs	Goals	Apps	Subs	Goals	Apps	Subs	Goals	Apps	Subs	Goals	Apps	Subs	Goals
TOTTENHAM HOTSPUR																		
1978/79	1															1	0	0
1979/80	7	3	4													7	3	4
1980/81	17		1	8	1	1										25	1	2
1981/82	32		3	7			8			8		1	1			56	0	4
1982/83	26		2	1			1			1			1			30	0	2
1983/84	30		1	3			3		1	9		4				45	0	6
1984/85	38		4	3		1	3			7		1				51	0	6
1985/86	23		4				3	3	1				2			28	0	5
1986/87	20	4	1	1			2	3	1							23	7	2
TOTAL	**194**	**7**	**20**	**23**	**1**	**2**	**20**	**3**	**3**	**25**	**0**	**6**	**4**	**0**	**0**	**266**	**11**	**31**

Tony played in the Charity Shield in 1981/82, 1982/83 & the Super Cup in 1985/86

	League			FA Cup			League Cup			Europe			Other			Total		
	Apps	Subs	Goals	Apps	Subs	Goals	Apps	Subs	Goals	Apps	Subs	Goals	Apps	Subs	Goals	Apps	Subs	Goals
SHEFFIELD WEDNESDAY																		
1987/88	12	6		4												16	6	0
1988/89	9	8	1		1											9	9	1
TOTAL	**21**	**14**	**1**	**4**	**1**											**25**	**15**	**1**
SWINDON TOWN																		
1989/90	6	5			3											6	8	0
TOTAL	**6**	**5**			**3**											**6**	**8**	**0**
CAREER TOTAL	**221**	**26**	**21**	**23**	**1**	**2**	**24**	**7**	**3**	**25**	**0**	**6**	**4**	**0**	**0**	**297**	**34**	**32**

Tony also made 163 appearances, scoring 23 goals, for Goole Town FC 1974/75 to 1977/78

Appendix 3: Tony Galvin's International Record

Date	Opponent	Venue	Score	Competition
22/09/1982	NETHERLANDS	A	1-2	UEFA European Championship Qualifier Group 7
30/03/1983	MALTA	A	1-0	UEFA European Championship Qualifier Group 7
12/10/1983	NETHERLANDS	H*	2-3	UEFA European Championship Qualifier Group 7
04/04/1984	ISRAEL	A*	0-3	Friendly
08/08/1984	MEXICO	H	0-0	Friendly
12/09/1984	SOVIET UNION	H	1-0	FIFA World Cup Qualifier
17/10/1984	NORWAY	A	0-1	FIFA World Cup Qualifier
14/11/1984	DENMARK	A	0-3	FIFA World Cup Qualifier
05/02/1985	ITALY	H	1-2	Friendly
01/05/1985	NORWAY	H	0-0	FIFA World Cup Qualifier
26/05/1985	SPAIN	H	0-0	Friendly
23/04/1986	URUGUAY	H	1-1	Friendly
25/05/1986	ICELAND	A	2-1	Independence Friendly
27/05/1986	CZECHOSLOVAKIA	N	1-0	Independence Friendly
10/09/1986	BELGIUM	A	2-2	UEFA European Championship Qualifier Group 7
18/02/1987	SCOTLAND	A	1-0	UEFA European Championship Qualifier Group 7
01/04/1987	BULGARIA	A	1-2	UEFA European Championship Qualifier Group 7
29/04/1987	BELGIUM	H	0-0	UEFA European Championship Qualifier Group 7
28/05/1987	LUXEMBOURG	A**	2-0	UEFA European Championship Qualifier Group 7
09/09/1987	LUXEMBOURG	H	2-1	UEFA European Championship Qualifier Group 7
14/10/1987	BULGARIA	H	2-0	UEFA European Championship Qualifier Group 7
23/03/1988	ROMANIA	H	2-0	Friendly
22/05/1988	POLAND	H	3-1	Friendly
01/06/1988	NORWAY	A	0-0	Friendly
12/06/1988	ENGLAND	N	1-0	UEFA European Championship Finals, Group B
15/06/1988	SOVIET UNION	N	1-1	UEFA European Championship Finals, Group B
18/06/1988	NETHERLANDS	N	0-1	UEFA European Championship Finals, Group B
16/11/1988	SPAIN	A	0-2	FIFA World Cup Qualifier, Group 6
06/09/1989	WEST GERMANY	H	1-1	Friendly

Substitute * Goal **

Bibliography

Batters, D., York City: A Complete Record (Derby: Breedon Books Publishing Company Ltd, 1990).

Charlton, J. with Byrne, P., *Jack Charlton: The Autobiography* (London: Partridge Press, a division of Transworld Publishing Ltd, 1996).

Cloake, M. and Powley, A., *The Boys from White Hart Lane* (London: Vision Sports Publishing Ltd, 2008).

Elton, C., Hull City: A Complete Record (Derby: Breedon Books Publishing Company Ltd, 1989).

Freeman, P., with Harnwell, R., Stockport County: A Complete Record (Derby: Breedon Books Publishing Company Ltd, 1994).

Jarred, M. & Macdonald, M., *Leeds United: A Complete Record* (Derby: Breedon Books Publishing Company Ltd, 1986).

Jarred, M. & Macdonald, M., *Leeds United: The European Record* (Derby: Breedon Books Publishing Company Ltd, 2003).

Goodwin, B. *Spurs: A Complete Record* (Derby: Breedon Books Publishing Company Ltd, 1991).

Rowan, P., *The Team that Jack Built* (Edinburgh: Mainstream Publishing Company (Edinburgh) Ltd, 1994).

Saffer, D., *Leeds United's Unsung Heroes* (Skipton: Vertical Editions, 2017).

Saffer, D., *Revie's Boys: The 75 Players Under Don Revie at Leeds United* (Skipton: Vertical Editions, 2011).

Sutcliffe, R., *Bremner: The Complete Biography* (Ilkley: Great Northern Books, 2011).
Thraves, A., *Daily Mail: The History of the Wembley FA Cup Final* (London: Weidenfield and Nicolson, Orion Publishing Group Ltd, 1994).

Cork Examiner
Daily Express
Daily Mail
Daily Mirror
Daily Telegraph
Evening Standard
Green Post (Yorkshire Post Newspapers)
Football Post
The Guardian
Hull Daily Mail
Irish Independent
Irish Press
Irish Times
London Daily News
News of the World
Sheffield Star Green 'Un
The Sun
Sunday Express
Sunday Mirror
Spurs News
Sunday People
The Times
Tottenham Weekly Herald
Yorkshire Evening Post
Yorkshire Post

Charity Shield programme (1981, 1982)
FA Cup Final & FA Cup Final replay programme (1981, 1982)
League Cup Final programme (1982)
Sheffield Wednesday programme (27 August 1988, 19 August 1989)
Tottenham Hotspur testimonial programme (Tony Galvin)
UEFA Cup Final first and second leg programmes (1984)
UEFA Euro 88 programme (England, Netherlands, Soviet Union)

Shoot magazine
Glory Glory ... Tottenham Hotspur: 1981 FA Cup 25th Anniversary (Tottenham Legends (1981) Ltd)
Tottenham Hotspur FA Cup Finalists 1981 (Tottenham Hotspur Football and Athletic Company Ltd)
www.swindon-town-fc.co.uk
www.extra.ie